# TRADITIONAL NAVAJO TEACHINGS
## A TRILOGY
## VOLUME II

# *The Natural World*

Robert S. McPherson and Perry Juan Robinson

Robert S. McPherson is Professor of History Emeritus at Utah State University—Blanding Campus and author of numerous books about the history and cultures of the Four Corners Region.

Perry Juan Robinson is from the highly traditional area of Piñon, Black Mesa, Arizona, with a strong family heritage of practicing medicine people. He has been a member of the Navajo Nation Medicine Men Association for over twenty years and continues to work as a hataałii.

Cover Art: Charles Yanito
Cover Design: Chris Monson
Interior Design: Chris Monson and Kerin Tate
Map Design: Erin Greb
Copyediting and Indexing: Kerin Tate

Other books of related interest by the author:
*Traders, Agents, and Weavers: Developing the Northern Navajo Region*
        (University of Oklahoma Press)
*Both Sides of the Bullpen: Navajo Trade and Posts of the Upper Four Corners*
        (University of Oklahoma Press)
*Viewing the Ancestors: Perceptions of the Anaasazi, Mokwič, and Hisatsinom*
        (University of Oklahoma Press)
*Under the Eagle: Samuel Holiday, Navajo Code Talker*
        (University of Oklahoma Press)
*Dineji Na'nitin: Navajo Traditional Teachings and History*
        (University Press of Colorado)
*Navajo Tradition, Mormon Life: The Autobiography and Teachings of Jim Dandy*
        (University of Utah Press)
*Along Navajo Trails: Recollections of a Trader, 1898-1948*
        (Utah State University Press)
*A Navajo Legacy: The Life and Teachings of John Holiday*
        (University of Oklahoma Press)
*Navajo Land, Navajo Culture: The Utah Experience in the Twentieth Century*
        (University of Oklahoma Press)
*The Journey of Navajo Oshley: An Autobiography and Life History*
        (Utah State University Press)
*Sacred Land, Sacred View: Navajo Perceptions of the Four Corners Region*
        (University Press of Colorado)
*The Northern Navajo Frontier, 1860-1900: Expansion through Adversity*
        (University of New Mexico Press)

# Contents

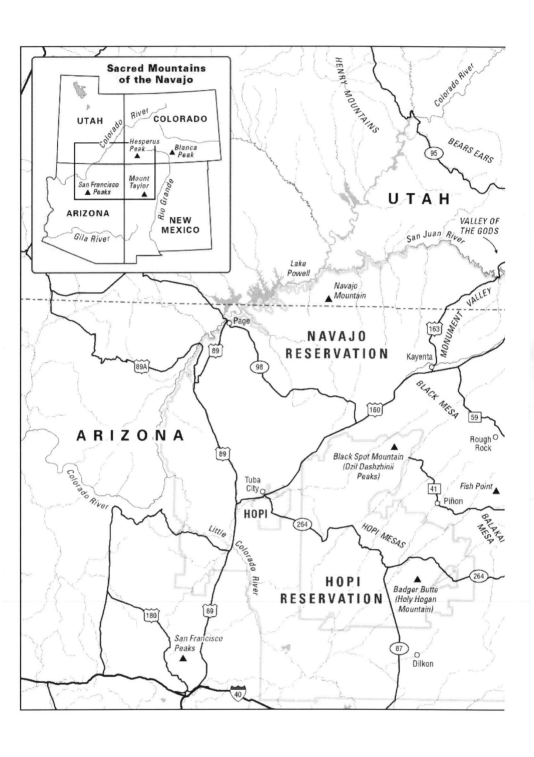

Sacred Mountains
of the Navajo

UTAH
COLORADO
River
Colorado
Hesperus
Peak ▲
Blanca
▲ Peak
San Francisco
▲ Peaks
Mount
Taylor ▲
Rio Grande
ARIZONA
NEW
MEXICO
Gila River

HENRY MOUNTAINS
Colorado River
BEARS EARS
95
UTAH
VALLEY OF
THE GODS
San Juan River
Lake
Powell
Navajo
▲ Mountain
MONUMENT VALLEY
Page
163
89
NAVAJO
RESERVATION
Kayenta
89A
98
BLACK MESA
160
59
ARIZONA
Rough O
Rock
89
Black Spot Mountain
(Dzil Dashzhinii
Peaks) ▲
Colorado River
Tuba
City O
41
Fish Point ▲
Piñon
HOPI
264
BALAKAI MESA
Little
Colorado
River
HOPI MESAS
180
89
HOPI
RESERVATION
▲
Badger Butte
(Holy Hogan
Mountain)
264
87
Dilkon O
San Francisco
Peaks
▲
40

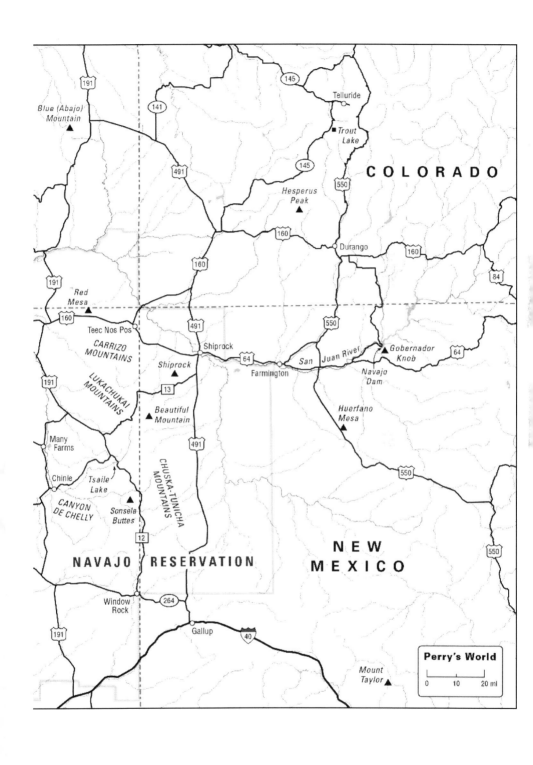

# INTRODUCTION

# *Thinking about the Natural World in Spiritual Terms*

Since the beginning of time, the Navajo people have enjoyed a close relationship with the land and all things above, below, and within. Those outside of the culture who have studied these people often refer to their interaction with the environment as a "land-based" religion. The phrase rolls off the tongue easily but puts Navajo beliefs and practices in a simplified realm that hardly speaks to the richness of what this phrase entails. In the previous book, *Traditional Navajo Teachings—Sacred Narratives and Ceremonies*, the reader encountered part of this complexity, especially in chapter 8, which looks at the ties between land, animals, and beliefs made manifest in the Bearway ceremony. This next volume takes those themes to a new level as different aspects of the environment are brought together to express the nature of relationships spread throughout the universe, near and far.

Let's start with something simple—two imaginary boxes. In one, place western worldview with all of its values, education, and philosophy, then do the same in the other for the Navajo. Distill each to their underlying core, after recognizing there are exceptions, and one can see two distinct ways of looking at the same thing. Western civilization views the contents of its box through scientific eyes that evaluate the world as an entity that functions through physical law. Those laws are rooted in hypothesis and theory that are observable with results that are reproducible and proven. By understanding physical laws through experimentation, Western society has been able to conquer certain diseases, place a man on the moon, and conduct heart transplants—all of which were made possible by a foundation of evaluation laid by the Greeks long before the time of Christ. By using observation, question, hypothesis, prediction, test, and refinement, many of the world's physical laws of functioning have been unlocked, understood, and then applied to improve the human condition. There is, however, no place for the unmeasurable or spiritual.

In our second box, the Navajo worldview observes the same physical phenomenon but applies, at times, a different explanation as to why something occurs that is not based in physical laws. No doubt there is an understanding that broken bones need to be set, that illness can cause death, that birds fly south for the winter, and that gravity holds people to the ground. They are keen observers of the physical world with its cause and effect. But the explanation of why these things happen may be far different from those of their Western counterparts; the Navajo view is often rooted in religious, spiritual, and unobservable explanation. The ultimate reason for a phenomenon is based in the teachings and stories of sacred narratives and not just in a physical law, although some of these laws are well accepted and understood. A different set of glasses is necessary—just as bifocals for reading provide a different view than sunglasses for jogging.

People unfamiliar with Navajo thought and dependent upon encountering the world solely in physical/scientific terms may balk at Diné explanations of why and how things happen. The purpose of this introduction is to provide a clearer understanding, one that is just as rational and utilitarian, given the beliefs from which this thought is derived. To distill a highly complex series of teachings into a few pages is unrealistic, and so four major tenets are examined to lay a foundation for what will be discussed throughout this volume. These are (1) inner forms, (2) centrality of relationships, (3) classification of entities, and (4) power through sacredness. Each of these could be a book in itself, since they are central roots to Navajo action. Here, these principles will be applied in discussing everything from wind and stars to frogs and water. The final volume in this series examines how these same principles, along with others, apply to the human body and stages of life from birth to death. With each of these steps, a clearer understanding and greater appreciation for what Perry Robinson has shared will grow.

## *Inside the Inner Form*

Soon after the emergence from the worlds beneath and at that place, the holy people took an active part in physically and spiritually forming the new world they now inhabited. They started to plan, then prepare their environment by first creating everything spiritually. Thinking, then speaking, it into existence was at the center of it all. Through words and by meshing mists and other physical elements, the first spirit/soul (bii'gistíín or ii'sizíinii—Inner Form That Stands Within) developed, as the holy people created all things animate and inanimate. Medicine man River Junction Curly described the process as follows: "With everything having life, with everything having the power of speech, with everything having the power to breathe, with everything having the power to teach and guide, with that in blessing we will live."[1] As these spiritual entities, created in human form, came into existence, they needed a physical body and location to inhabit. Some of these beings were placed in the mountains, others in animals and insects, still others in clouds, water, rocks, and even the cardinal directions. There was no place and nothing that did not receive an inner form; regardless of its outer shape, there was inside of each a humanlike spirit that could respond and interact.

Father Berard Haile, O.F.M., as a Roman Catholic priest living at Saint Michaels, Arizona, had an intense interest in the spiritual knowledge of the Navajo people he worked among. Through his superior understanding of the language and years of interviews, he learned of how the inner form operates in every aspect of the Navajo universe. After referring to the outer form of whatever it may be, he continued, "In native conception the phenomenon itself [outer form, i.e. mountain, plant, animal, and so forth] is not animated, but a personification, as it were, is placed within it, human-like in most cases, but always retaining its distinct individuality. This inner form, personality, or whatever else we may choose to call it is, in popular opinion, frequently equated with the soul of the natural phenomenon, just as the human forms of plants and animals are rated. The reason is that these beings do not differ from human beings, specifically the Navajo, who live by similar inner form."[2] He went on to say that during the time of creation, there were many of these inner forms that were created and paired as male and female, that their outer forms could be removed to reveal a human being, and that in sandpaintings both the inner and outer forms are portrayed to underscore both the physical and spiritual nature of the curative process. The spirit matter itself is indestructible, so when a person, for instance, kills an animal, as with a human being, their "soul" is released but continues to exist in a spiritual state.[3]

Each of these spiritual entities has a personality that can be either good or bad, helpful or harmful, easily approached or difficult. They have their likes and dislikes, and since each was created through songs and prayers, these become the way to ask for their assistance in using the special or unique powers they hold. While they are all part of this earth under the control of White Shell/Changing Woman and were created through an extended Blessingway ceremony by the holy people, many of the teachings about them are found in the chantways and are tied to specific rituals. Thus when one analyzes the prayers and songs used in healing, what is accessed is the inner form of a particular place or object that is dressed in human attire, even though it may be referred to as a mountain or a fire poker. For example and for the sake of brevity, take a short excerpt from a lengthy chant given by Slim Curly. In addressing the inner form of Blanca Peak, mountain of the east, he sings:

> A beautiful one gazes upon me with it [garments].
> Now I am Changing Woman's [Earth Mother's] child as a beautiful one gazes upon me with it.
> Blanca Peak, a beautiful one, gazes upon me with his white shell moccasins.
> Blanca Peak, a beautiful one, gazes upon me with his white shell black seamed moccasins.
> Blanca Peak, a beautiful one, gazes upon me with his white shell leggings.
> Blanca Peak, a beautiful one, gazes upon me with his white shell legging trimmings.
> Blanca Peak, a beautiful one, gazes upon me with his white shell kilt.[4]

This continues with a varicolored sash, white shell garment, arm fringes, necklace, ear bands, white shell face (mind), white shell voice, and head plume (holy feather—ats'os diyinii). The power of the image and the power of the prayer are increased through repetition, while the power of the inner form that is viewed as a holy person is summoned to bless the life of the individual receiving the benefits of the song.

A final example illustrates the important points of how, in this case, the inner form of an agate, often referred to as a mirage stone, came into existence and was given important powers, assigned a specific location, and instructed on how to interact with the earth surface people. What happens in this comparatively, brief explanation provided by medicine man Frank Mitchell can be applied to countless other "things" in the Navajo world, each with its own powers and responsibilities.

> The four Agate People which had been made were addressed, "You too, that by which you are useful, that for which you have been made, in times to come, it will become known by means of which things you will be useful," they were told. "You who are men and you who are women, it will now be made known to you how you are to be useful ones. You see in regard to these people with whom you have been made, the manner of their future usefulness is entirely known. Along the same lines you will be

*Everything in the Navajo universe has an inner form and an assigned place, power, and means of communication. Many of these inner beings have a human spirit that can think and react to what is right and wrong. While they do not have the same robust overall capacity as earth surface beings, some hold as much or greater power within their own realm. (Drawing by Kelly Pugh)*

useful, you are being made successively only for that purpose. You in particular who are men, will be man's heart in days to come, by your aid man's mind will be firmly set, by your aid his heart will be strong, you have been made for that purpose. And you who are women are similar, you will be the heart of women without exception, by your aid her heart will be strong. In times to come you will be useful in this very way to all people without exception who grow up in succession," they were told.

"And the place where you will live will now be made known to you. Here on the east side you will have a home of dark agate, in which you will live. In days to come you will be existing with the earth surface people [not yet created] as they come to be born, and when they die, it [agate heart] will return to its proper place again [to you]," they were told. "And the means of breathing of the people that have been made, that same will be your means of breathing. And the same [power of] speech given them will be your speech. Thereby you will be long life and thereby you will be happiness [in nature]. Therefore there will be some songs for you and there will be some prayers for you. That is the purpose for which you have been made. Therefore you must help people to become strong with your aid. Now you may go," they were told. It seems the so-called Agate [butte; perhaps Santa Fe Baldy peak] was set down for them into the interior of which they entered. So this happened, they say. It seems that again four different kinds of people had been made.[5]

This is why today, a Navajo person undergoing a chantway ceremony may place an agate in their mouth or keep it in their corn pollen pouch to give power and strength to the contents within when eaten.

## *Relationships*

What then, does all of this mean in the life of a traditional Navajo? Anthropologists and cultural historians might identify the belief of things having an inner form or spirit as animism and animatism, but a Navajo would describe it as living in a world of relationships (k'é). The scientist and anthropologist leave no room to recognize the operation of spiritual forces in the universe—accepting only that others believe in them. Their existence is unprovable. At the other end of the spectrum, medicine man Claus Chee Sonny states, "Through these stories, songs, and prayers I have become attentive to the fact that the land asks me that it be properly managed and that all of the fences might be repaired. Likewise, the home speaks out on behalf of itself to be repaired and to be cared for. The livestock does the same. Even the children let you know that they need help."[6] Chapter 5 of this book is devoted entirely to animals with antlers, primarily deer. Sonny, in describing extensively some of the do's and don'ts of deer hunting, outlines a number of teachings given by the deer to ensure they receive proper respect, for which they are willing to surrender their life to a hunter. There are many, but a few include the following: don't speak disparagingly of the animal because they have excellent hearing; when a deer is killed, a prayer is given; do not just throw the bones away anywhere, but rather use them as a tool or dispose of them in the woods with an offering; skin and dress the animal correctly, according to a set pattern; and pay attention to Talking God and Black God, who control them. "If you do everything right . . . you will always have enough meat to eat. It does not matter how many people there are. You will always get enough if you hunt right, if you prepare the animals correctly, if you bring them home properly, and if you dispose of the bones in the prescribed manner."[7] It is all about relationship.

For those who do not believe that everything has an inner form and is a spiritual creation, this type of belief and behavior may be hard to accept. Christianity, which emphasizes man's relationship to man and man's relationship to God, lightly passes over the fact that the first chapter in the Bible, Genesis, is about the spiritual creation and the second chapter about housing those spirits in physical forms. Readers often slide over the entire creative process being carried out through words and language; they struggle with the story of Balaam, who after beating his donkey for disobedience, had its mouth "opened by the Lord" then heard the animal say, "What have I done to thee, that thou hast smitten me three times"; Moses parting the Red Sea waters through word and action is just accepted as an interesting folk tale; and Elijah sealing the heavens through prayer that caused a drought and being fed by ravens while in hiding is simply impossible. There is no explanation as to how Christ calmed the sea and storm, withered a fig tree by speaking to it, cast evil spirits out of people and into swine, or walked on water. To many this is all religious fantasy from the past. Even Saint Francis of Assisi talking to birds, and in another instance a troublesome wolf, is hard to accept without an understanding of spiritual constructs.

Some may ask why these things do not happen today. Perhaps they do. Without going into detail concerning recent animal studies and communication and to avoid the appearance of trying to convince reluctant readers, let me recount an experience of nature writer and zoologist Farley Mowat in his book *Never Cry Wolf*.[8] While on assignment in the Canadian Arctic to study wolf habits and characteristics, he befriended an Eskimo (Inuit) named Ootek, whom he hired as his assistant. The two became good friends and fieldworkers and eventually dissolved a lot of their initial communication barriers. At one point, Ootek, who understood the language of the wolves, gave very specific information he received from them about the movement of the caribou on their migratory amble to their winter ranges.

It was enough to send the Eskimo man off to hunt for meat and in three days, he was back, having found the caribou where the wolves had said they were. On another occasion, thanks to the wolves' howling, he learned of three other natives traveling through the area, found them, and brought them in to camp. Ootek clearly understood the animals' communication.

In Navajo thought, trees, rivers, and other inanimate objects as well as those things classified by Anglos as living, comprehend communication when the right words, prayers, and songs are used. Rivers can either help or hinder when being crossed, they have specific sites where information is delivered through shifting sand patterns, and they can provide protective power when entering hostile territory. If a certain stone or rock slab falls from a cliff, it can be a sign that something foretold is about to happen; the flight patterns of birds may provide an answer to a troubling question; and the wind or stars may have something important to make known. Those who are trained and practiced in receiving these messages can do so for the benefit of others. A whirlwind or dust devil may have a negative force that can be controlled by words and action; a tree may take on a very personal relationship through a ritual adoption; and clouds and rain can be persuaded to bring their healing moisture to the earth. All of this is possible for those who understand the language, form a proper relationship, and maintain respectful procedures. This brings harmony through the peaceful order of words and avoids evil chaos and negative outcomes.

## *Classifying the World*

Not all things are created equal. The inner form of a man is more sophisticated than that of an ant, although each has its own power and position in the universe. As with many practices in culture, there are ways of thinking about things that never reach the conscious level but are just accepted as the way something is to be thought about. Perhaps the clearest explanation of this classified hierarchy of elements found in Navajo thought is given by Gary Witherspoon in his *Language and Art in the Navajo Universe*.[9] He provides a sophisticated explanation based in grammar, taxonomies, and syntax that can only be summarized here. For those who wish to delve deeper, see his chapter entitled "Classifying the World through Language," in which he goes far beyond the simple noun-verb-object forms discussed here.[10] According to Witherspoon, the Navajo language arranges the world into eight categories of nouns that can act upon each other. These include, in descending order of power: "Nouns denoting persons; nouns denoting the larger animals and medium-sized animals of special intelligence or relationship to man (such as the dog) and predators; nouns denoting medium-sized animals; nouns denoting small-sized animals; nouns denoting insects; nouns denoting plants and inanimate objects; and nouns denoting abstractions such as old age, hunger, disease, and so forth."[11] All of these have the ability to act upon or control those in a lesser ranking—even the inanimate ones. For instance, a rock can roll against a tree or person and make an impact. The verbs and the position of the object receiving the action is determined by which of the nouns has the greatest intelligence based in this ranking.

In Western thought, actions occur either because of natural laws or because of luck or randomness, while in the Navajo world, since everything has an inner form, actions are based in thought and who controls or allows a particular action to take place. "All movements, events, and conditions are ultimately controlled by the thought of one or more beings. Although entities without the capacity to think have the ability to move, their movements are caused and controlled by some being who has the power to think."[12] Thus, everything that happens is brought about through a thought-filled, controlling agent. Thinking can turn a neutral object into something that is either good or evil, depending upon whether the thoughts create order, which is often maintained through ritual, or through chaos, which leads to destruction and outcomes that are bad. Evil depends upon things that are out of control, ritual reestablishes order. The one with the higher intelligence can exert the greater control over both good and evil. "Beings and entities in the Navajo world are categorized and ranked according to a scale based on who can control whom. Beings of lower intelligence cannot control or act upon beings of higher intelligence, unless the beings of higher intelligence willfully or inadvertently yield to the control of beings of lower intelligence."[13] In simpler terms, a horse does not kick a person, that person allowed the horse to kick him.

There are also two categories of beings—animate and inanimate, each of which is subdivided into two parts. Within the inanimate category, there are those that have a physical, material presence such as rocks, trees, and mountains, and those that are incorporeal or an abstraction such as hunger, emotions, and the cardinal directions. Since they have no mass or intelligence, these are the least powerful. What if two entities on the lower scale in the physical world collided, say a rock rolled into a piñon tree? How would the verbs in a descriptive sentence assign the role of acting and being acted upon? Primarily, the object showing the greatest motion or action is credited as being the one doing the acting and so is in control. If the rock or tree fell on a human (as an Anglo person would think of it) then that person would have submitted or allowed themselves to be acted upon by these objects.

Moving to the animate classification, there are two ways of thinking about those that communicate through sound. They are separated into being either speakers or callers. Man, of course, is a speaker, while animals such as birds, dogs, and deer are callers because of the noises they make. While their inner form can understand and react to what is being said to them, their ability to speak and "control" their universe is limited. Unlike the wolves described by Ootek, who interpreted what these animals were saying, the holy people at the end of the creation period forbade the removal of outer forms and the use of human language by animals except under very special circumstances. While the creature can understand the prayers and songs given to them, the communication is only one way and is answered through their actions or by results. In summarizing this way of thinking about and categorizing the world, Witherspoon concludes by pointing out "the tremendous emphasis Navajos place on language as a means of controlling the universe. It is through language that man acquires human status. It is through language that man acquires the capacity to control the holy people, the inner forms of powerful natural forces and entities that control and maintain the operation of the fifth world. Without language man is greatly reduced in stature, and his control of the world about him is greatly impaired. He becomes the acted upon rather than the actor, the created rather than the creator, the object rather than the subject."[14]

## *Power through Sacredness*

In the Navajo world, relationships with entities ranging from rain to ants are approached through humility. A person must be inoffensive if the spirit within that entity is going to submit to what is being requested. The importance of relationship cannot be overstressed. The quality of that relationship is expressed by maintaining its sacred nature. What does that look like and how is it achieved? The Navajo view the world as one large spiritual being loaded with millions of other smaller spiritual beings who hold power. As each of these beings live their life upon this planet, they can either be treated as a sacred spiritual entity or just a profane element with no particular significance. Both the sacred and profane must exist in order to highlight and give contrast to the other. Romanian-born Mircea Eliade (1907–1986), a historian of religion and culture, spent much of his life defining the quality of the spiritual experience, what it means to be a religious man, and how different faiths share many similarities. His description found in *The Sacred and the Profane: The Nature of Religion* accurately portrays the function and practices found in Navajo beliefs and so is used here as a framework for discussion.[15]

Religious man recognizes that this world is a spiritual creation formed and operated by higher, often intangible powers—be it a single God, a multiplicity of gods or holy beings, or some power of a higher order than humans. This god or gods can be helpful and loving or terrifying when not respected. Man's duty is to follow this being's directives through an attitude of awe and obedience. There are specific places where one can go to address this being; it may be the holy one's dwelling, a place where he or she is known to have appeared before, a designated meeting spot, or a site agreed upon, but wherever it is, the god will make itself known or appear through what Eliade calls a hierophany or a manifestation of the sacred.[16] Examples of this in Navajo beliefs are as common as the Four Sacred Mountains, where specific holy beings dwell, a river that has spiritual entities living within, a rock formation whose inner form can be appealed to for protection, or the multitude of places mentioned in the chantways where supernatural people have appeared and are known to frequent. As a "land-based religion," this turns those spots into sacred sites where mortal man can commune with powers greater than himself.

When approaching one of these sites, the person must change his behavior in keeping with the dictates of respect and living with awe. There must be a clear demarcation between the place that is sacred or controlled by the holy being and that which is profane or unremarkable. Preparing to encounter a deity at this spot may require removing one's sandals as Moses did when nearing the burning bush on Mount Sinai; or using an altar bar in a Roman Catholic church to separate the priest in his sanctuary from the parishioners seeking communion; or praying at the temple wall in Jerusalem where special attire and actions are required. At each of these spots there has to be a clear delineation identified as a threshold, separating the sacred from the profane. Once it is reached, behavior changes, different requirements come into play, and interaction with God or the gods is possible. They are present.

In volume 1 of this trilogy, *Sacred Narratives and Ceremonies*, Perry Robinson provided a number of examples. For instance, his climbing of Mount Hesperus with three other medicine men started with song and prayer once they reached the base of the mountain (threshold). The appearance of a crystal (hierophany), which he now uses for divination, showed that the holy people were there and mindful of his need, while his selecting of a companion stone during his descent was a continuation of the sacred experience. Another example is the preparation of a hogan for a ceremony. The hanging of a blanket in the door, the invitation for the holy people to look through the smoke hole to view the preparations, their entrance into the hogan through the doorway, the participants sitting away from the wall so that the gods can walk behind them, the planting of the prayersticks as an invitation, the sprinkling of the sandpainting with pollen, and the seated patient in the midst of the sandpainting, allows the holy people to go with that person back in time to when the first cure was performed. Participants, as soon as they come into the hogan—even though it may have been used the day before as a regular home—now enter that sacred space where the holy people will effect a cure for the sick person. Defined procedure and proper respect has transformed profane space into the sacred.

In summarizing the beliefs about sacred geography and all that stands within, there are some final points to underscore. When talking to elders about a ceremony, they will often refer to exact locations, identifying where the songs start and end with a host of sites mentioned in between. As the ritual unfolds, these places are tied to specific events in a narrative, just as a movie goes from scene to scene in an evolving story. In each of those settings, there are powers and holy people who can lend their strength to the outcome of the ceremony. It is not a matter of simply creating a stage for the event, but rather evoking the power of place and personalities to be involved in the healing. The songs describe and invite the powers to attend. Speaking of the spiritual essence of the mountains, discussed in the next chapter, Frank Mitchell details exactly what is available and how they can help, each having their own abilities. These geographical forms are not just a mass of rock, dirt, and plants, but something that has knowledge and is approachable. Mitchell put it this way: "You see they were made alive by means of these inner forms . . . and the same applies again to the songs used in bringing them into being, and the prayers of their origin, and the songs used to bring their names into being, and those used to bring their head plumes [for spiritual communication] into being. For all of this they have songs and prayers, they say."[17]

What follows is a more detailed description and explanation of how the Navajo perceive the operation of the physical world. Starting with one of the most frequently discussed topics, that of the Four and Six Sacred Mountains, as well as important rock formations, the reader will then encounter teachings about water in its various forms and the beings who control them. Everything from rainmaking to its relationship with fire to its universal acknowledgment of the individual is discussed. The sky, sun, moon, and stars are tied in with string games, seasonal changes, and winds, illustrating the power of the holy people in controlling the weather and atmospheric conditions that bring life. Chapters 4 and 5 look at plants and herbs—those in the forest and those domesticated—and how they heal, feed, and protect the earth surface beings by providing agricultural products, medicine, and shelter. Animals of all sizes—from those with antlers to birds, reptiles, and insects—will complete the study of the physical world of the Navajo. Each chapter provides insight into the relationship of these people with sentient beings in their universe.

As in all three volumes of this trilogy, each chapter has two parts. First is the chapter introduction that I have written, followed by the bulk of the chapter by Perry, which I have transcribed from interviews, organized, and edited. The change in author voice is noticeable, but we have placed a divider to visually separate the two texts. The introductory material provides supplementary information and sources for further reading. It also mentions differing views, as Navajo traditions, teachings, and stories can vary and may be at odds with information shared in other accounts.

CHAPTER ONE

# Mountains, Mesas, and Medicine

## The Living Inanimate

T he quality of life on the Colorado Plateau, part of which is home to the Navajo, depends on the mountains and the moisture they attract. This high desert country is divided and defined by the availability of resources like water, trees, grass, animal life, mineral deposits, and medicinal plants important for survival. Those are the physical things. But there are also spiritual powers, religious teachings, and traditional stories that define where one goes and what will be encountered once at those locations. Indeed, embodied in the mountains are some of the most important elements found in Navajo culture. There are few chantways that do not, in some way, use the mountains as a backdrop to the main storyline of the teachings or enumerate the powers and holy people located there. One prime example of this is found in the Blessingway narrative, in which the creation and assignment of qualities to the Four Sacred Mountains is foundational. Those mountains with their powers circumscribe the land, its people, and the cultural practices that make all three unique. No place is this encapsulated more fully than in the mountain soil bundle (dahńdiilyééh) that should reside in each Navajo home and is the only absolutely essential piece of ritual equipment needed to perform the Blessingway, a ceremony of well-being.

In this chapter, Perry provides a potpourri of traditional teachings about the mountains. Whether referring to them as hogans, pairing them in male and female relationships, tying them to weather phenomena, connecting them as unifying elements of water control, identifying them as homes of the gods, or celebrating their powers as medicine that mends character

14

disorders, mountains serve as one of the most unifying symbols in Navajo culture. Since the creation of this world, nothing has been more ubiquitous than their role, as witnessed by their being on today's tribal seal. To provide context to what Perry offers, there are five related topics to be touched on here: (1) Navajo perception of the mountains as part of Mother Earth (2) the holy people assigned to them and their personalities (3) their comparison to hogans (4) how their powers are accessed and (5) the role of the mountain soil bundle.

The Blessingway story provides the lengthiest discussion about the Four Sacred Mountains. Although each version of this narrative may offer different information and new interpretation, most accounts teach about how First Man and First Woman, two spiritual beings who have both good and harmful qualities, brought soil from the worlds beneath from each of the prototype mountains below. These soils they placed in the cardinal directions, then enlarged them by blowing into their mass. To the east in Colorado sits Blanca Peak (Sisnaajiní—Descending Black Belt Mountain), whose inner forms are Dawn Boy and Dawn Girl, and whose entrance is guarded by Bear. South in New Mexico is Mount Taylor (Tsoodził—Big Mountain, also Tongue Mountain), whose inner forms are Daylight Boy and Daylight Girl, with Mountain Lion standing guard. Mount Humphreys in the San Francisco Peaks (Dook'o'oosłííd—Never Thaws on Top) of Arizona has Evening Boy and Evening Girl guarded by Big Snake, while Mount Hesperus (Dibé Nitsaa—Big Sheep) is the mountain of the north with Night Boy and Night Girl guarded by Porcupine. These four mountains, along with Huerfano Mountain (Dził Ná'oodiłii—People Encircling Mountain) with Mirage Boy and Mirage Girl, and Gobernador Knob (Ch'ool'į'í—Spruce Hill) with Dusk Boy and Dusk Girl, comprise the six Chieftain Mountains of the Navajo.[1] As Perry points out, there are materials, colors, qualities, and ways of securing them to the earth that are unique to each of the mountains with their inner forms.

The last two—Gobernador and Huerfano—were made from soils taken from the main four, then placed in two key locations on Mother Earth. Just as Mount Taylor (mountain of the south) is called Tongue Mountain because it represents that part of the body of Mother Earth, so too were these two formations placed in critical body parts. The holy people emplacing them decided, "They will be set upon the heart and lungs of the earth. Huerfano Mountain will be set upon the lungs, it will be its own lungs [and] Gobernador Knob will be set on its heart. . . . It will be like its own heart. . . . Therefore, this one [Gobernador Knob] will be in charge of the Blessingway, the other will have charge of Injuryway."[2] Gobernador is also called Mountain Covered with Hard Goods, while Huerfano is Soft Goods Mountain, each of which are represented as the southern and northern door posts (respectively) found in a hogan. Other qualities of male and female rain, types of vegetation, and powerful stones are also assigned to them.[3]

As with humans, every mountain has its own responsibilities. From the beginning, each of them received from the holy people assigned tasks and unique powers. In the Blessingway, these are often enumerated and given detailed description, creating a mental image of a helpful partner. The songs and prayers offer a recounting of what these powers are. As Frank Mitchell points out, "From the time that thinking began about them, the lines of their songs are strung out, and songs of talking about them string along, songs of placing them run along. There is a song of how they are being dressed, a song of how they have been dressed up. Then there is a song of how they moved, another song when they raised themselves, another song of how a smoke was prepared for them, another song of how they smoked and another song expressing their gladness."[4] As a patient listens to an explanation of the mountains' powers and the help they provide, he or she mentally sees and understands the forces that are at play in the healing process. Slim Curly describes how the holy people living in these mountains and elsewhere assist those who petition them. He recognizes that these powerful beings stay in their assigned location, but they have many messengers who travel about and report back with their findings. "These messengers sit facing you while you pray. This news they bring back to the homes of their chiefs where they relate of you, 'Clearly he is pleading when he says, I have made your offering.' Therefore, you will treat it with every respect."[5] Thus Talking God, who lives in Blanca Peak, and Calling God, who lives in the San Francisco Peaks, remain in their hogans, await the news, and provide the cure.

Filled with spiritual powers and important teachings that affect every aspect of life, these six Chieftain Mountains are central to Navajo well-being. Indeed, one medicine man insisted they were comparable to a governing body for the Navajo in the way the federal government is for Anglos. "The white people all look to the Government like we look to the Sacred Mountains. You white people hold out your hands to the Government. In accord with that you live. But we look to our Sacred Mountains . . . they are our Washington. . . . They existed in the underworld and the Blessingway stands for them. There existed those things with which they are adorned; they were placed for us, and according to them we live."[6]

Perry explains that the Six Sacred Mountains surrounding Navajo land represent the foundational posts of a Navajo hogan whether it is conical (male) or rounded (female), just as Gobernador is conical and Huerfano more round. The holy people created the first hogan and live in similar structures that are mountains today, while the Navajo mirror these structures in the homes they build. In order to have the blessings and powers found in the Chieftain Mountains, they must intentionally be brought into a person's home. Perry explains how these qualities are summoned by "dressing the mountains" or main posts through prayer and offerings during the construction of the hogan. Every structure has a post placed in each of the cardinal directions that represents one of the sacred mountains, bringing its powers and blessings into the home. The two posts in the east-facing door represent Huerfano and Gobernador.

Yet to keep these powerful forces for good as a part of the hogan and to have them available to bless the family residing within, a mountain soil bundle (dahńdiilyééh) with portions of mountain soil (dziłleezh) and other materials bring the blessings from each into the home. Within the main bundle made from unwounded buckskin (dook'aak'éhii) are four individual pouches, each with soil from one of the mountains. Each represents the specific powers associated with the mountain from which it comes, illustrating the principle called synecdoche found throughout Navajo ceremonialism. Specifically, the part represents the whole. For example, an eagle feather might hold the power of the bird, water from a specific spring a healing liquid, a rock from a particular formation the inner spirit within, or a piece of hair an enemy warrior. In this case, the soil brings a large number of powers to bear that are specific to the direction and the essence of the mountain. That is why each pouch is identified by a marking or attachment on its opening to indicate which mountain it came from, to assist in keeping the soils separate, and as a way of focusing each of those powers.[7] Other sacred objects are also included. The importance of this bundle is captured in the Navajo phrase, "It is in front of life" (Iiná bitsiji silá), meaning that it is a safeguard and powerful force for good. As one medicine man said, "That dziłleezh includes everything standing for the holy people, the holy places, the earth people, and the air. It is our means of communication with the holy people in all four directions and other places. When we use it to say our prayers, even our morning prayers at home for long life, the holy people hear us and our problems get answered."[8]

Once the bundle is put together and "activated" through prayer, song, and pollen, it is not only considered alive, but also representative of the well-being of the individual and family who own it. Likewise, if a person does not respect it, fails to use it properly, does not feed it with songs and prayers and pollen on a regular basis, does not have a renewal ceremony (Dziłleezh biinit'etł$\acute{\text{í}}\acute{\text{í}}$) as recommended every two to four years under normal circumstances, or acts inappropriately (cursing, fighting, and so forth), the bundle may withdraw its powers. Very human emotions of feeling neglected, experiencing happiness, resentment, and appreciation are all felt by a mountain soil bundle. As with a human being, a piece of turquoise is tied to the pouches' exterior to bless the container and to connect it to the holy people.[9]

Charlotte Frisbie, who has studied medicine bundles extensively, shared an account of creating one, given by Frank Mitchell in his autobiography.[10] A brief summary is given here with the understanding that the length of time and some of the procedures will vary with different medicine men during different time periods, this one starting in 1925 and continuing for a total of three years. Mitchell noted that the ceremonial preparation of the individuals involved, the procurement of unwounded buckskin, travel, and other procedural necessities were the reason it took so long. By the end of the experience, he had visited four of the six Chieftain Mountains and had served as the appointed leader on one of the trips. Mitchell had learned the collecting ritual from his father. His wife, Tall Woman, a highly traditional person who supported her husband's practices as a hataałii, prepared the ceremonial food needed for each of the expeditions.[11] Along with normal Navajo fare, the participants ate corn bread mixed with wheat, barley, and wild plants that represented all of the vegetation found on earth. Clothing was repaired, jewelry and traditional garb obtained, ritual equipment prepared, sweat baths taken, and abstinence in sex followed. Once the trip began, the men sang travel songs until they reached their destination, where special songs about the mountains accompanied by prayer were offered as they climbed the formation until they reached the first water. There the men bathed, dried themselves with cornmeal mixed with ground mirage stone, then donned "clothing something like you see on Yé'ii Bicheii dancers. You know, when the Yé'ii Bicheii is ready to dance he is all decorated with silver belts and bracelets and beads. That is the way we dressed on the mountain."[12]

As the medicine men ascended, they also left offerings of sacred stones (ntł'iz) at a water source and again when they took small portions of dirt for their bundles. Once they had obtained what they needed, the area received an offering that was then covered over to hide any disturbance. Mitchell recalled, "After we made the jewel offering to Mother Earth, we said a prayer up there on each mountain to thank her for what we came for and for the protection that we would have because of that. We were praying for the whole Navajo tribe, because the ceremonial singers are the ones the people look to for protection."[13] Once this ended, the singing resumed until they reached the bottom of the mountain, where each person blessed himself with pollen before getting dressed into ordinary clothes. When the men returned to their communities, the people knew what they had accomplished, and so frequently requested that they perform ceremonies on their behalf. The power of the mountain was now present.

Perry adds his understanding about the mountains and why they figure so prominently in Navajo life. His knowledge has been passed down through his family for generations and is now available for others to understand the importance of these hallmarks on the land.

## *Mountains, Directions, and Colors*

There are many important teachings about the Four Sacred Mountains, most of them coming from different narratives with each having its own emphasis. There is a general belief that materials from the worlds beneath this one were brought to the surface of the earth and placed in the four directions. One of the stories from part of the Enemyway called the Flintway (Béshee Biką'jí), speaks of when the people and creatures moved from the First or Black World through the remaining three. There was a young man who always sat behind the people. He decided to take a pebble or shell from each world—black, blue, yellow, and white—each representing the travel of the creatures and what they had passed through. The holy people placed the stones and shells in the four directions—white shell to the east, turquoise to the south, yellow abalone shell to the west, and black jet to the north, because there was no light in the northern region. When bad things happened, the creatures had to stay sitting in the Black World to the north. These stones or shells later became the mountains, each with their own songs and prayers given to them by the holy people when being put in place.

The gods and the creatures really wanted to talk about the structure of how their lives should be, but the stones, small at this point, were sitting too close. The holy people wished to move them away, make them bigger, and give them powers that would help humans by providing good things. As the gods sang about it, they emplaced a lot of blessings. To the east they put the dawn, representing elements of the morning—a new beginning, morning flowers, and bird calls heard only during that part of the day. White was its color, and the Chuska Mountains, one of its representatives with its aspen trees sparkling white with color, served as a reminder that in the future, White Shell Woman would be born. Critical thinking was part of its power. As the holy people talked about the south and the Blue World they thought of blue birds, blue flowers, blue spruce, and turquoise. The south would be important for the planting of crops and of life, where skills, work, and focused thought on survival should exist. A lot of preparation was necessary. To the west, the holy people talked about families, relationships, organizations within society, and how each should function. The north had thunderstorms, rain, and darkness, but with these also came good things that helped. The night gives pleasant sleep and rest that rejuvenates, something everybody needs. Thus, there were many benefits placed in the four directions with colors to remind everyone. Once the holy people started singing, they put these qualities in place and caused the mountains and their waters to become wider, bigger, and more distant. All of the beings from the Four Worlds adopted each other and became one people.

These same beings, as they moved upward, carried mud on their shoes embedded with pebbles from the different worlds. By the end of the Fourth World, the people and creatures emerged to this earth, where they stood on a small island surrounded with deep water. They asked how the water could be drained to create more land to live upon. They talked about it until a young man spoke saying, "I have a pebble that I brought from the Black World." He showed it to those about him; another person chimed in that he had one from the Blue World, another with shell from the Yellow World, and yet another from the White World they were now in. With four colors in hand, the holy people sang songs that turned these objects into spinning rocks and shells that could cut through the surrounding mountains. The first one they let run to the east to make a passage for water to drain in that direction. They next, in a clockwise manner, set the other rocks in motion to the various directions. Each spinning rock or shell they called a holy one as it cut through the mountains and caused the water to flow out and away.

Once they completed their task, just as in the Enemyway and other ceremonies, the rocks returned with their medicine and power and crossed over in the opposite direction, after meeting at the center. This is why a person praying brings small crushed black, blue, yellow, and white rocks or shells mixed together as an offering in a ceremony. These are small granules, a combination called "precious stones" (ntł'iz). The holy people brought all four rocks back into the center, representing what they identified as the crossing of the ceremonies for the first time. The rock that cut across Blanca Peak was the black rock and represents that mountain; to the south sits Mount Taylor, which is tied to turquoise; the San Francisco Peaks to the west are yellow in color and made of abalone shell; and the one to the north, Hesperus Peak, is represented by white shell. The black and white are reversed in this case because that was how the ceremony was set. Even though we place the black rock from the north and the white to the east, as far as the ceremony is concerned, they always reverse each other right there, because the black portion of it stands before us all the time as our protector, while the white one brings peace back to the earth. The north is the direction where the evil one comes from, and so we put the white one there.

*Navajo artist Harrison Begay captures some of the many aspects of the sacred mountains. Each holds its pairs of males and females, provides water from a bowl (tó'ásaa) located within, provides a home for mountain animals and birds, works with the sky to bring moisture and rainbows to the land, and offers many blessings to the People.*

## *The Chieftain Mountains*

Each of the Four Sacred Mountains has special powers and teachings. Starting with Blanca Peak to the east, it is a male mountain fastened to the earth with a sash belt and is associated with childbearing. Traditionally, a belt was hung from a post or beam in the hogan to facilitate the birthing process. This mountain serves as a doorway to life with its many unknown experiences that entice people to begin learning. It also represents the family and togetherness, just as a belt surrounds a person and holds them in a complete circle. This mountain is always considered the doorway open for children and the things associated with new beginnings. White Shell is connected to light, sunlight, and the east. The holy person who is found in this direction is Black Body Person (Bits'íís Diłhił) and is there for protection; there are also unknown elements of life that create new beginnings and enable learning. Early radiant morning sunlight symbolizes this direction. When Changing Woman and the other holy people were first forming human beings, they went in search of the spiritual forms of sacred boy and sacred girl who lived in the air to the east. Talking God sent someone to bring back Black Body Person, one of the Air People (Nílch'ih Diné), to provide spirits for two males. Those for females came from (Holy Wind Girl—Nílch'ih Atééd). The ceremony took place at Blanca Peak as two ears of white corn and two ears of yellow corn were placed beneath a buckskin. The holy people sang songs and offered prayers, the four Holy Winds went under the hide and entered into the corn, turning it over and forming White Corn Boy and Yellow Corn Girl, the first teenagers or young adults to ensure the continuation of physical life. This process helped avoid incest from within a family. In the east, there is always a god who sits there to control and work with the unknown that requires miraculous supernatural power (álílee k'ehgo) to intervene. When the holy people answer prayers and songs in a supernatural way, the power to do so comes from this mountain. Black Body One is the holy person who resides in Blanca Peak, but his influence is like a rainbow that spans from east to west as he responds to prayers performed in a holy way.

Mount Taylor is fastened to the earth with a flint knife; is a male mountain, viewed as a doorway to the south; and is represented by turquoise, which brings rain. This stone sits as a water offering with blue twilight and is concerned about daily life. When the sun is out and there are no clouds, the clear, blue skies are considered the promise of a good day with no interference. Nothing bad will happen, a person will have a productive time because of the sunlight and good air coming from the Blue Body Person stationed in that mountain. There is a turquoise cane fastened to the mountain's doorway. It also has its own blessings that can be prayed to for help in different activities and new experiences faced each day. This direction is always about something new that is going to occur, not in a miraculous way, but in the normal flow of everyday life. For instance, in the girl's puberty ceremony (kinaaldá), the young woman runs to the south after being told to think about turquoise. This stone, when given to a young adult, provides their identity to the holy people. Snakes and all the creatures that crawl or walk upon this earth recognize the person who wears it, thinking, "He's my brother, my grandchild, or my grandfather." They will know you by it and get out of your way if they are in your path. Rattlesnakes and other harmful creatures will say, "This person's wearing turquoise. Let's make way for that one," and back off. Deer will welcome you saying, "Here comes our grandson. Let him go through."

San Francisco Peak is fastened to the earth by a sunbeam and is associated with adulthood, physical strength, and the winds. The abalone shell that represents the mountain is female. A person driving from Tuba

City who stops at the junction leading to Flagstaff can look south to see this mountain and see the outline of a woman lying down. Her hair spreads out to the east, like a wave of water that falls from her forehead and flows toward Phoenix. Tracing the outline of her face, one starts with her forehead, then nose, lips, chin sticking up in the air, and throat. Her body is that of a pregnant woman with knees propped up and torso lying toward the west as she faces east. The main part of her body is the San Francisco Peak range, her breasts are prominent, and because she is trying to give birth, her legs are bent to the side toward the Grand Canyon. A lot of prayers and songs are associated with this form. If a woman is pregnant and needs help, medicine men go to the mountain to make offerings.

No bears are supposed to live on it because they were told to live on the male mountains, like the Chuskas on the east side of Navajo country. There is a long story about why this is so; it is connected to the Evilway (Hóchxǫ'íjí) ceremony. A young, attractive woman who lived with her twelve brothers had many suitors. Through trickery, Coyote was able to marry her and teach her how to transform into a vicious female bear. Her brothers were very unhappy living with Coyote and so forced him to leave their home, which angered the sister. She eventually killed all but the youngest of her brothers. This survivor subdued her, and rather than killing her, provided a chance to live another life. He gave her a sacred flint knife to put around her neck and said, "If you want to live, it's going to be this way. You are going to have to go to the east and not return to this mountain." She had to move away from the female mountain (San Francisco Peaks) and could no longer live as a woman, because these mountains were still associated with women and their needs including the peaceful Blessingway ceremony.

Hesperus Peak is a female mountain made of jet; fastened to the earth by a lot of jet bows and black flints; decorated with white and black feathers; and associated with winter, old age, and things that come from the ground. This mountain is considered female because the water that flows from it gave birth to the four sacred rivers. Its water represents the first water [amniotic fluid] when a child is born. That water bursts and runs from Mount Hesperus, flowing all the way to the Grand Canyon moving south and is considered female water (tó yisdzáán). The mountain is also associated with storms. White Body God lives there on top, makes thundering and wind noises, and is represented by the white spruce and aspens with their white bark. They are considered gods who say, "I have many colors that I will show you. As the seasons shift, the color of my skin or leaves tell you that a change is beginning and that you also must change." They sit on the mountain and serve as teachers.

*A mountain or rock formation may have multiple stories and powers. The San Francisco Peaks, here, provide an example of how this landform supports teaching. Viewed as a pregnant woman, the mountain is connected to childbirth and female concerns and is a place women can appeal for help. Starting with the snowcapped peak as her abdomen, can you spot the physical details Perry mentions? (Photo by Perry Robinson)*

The north also has a lot of powers concerning darkness and the people who have left this world. The Evilway and Enemyway, which deal with negative aspects of life, refer a lot to this direction, but the mountain helps to turn it into a positive situation. Hesperus Peak is considered a great talker because thunderstorms and inclement weather come from that direction, making noises that connect with the heavens and lightning that strikes the earth with a flash anywhere it chooses. That is how powerful this mountain is, and so people use it as a protector. A person having a Protectionway ceremony goes there to pick herbs for it. Even the rocks from this area are heated for use in a sweat lodge and mixed with lava stones from Mount Taylor, which are said to be the blood from one of the monsters killed by the Twins. The rocks from Hesperus and Mount Taylor are combined in the sweat lodge to ensure protection. Thus the mountain of the north, even though it is female, deals with men's issues and things that are dark and black like war, hunting, and evil, requiring protection.

The bow and arrow serve as a good example. When Monster Slayer and Born for Water finished killing the monsters, they returned the four sacred arrows made of two types of lightning, sunbeam, and rainbow to Sun Bearer.

Left behind on earth, however, were four different types of colored flint fastened to the mountains. To the east was white shell, to the south turquoise flint, and to the west abalone flint, while at Hesperus was jet. First Man wished to have weapons just like those returned to Sun Bearer and so asked other holy people, "How do we develop a bow like the gods have?" The holy people sang about it, asked questions, and then decided to go to the mountain in the north and talk to Thunderstorm, who lived there. Before leaving, they cut willows so that Thunderstorm could bless the wood and leave sacred markings on the bow in four different corners. Since Thunderstorm had his own bow and arrows that he shot from the sky to the ground, he willingly shared the design and assisted them. Therefore, the bow and arrow came from the north and Mount Hesperus.

To show proper respect for this, when a bow is brought into a hogan, it is kept on the north side of the house and is not brought into other family areas. Some hogans have a bow and arrow hanging above their door, which is located in the east. This is put there for ceremonial purposes to keep evil away from the home—a form of local protection. But the bow and arrow used for everyday hunting, warfare, and physical safety, is kept in the northern part of the hogan. The quiver, made of mountain lion skin and arrows, is also kept there. When a man gets ready to go out of the home with this weapon, he puts it on his shoulder and walks directly from the north to the outside, and when he returns, he hangs it in the proper place.

A man never left his quiver behind in the old days since he did not know who might meddle with it; no one else should touch it because it is sacred. Traditionally, Navajos made quivers out of cougar skin, an animal associated with the mountains. The hide was considered a trophy and proof that the owner was a successful hunter. These animals have great power by possessing wisdom and being masterful hunters. The holy people gave this animal the name of "The One Whose Paws You Cannot Hear" (Kétł'ááh doo hodiits'a'í). If a person is able to kill one, then he is a better hunter, and so the cougar blesses him. By having a quiver made of this skin, the owner obtains the powers the animal possesses.

The mountains are paired with the two females and the two males working together—San Francisco Peak with Hesperus and Blanca with Mount Taylor. The females are involved with daily life, the tangible things needed for existence, and other women's concerns—just as in Navajo society. The hogan is divided into the same use areas, with the women working, sleeping, and tending children in the east and south sides, and with the men more in the west and north. These powers are brought together through the creation and use of a mountain soil bundle (dahńdiilyééh). One is made from soil taken from both male and female mountains, and like a family that combines both sexes, together they bring the blessings from each

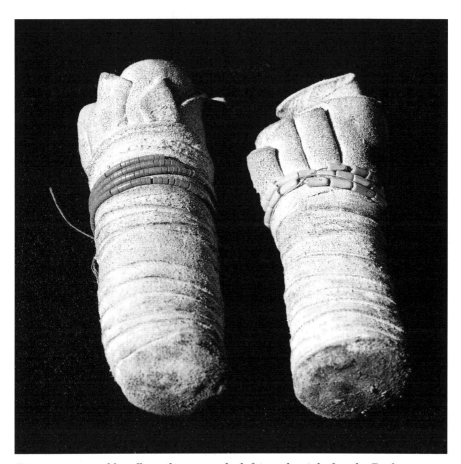

*Two mountain soil bundles—the one on the left is male, right female. Each contains soil from the four sacred mountains wrapped in unwounded buckskin. In the male bundle is a black and red mirage stone and abalone shell, in the female a white stone and white shell. One of these dahńdiilyééh ("hold it up") bundles are held by the person for whom the Blessingway is performed, bringing all the powers of the mountains to enrich the home and the individual. (Photo by Kay Shumway)*

into a person's home. This medicine bundle is used to pray with on behalf of the family or oneself, or to obtain what is needed to exist. The stories of the four directions tie into it, bringing the sacredness of the east, south, west, and north into that bundle.

The bundle also connects to the first four posts placed in the ground when erecting a hogan. Each log (the two sides of the doorway are considered to be one, standing for the east), represents the mountain in one of the four corresponding directions, with the home at the center. After the posts are secured in the ground, they are blessed with corn pollen, the prayer being called "Addressing the Mountains." This is done to summon their powers through the holy people and into the home. Anywhere a person sleeps, walks, or lives is considered part of the home and a central place within the four directions. These directions should remain uppermost in a person's thoughts as he carries them through daily life. The hogan faces east, has four areas, is blessed with corn pollen in four directions, and is prayed to for the holy people's presence.

All of this, symbolized in the four posts, is similar to the four mountains, which are said to form a large hogan that encompasses the Navajo Nation. The doorway to the east is comprised of Gobernador Knob and Huerfano Mesa, which represent the post on each side. Then one moves in a clockwise direction, just as in a ceremony, to Mount Taylor sitting in the south and then to the other directions, forming a circle where the people live. The songs in a ceremony are mentioned in the same order. As in the hogan doorway, the north mountain (Gobernador) represents hard goods, and the mountain to the south (Huerfano Mesa) stands for soft goods.

The Four Sacred Mountains are also referred to as the four mothers, while any Navajo person is referred to as their child located in the center of a hogan formed by the mountains. Regardless of where an individual may be on the reservation, he or she is the center of attention of these mothers. In spite of two of the mountains being male, all are referred to as female because they are part of Mother Earth. This is the way medicine men talk and pray about it, but if they are visiting one of the mountains, then it is described by its male or female name, just like humans. Water is also discussed in this way—Mother Water is a female even when there are male rivers. Rivers, like mountains, encircle Navajo lands encased in the center.

## *Mountain Tobacco*

Each individual is responsible for maintaining his or her life, focused in the teachings of the People. Mountain tobacco, representing the Four Sacred Mountains, helps a person to symbolically maintain that mindset. It should not be constantly used in an addictive manner; rather, it is to gather one's thoughts and to foster contemplation for a sacred reason at a special time. Mountain tobacco is used sparingly, even though a person may use it for purification and may carry a tobacco pouch daily. For the man who smoked excessively in the past, the animals smelled him, the enemy smelled him, and he was quickly defeated, turning what should have been a help and blessing into something dangerous. This is true with overdoing anything. Here, smoke is about feelings and inner thoughts and is especially helpful in straightening one's mind or healing mental illness. One's thoughts act very much like smoke—difficult to measure, control, and direct. They are intangible, carrying a lot of feeling with them.

The Mountain Smoke ceremony is about rearranging one's perspective and is based in a story about when the mountains became confused as to their location. At one point, the holy people had moved all of these formations around—the ones in the east changing places to the south, the south to the north, others going in a circle. They began to talk to each other and say, "What's going on? I'm not where I'm supposed to be." This is where a lot of the songs called The Mountains Have Gone in Different Directions (Sin ałtaanáskai sodizin) came from. The holy people had to reposition them to their initial place. These are the songs also used in rededicating a mountain soil bundle in which the covering is untied and the contents dismantled. After the first song is completed, a second one begins the process of putting elements back where they belong. The song tells them that this is their place where they are supposed to be. This is what the songs are all about—being centered, doing what is right, and remaining where one is placed.

The mountains acted like people who get lost. The holy ones and mountains were helping each other saying, "Look over here, my son. I'm over here. Walk toward me. I'm your mother. I'm the one who is sitting on the east side. I'm this colored holy person. I'm the White Shell Woman here with the white mountain. Son, come back over here and I will give you direction again." That was how they were talking. During the ceremony the songs are sung—Shiyáázh o'óóh oo ei'ąą Shiyáázh o'óóh oo ei'ąą Shiyáázh iowąą iowąą Shiyáázh o'óóh oo ei'ąą Shiyáázh o'óóh oo ei'ąą Shiyáázh ei'ąą iowąą iowąą—the mountain is talking to the lost person saying, "Son come over here. Come back this way. I'll give you better direction. You are lost; your other mother is sitting over there. The other one's sitting over there." The lost child looks around and says, "Oh, yeah. This is my other place and I belong here. Okay, now I'm back in order." This is how the mountain soil is put back together, the songs and prayers concluded, and the bundle tied. During the ceremony a pipe with white tobacco is lit, and its smoke is blown on the first mountain placed in the east. After the mountain to the south is located in its proper position, blue tobacco smoke is blown on it, as is the smoke from yellow tobacco on the western mountain, and black tobacco on the northern mountain. Following the ceremony, the four different colored tobaccos are mixed and placed in a bowl. Anyone participating may take some of the mixture and put it in their tobacco pouch as part of their blessing for future use. Now they have holy tobacco to smoke.

The teachings from this ceremony also apply to individuals. People warn, "This can happen to you. You may become disoriented one day and

*There are various types of tobacco such as mountain tobacco, water tobacco, and so on. Each medicine man will designate the contents of the one he uses, depending upon the ceremony and his training. For instance, Perry specializes in the Enemyway, and so the mountain tobacco pictured here is a mixture of various plants, in some cases up to eighteen different species, and has a strong odor. (Photo by Kay Shumway)*

lose focus of where you belong. But with this mountain smoke and the mountain songs, you will return and be put back in the proper order." In the old days, Navajos traveling a long distance would sing mountain songs, which helped them to stay on the right path. For instance, when I travel to Colorado, I always try to slow down, maybe park somewhere, and sing to Dibé Nitsaa (Hesperus Peak). My song reminds me that I am their child and they are my mother, saying, "I am here. I am singing your song. I am your child sitting here. I am singing your song. Today I am going to have a good day. Today I am going to get something nice with blessings coming my way. I am going to have a good evening and sleep well tonight with my family." When people introduce themselves by singing the mountain songs as they travel near the mountain, they receive protection and better guidance about a lot of things. If they actually go over the mountain, then they should take their corn pollen out, pray, and excuse themselves for traveling on top of this holy one. The same is true no matter which of the Four Sacred Mountains are approached.

# *Gobernador Knob and Huerfano Mesa*

While these mountains are literally central to Navajo thought and being, there are other mountains and formations that have their own powers and responsibilities. Two of them, previously mentioned, are actually mesas— Gobernador Knob and Huerfano Mesa. Medicine people say that when the Yé'ii Bicheii start to emerge in the late fall, they stamp their feet on the ground and dance, moving the earth while one Yé'ii Bicheii sings and makes noise. Then they all say "Whoo-oo-whoo!" which wakes up Huerfano Mesa. The land form starts to rise and turn. If a person goes to the top of the mesa, they can see its form is a circle that comes together. But you have to be at the very top to completely see it. Your mind and eyes work with it; this is why the mesa received its name and is said to be the only mountain that can take people to the spirit world to see things. This place is very sacred and where a medicine man who has lost his focus and forgotten his songs and prayers can sit on top and be renewed, remembering what he has lost. The turn of the mountain will rise with him to a certain level so that the holy people will sit with him and make the necessary corrections.

This practice originated with Monster Slayer and Born for Water, who sat on top for this purpose. They would bathe in one of the rocks that had a large cavity, maybe ten feet wide, that collected water. This big bathtub is a very sacred place. There is a story that few people talk about concerning this mountain and the time that the Twins were still virgins. One day, Monster Slayer and Born for Water sat upon the top of Huerfano Mesa and saw a flash of light from the south. Monster Slayer glimpsed it first, rubbed his eyes, asked his brother if he had seen it, and then wondered who could be signaling them. Born for Water looked and saw the repeating flash. Monster Slayer told him to remain on the mesa while he went to investigate, but once he reached the spot, he found nothing.

He was quite sure he was at the right place, where a wooded area and little mountain came together. Suddenly a bird started singing but was not visible. A nearby tree split open, revealing a blue bird who, when it spread its wings, sent out a blinding flash of light. Monster Slayer immediately covered his face with his hands, but peered through his fingers to see the light dimming. The bird now changed into a naked woman with dark blue hair. The warrior admired her physique, then asked if she had been the one flashing him. She answered that she was; he really liked that. The two continued talking, the woman covered herself after descending from the tree, and the pair spent the afternoon walking and courting. Meanwhile, Born for Water sat atop Huerfano Mesa waiting.

That night, the couple slept together, but in the morning Monster Slayer decided he needed to return to his brother. The woman, however, had different plans, saying that he was now her man. He explained that he was a god and could not be controlled by others, but she insisted. She grabbed his testicles and told him that he may want to go now but that he would return one day. The woman then let go, allowing him to painfully walk back to his brother on the mesa and report what happened. The next day there was another flash—this time yellow—coming from the same area. Born for Water went to investigate and found a warbler bird woman with blonde hair and yellow feathers, whom he slept with that night. Now both of the Twins had lost their virginity. This story is about intimacy and how these women stole the warriors' virginity, giving rise to the saying that the men and women had "stolen each other."[14] The Blue Bird Woman, the Yellow Warbler Woman, and the Twins stole each other and walked away. Elders in the past spoke of how, in the future, children would be like this, would not marry or sit still, would be interested only in sex before going off on their own.

This is the teaching of this mountain that talks about the problem of freely giving away what should be intimate and maintaining one's virginity. When people have sexual problems, they may go to this mountain to work at fixing them, because that is where the teaching and medicine lives. Both men and women have a part in healing the relationship. This story comes from the Coyoteway and is not often discussed by everyday people, even though there is a great need for its teachings. If there is a problem with incest or other forms of inappropriate sexuality, this story provides guidance that can be shared in a sweat lodge ceremony. That is the only time it is told.

## *Other Formations*

Each of the mountains has its own stories with people from different regions having their own versions. For instance, Navajo Mountain (Naatsis'áán—Head of Earth Woman) on the Utah-Arizona border is connected with teachings about the water monster (Tééhooltsódii). That is the one I know. Even the Navajo names of the mountain can be understood in three different ways—one meaning "Head of Earth Woman," another "To Walk on Top," and a third "Underneath There's a Channel." This last one ties in to my knowledge about the underground water flowing from the Navajo Dam area in New Mexico to Navajo Mountain and Rainbow Bridge, where the water monster and the Rain God dwell. It is also said to be the head of another giant female figure whose body is Black Mesa, with legs and feet extending to Balukai Mesa. Another connects Black Mesa or Black Mountain as the home of Black God (Haashch'ééshzhiní bighan), who lives on top of this formation. When he hears songs and prayers for water, he asks Navajo Mountain to assist, so she sings the songs and determines if there will be rain. If clouds cover the Head of Earth Woman, then there will be snow or rain. The rain god who sits at Rainbow Bridge actually sends the moisture.

There is another story that I am not familiar with about a scalp with attached feathers that was cut off and placed to the north beyond the San Juan River so that its harmful influence would not return. Part of it separated and became Navajo Mountain while the remainder went across the river and formed the Henry or "No Name" (Dził Bizhi' Adani) Mountains. This range is not a good place for a Navajo person to go. Since it does not have a name it is lost; people who die and have no sacred name go there. I do not know the rest of the story, but I do know that because it was put in the wrong spot, it could not receive a name. This is how these two mountains are related. My information comes from the Enemyway, but I am sure that other people from different areas will have their own thoughts.

I have a little knowledge of Blue Mountain (Dziłditł'oi—Furry Mountain) based upon teachings about a doe and a black horse with white face and legs. These two animals joined together and were running across the top of the mountain, but the horse got bogged down and froze in the snow on the east side, while the doe sits on the south. The deer's colors only show up in the fall, when the tan markings of the face, the two tips of the ears, yellowish color of her body, and tail are visible. The story about these two is called The Sacredness of the Horse (Yoołgai Yikáá' siziní—The Mountain Has a Horse on It) and is tied to the songs about this mountain. As the water flowed from the mountain to its base, many baby horses came out of it and started walking in different directions. The La Sal Mountains (Dził' Ashdlaii—Five Finger Mountains) also had horses that joined the others and moved to the San Juan River, where they met the Navajo people, who surrounded and chased them across the water. This is how the horse came from the north.

Blue Mountain is connected with the Bears Ears. My understanding about this formation comes from the Bearway ceremony. The story behind it tells of a time when an incurable sickness plagued the people. They had no defense against it and so prayed to the holy ones, which included the Water People, for assistance. From the north arose big black clouds and a violent storm that revealed a large black bear coming to help. As the wind and rain grew fiercer, he enlarged and began emerging out of the earth. The People were singing protection songs as his head poked above the ground. He slowly turned around so that those he would be protecting would be behind him. His eyes and ears faced north, and he was able to see the approaching sickness and hear the prayers, but the songs summoning him were never finished. Now, only part of this animal is visible, but he still defends Navajo land from evil to the north. He is a holy one, so that when a Bearway ceremony is performed, we sing "On the north side he lives to spot things" (Sa sǫ diłhił dził diłhił yikáá'jį' hanádááh k'eet'ą́ą́ yáłti'ii yooléélgo ch'ó yáázh diłhiłii yił yah anádááhii). That is where the prayers are sent. If somebody asks me to perform a Bearway, my words go directly to the Bears Ears, where the prayers and songs start before moving on to other places. In the prayer he says that he has to face north so that he will have the people behind him for protection and that is why he slowly rotated in that direction—"that way my children will stand behind me, and I will be on the opposite side, facing my enemy." Anything that we talk about in the prayers is set behind him, keeping the bad things beyond the Bears Ears in a place where they will not have the power to return. Herbs used in the Bearway are also collected in this area. I have been told that in the past there were certain rock formations where people would go to perform this ceremony, but that knowledge has been lost, and I was never introduced to it.

*The Bears Ears has a second story about why this formation appears as the top of a bear's head. Seen on its east side, one can spot its ears (actually composed of only one of the two ears seen from the south), long snout, and nose. This formation faces north to protect the People from evil coming from that direction. (Photo by Kay Shumway)*

Black Mountain (Dziłíjiin, also called Black Mesa)—bounded by Chinle, Rough Rock, the Hopi Mesas, and Kayenta—is considered one of the most traditional areas of the reservation. People who live on Black Mesa speak of themselves as being above Chinle or above Rough Rock, whose people are unaware of what those living on Black Mesa are like. My father taught that the true version of the Navajo language is spoken here. "If you ever lose your language or how you should talk, go back to Black Mountain. You will get your voice back. Go back over there and you will get your medicine straightened out. Go back over there and you will gather whatever is supposed to be from the beginning. All the other areas on the reservation have just branched off from us; the main stalk or heart of Navajo land is what we call it."

This formation is also viewed as a large hogan that sits at the center of the Four Sacred Mountains with its door near Black Spot Mountain (haashch'ééshzhiní bidéídiníléí or haashch'ééshzhiní boghan), west of Piñon. Black God (Haashch'ééshzhiní), who controls many aspects of traditional practices, lives there with other Black Body Surface People. It is also thought of as a female formation located at the center of the Navajo Nation. Her vital organs keep the land functioning, with all of its coal being her liver. Recent mining of that coal has hurt the land and its people and is considered by some to be a huge violation against Mother Earth. My grandfather never liked it and thought all the minerals should have been left alone. Now, people have lost their land, family, health, and mind—everything—and have died from a broken heart because of the desecration and disrespect. Even its name was sacred because of the black spirit people living there who controlled many aspects of medicine found at this center.

The Chuska-Tunicha mountain range is the male partner of Black Mountain, and from it medicine men collect male water to be used in any ceremony that is considered male. For example there can be a Male Lightningway or Female Lightningway. Water needed for the male version comes from springs and other bodies of water flowing from the Chuska-Tunicha to the Lukachukai Mountains. To the east of the Chuska and Carrizo Mountains lies Shiprock, home in the past of two large monster birds called Tsé nináhádleehí (A Rock That Lays Eggs). These monster birds had two children. Monster Slayer killed the parents and then twirled each of the baby brothers around his head. One became an eagle, the other an owl. The two brothers still look similar, having the same beak and claws, but one has big eyeballs while the other has smaller ones that are protected so that he can see clearly when he flies high and fast. The owl lives and hunts when it is dark, but the eagle was told by Monster Slayer to travel only during the daytime. While the eagle can go through the thinnest air, high into the sky, and then quickly dive to the earth, his eyes will not water and the wind cannot burn them. The owl, on the other hand, sits still but can rotate his head around in all four directions. He does not have to move; his body sleeps, but his head is always awake, looking around. That is the magic that they have. Both of these birds, with their special powers, originated from this rock formation.

# CHAPTER TWO

# *Water, Rivers, and Rain*

## *Sources of Life*

Water, whether falling, resting, running over, or flowing under the land, remains one of the most essential elements of life for the Navajo living in their high desert environment. Little wonder that important holy people control it, there are ceremonies to summon it, and there are a variety of ways to think about it. In this chapter, Perry shares teachings seldom discussed and noticeably absent from the literature. What becomes apparent is that, as impersonal as it may seem to many, water can be both a close friend and a harsh taskmaster that fosters love and reverence while also chiding and teaching. Viewed as one of the four foundational elements of life—along with earth, wind, and fire—water exists to bless the lives of those who respect it.

Rain plays a prominent role in Navajo life and thought and so, not surprisingly, is carefully characterized through the nouns and verbs used to describe it. Rain is either male or female. The former arrives in a downpour that scours the ground and runs in rivulets over the land and into the canyons. It is torrential rain, accompanied by jagged lightning, rumbling thunder, and destructive power. Objects struck by violent male lightning are avoided. Female rain, on the other hand, is accompanied by heat lightning and is a gentle, soaking shower that nurtures crops and lingers over the earth. After rain hits the ground, there is vocabulary to describe what it does—following the earth's contours (Bits'íís Nooltłizhí' Ch'ikę́ę́h), forming temporary waterfalls off cliff edges and excavating pathways through desert soils (ni'biłha'doolkǫ'í tsíłkę́ę́), carrying debris and joining other running water (tó ałtah náshchíín), and getting captured in a rock cavity and never flowing (tó biyáázh). There is also Collected Water (tó áłah náshchíín), used in rainmaking ceremonies such as the one John Holiday describes below. Collected Water is comprised of a number of different types of liquid from springs, hail, and snow, and that found in the four directions sequestered in rock basins or depressions.[1]

As with every aspect of life, there are powers within water that can be influenced for good. When discussing one of the most important deities, Tééhoołtsódii (One Who Grabs in Deep Water), Perry describes this creature from the Second World. Anthropologist Gladys Reichard gives another description, saying this water monster "looks much like an otter with fine fur, but has horns like a buffalo. The young look something like buffalo calves, but have spots of all colors, yellow hands, and a generally strange appearance."[2] This holy one has its own prayersticks, and like its underwater associates, the other Water People (Tó Dine'é), it is generally viewed as quick to anger. "These are mean people . . . and that is why they have no guards; they don't need them. They get angry easily. If anyone talks to them, they get angry and fight. . . . These gods do not have tobacco pouches, only whistles. They carry fir medicine in the right hand for medicine, for a person who gets crazy or is hurt by water."[3]

One of the best illustrations of the water monster's personality is found in the story of the emergence when the trickster, Coyote, stole its baby. Details vary from version to version, but the general narrative shares many of the common elements as found in the one told by Sylvia Manygoats at Navajo Mountain in 1988.[4] It seems Coyote was tired of listening to a baby water monster constantly crying and fussing, and so he decided to act. Stealing and concealing the infant under a black cloud, he opposed the holy people, who warned him not to kidnap this infant or else there would be consequences. He paid no attention. Once the husband and wife water monsters realized the child was missing, they became incensed, especially when no one confessed to the deed. The skies in the four directions grew dark with moisture, the winds increased, and the water surrounding the land began to rise. The water monsters were determined to drown everyone for this crime. As the water spread over much of the land, the people panicked and began searching for an escape route. Finally they planted a fast-growing hollow reed that grew into the sky, allowing the people to crawl through it and away from the rising waters and into the world above. After Locust secured the right for the holy people to move on to this next level, the water monsters followed them, threatening to flood this world, too. In many versions, Coyote, after being pressured by the other holy people, relented and gave the baby back. In Mrs. Manygoats's version, when the male and female monsters reared their heads into this next world, the people placed an abalone shell basket filled with abalone pieces between her horns and a turquoise basket with turquoise pieces between her husband's horns as offerings. "Then they pleaded with the water monsters to let them take the baby with them, so that in the future the people may have plenty of rain, so that the rains may come all of the time."[5] The Tééhoołtsódii agreed, giving rise to the practice of offering "sacred stones" (ntł'iz) for an abundance of rain and a tempering of the elements.

How does this story play out in traditional daily life? Jim Dandy, a Navajo culture teacher raised in the 1940s, said that his grandmother often taught how to act around and with water.

> Do not play in the water, yíiyá (scary!). You should not be in the water when it looks like it is going to rain, and do not go near the water while clouds are forming because lightning will strike. These teachings began when Coyote angered the power in water and stole its baby. You should not go swimming, even if it has just barely rained, but rather stay away because of what Coyote did. A lot of times when someone's reservoir gets really full, people say that there is a lot of power in the water and so you should not play or swim in it. Also, you should not throw or splash water on people as a joke; that is like spitting on a person, neither of which is polite. The only time you can play with water is when you think it is going to rain, but even then there needs to be a prayer said. . . . When rain begins to fall, you should sit down, be quiet, and respectful. There is no hunting in the rain because having a weapon that is sharp is offensive to lightning and does not show respect to the water, while killing opposes life that comes with rain.[6]

There are many other taboos associated with water: one should only drink from a pool of water with some type of cup or dipper; never point at a rainbow with a finger but only one's thumb because the finger is straight like an arrow while a thumb is not; rain during a healing ceremony is beneficial unless there is thunder and lightning, which can be harmful; and when water is used to bathe someone ceremonially, once the washing is finished, the water cannot be disposed of so that it will flow toward the patient. All of these taboos result in sickness and possibly death, because the water has been disrespected and is angered.[7] The same holds true in crossing a river, swimming in a lake, eating fish and other water creatures, moving about during thunderstorms, and weaving while it is raining. Respect is fundamental in this relationship.

Maintaining the land through rainfall is an important concern for the Navajo. For those unable to use flood irrigation in river beds or channel irrigation through the fields, dry farming supported by what falls from the sky is extremely important. Perry's story about surviving a drought and having the holy people release rain upon the land is told in detail here and is mentioned at other times because of its importance. The same story, shared in *Grandfather Stories of the Navajos*, with variations, offers another version of the Navajo Ceremony for Rain (Níłtsą́ Bíkáh Nahaaghá).[8] Some of these elements are worth noting to confirm important concepts at work in the ceremony. In this second version, Gopher (not mole) serves as the go-between among the earth surface beings and the Water People. Frog serves as a spokesman, Coyote as purveyor of seeds (not ntł'iz), the visit to the water monster(s) on the twelve stairs (not ladders), and the eventual releasing of rain after people grew respectful of the holy people, are important aspects in bringing rain to a desert land.

An abbreviated account of an experience by medicine man John Holiday illustrates how many of these elements work together. The entire Southwest had been trapped in an extensive two-year drought (1930–31) known as Horses Died of Hunger (Łį́į́' Dichin Bííghą́ą́'). It had dried up existing water sources, shriveled the vegetation, decimated crops, and challenged herds of livestock. The people turned to various medicine men to summon the rains but to no avail. A crystal gazer identified that there was one person who could help, and so a delegation went to John Holiday's father's home to request assistance. His father pointed to John's grandfather, Metal Teeth, and said that he could perform the ceremony; following a discussion, the men agreed. John, who was twelve years old at the time and had been apprenticing under his grandfather, was shocked when his mentor turned to him and told him that he was the one who would perform it. With only a couple of days to prepare, the two went to work and rehearsed everything necessary and then traveled to Douglas Mesa to conduct the ceremony. Following the erection of the ceremonial hogan, holding different sweats, obtaining water from sacred springs in the four directions, and having a young male and female about John's age appointed to serve as Rain Boy and Rain Girl, the ceremony began. John recounts:

> We crawled inside the hot sweat lodge and sat down. Then out of nowhere, we heard a frog croaking. "Shine the light inside, open the blanket door. Let's see where it is coming from! These are the sounds of Female Rain Girl (Níłtsą́ At'ééd) and Male Rain Boy (Níłtsą́ Ashkii). There they are, sitting side by side in the farthest corner of the hogan. Catch them and throw them in the puddle outside!" they said. The men caught the two frogs and threw them in the puddle. The poor little frogs were taking a sweat bath too, but were removed and placed in the water with a splash! We continued our sweat while the frogs croaked in the puddle.
>
> After the ceremony, I went to the water to wash and did the sacred wash ritual on the young boy and girl. . . . After the bath everyone covered themselves with ground-corn powder and spread a large blanket outside for

the offerings of ntł'iz. This is the part of the ritual when the little stone offerings are selected and put together to take to a sacred spot, prayed over, and left. Before we went with these offerings, there was a request made by the men who came from faraway places. They wanted to take some of these sacred stones with them to their homes because it was not raining there, too. Grandfather said, "No, I don't do it like that. I place all the sacred stones in one place only." We took them to one little spot near the mesa where there was a small oasis of water. I said the prayers as we laid down the offerings, speaking to the four sacred points of the earth. While I was doing this, there was a sound of thunder, then another, but there was not a cloud in the sky and it was very hot. Suddenly a cloud began to form above us, and just as I finished the prayers, it started to rain! The clouds poured forth buckets of water. It was a longways back to the homestead, and our handmade moccasins became soaking wet. Streams of water were everywhere, going in every direction. Once we arrived home, we did the one night Blessingway. It rained so hard that it snowed, covering the sand dunes with a thick blanket of white moisture. Ribbons of water flowed among the sand dunes as it rained and rained for four days, proving our sacred songs and prayers a success. It was holy.[9]

John, like many medicine men, had other fruitful experiences in summoning rain to a parched land.

A final point is that Perry, here and elsewhere, mentions Navajo Mountain as a prime area for rainmaking, water-producing, and summoning the holy people associated with both. Karl Luckert in *Navajo Mountain and Rainbow Bridge Religion* provides a fascinating and complex study of how this area, with the male San Juan River flowing over the female Colorado River, creates water (as babies) and is connected to mountain and rainbow, earth and sky, for the welfare of man. Prayers, songs, and ritual come together in petitioning the heavens at the beginning of each summer for the moisture that the people will need to sustain themselves for another year in the dry deserts of the Southwest. Since the creation of Lake Powell and the tourist industry promoting Rainbow Bridge, much of this has stopped.

## *Controlling Water and Its Inhabitants*

Water is a very important part of Navajo life with many different teachings. No matter where the water is located—oceans, rivers, streams, ponds, lakes, underground, or as precipitation—it is connected and controlled. Whether on the earth or in the air, there is an all-directing water being or holy one called Chief of All Water or Living Being Over All (Tsoyánádleeh), who lives in the underworld and manages the different water systems on, under, and over the ground. His reach is spread to all water, which is maintained mostly on the surface, where it is circulated and regulated. He and his brother, Tééhoołtsódii (One Who Grabs in Deep Water), are water gods who work together in and under the water. Tééhoołtsódii takes orders from his older brother but is the main influencing force. He controls rain and surface waters and is represented in Navajo ceremonies as Water Sprinkler (Tó Neinilii), whose mask is painted blue with white trim, whose horns symbolize power, and whose body is covered with stars. He and his brother look quite similar. The Water Horse (Tééh łį́į́') is the pet of Tééhoołtsódii and guards his home.

Another holy being that lives in the water is Child of the Rainbow (tó biyáázh). Its body is silver with rainbow colors running beneath, just like a fish. This creature's face is a combination of an amphibian and a fish with wide eyes, nose, and mouth adapted for use underwater. A Child of the Rainbow flashes when it moves. Sometimes I try to figure out how it really looks, but the best description I can find in the songs is that it has a silvery color on its sides and a rainbow on its stomach, just as frogs and fish have iridescent coloring beneath. All of the fish and other creatures that live in the water are related as brothers and sisters and are considered water's children. Their story goes back to Shash Agháanii, when the water from the lake leaked into the ocean and a water horse (tééh łį́į́') came back to live in the water. He was to serve as a messenger to his master and be the keeper of the lake. People started to disappear when they entered those waters and became fearful. The water horse promised not to be a problem, so as a sign of his good will, he became connected to the sacredness of the rainbow. Navajo people now walk into the rainbow, a symbol that represents being safe, protected, and prosperous. All the colors stand for peace and security. As part of this agreement, there were the rainbow's children such as geese, ducks, amphibians, different kinds of fish—especially the rainbow trout, eels, and snake-type fish. They all have the same shape, facial features, and eyes. One or two may represent the entire group, they say.

These creatures' connection to the rainbow can be seen in their outer skin or feathers that have an iridescent sheen. For example, the mallard duck carries the rainbow on the top of its wing and underneath its bill. Ducks live in the water above amphibians whose feet are similarly webbed, while the duck's head belongs to the sky, where it flies. Ducks are considered sacred because of their ability to operate in both worlds. Geese have rainbows on the tips of their tail feathers; remember they are also the ones who give directions as messengers by the way that they fly to a person who is searching for an answer. The rainbow always sits in a ceremonial place, as

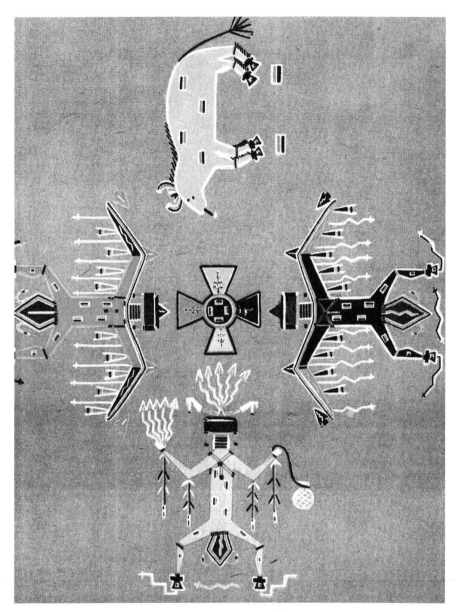

*Water Ox (Monster) and Water Horse are extensively associated with water. The thunder beings have wings instead of arms, their feet are cloud symbols that rest on short rainbows, and the tails have rain designs, while the curves at the bottom represent reverberations of thunder. The wings hold rainbows and thunder. Water Monster and his horse stand upon and bear short rainbows; lightning and a water bowl are controlled by the monster.*

can be seen in sandpaintings. They are always drawn in sets of four, and when mentioned in songs, they are asked to share their healing power.

It does not make sense to eat the power that heals a person seeking a cure. Geese, ducks, fish, and amphibians are not supposed to be eaten because of the powers found in them and their ability to reflect back the rainbow. If for some reason a person started eating one of these creatures, the thunderstorm would not hesitate to harm him. Through thunder and lightning they talk to that person and make them sick for playing with their medicine. That is why the old people in the past would not even think about bothering rainbow children. Today, things have changed. All kinds of fish are readily available in the market, so much of this teaching is ignored.

There are many different types of water, and all are related. Ocean water (tónteel) is considered male, while fresh water is female. Fresh water can be further separated into male and female water due to source—rivers, streams, and so on—or location or ceremonial function. Fresh water is female (tó yisdzáán) because it nurtures people, grows food, and allows us to create a home near where it is available. Water that comes from the ocean is used only for certain ceremonies and is considered to be undesirable because it is powerful, rough, and violent. It is associated with tornadoes and hurricanes that live on the ocean. Their winds and water have an angry attitude that brings destructive storms and other forms of harmful weather. There is nothing really good about ocean water because it is rough, has a bitter taste, and is not even really considered water. Because sea water has this bad temperament, Navajos use it in the Windway or Hailway ceremonies to work against the strong winds of an illness caused by storms, lightning, rain, and dark winds. It has male power used in male ceremonies to push or blow a bad influence away from a person who needs healing and to get rid of something. The patient washes in sea water and makes an offering back to the ocean. My grandfather used to have a ceremony that used ocean water, but I never really questioned him about it. He rarely performed it. Regardless, whether fresh or salt water, bodies of water are holy ones.

## *Drought and the Message of Respect*

There is a very old story about when the gods stopped sending the rain and snow, giving rise to a terrible drought. There was no moisture, so the green plants died, birds stopped flying, and chaos was everywhere. The dry spell dragged on as the people suffered with no end in sight. The animals talked among themselves, asking what had happened and where the water had gone. Ceremonies did not bring it back; nothing seemed to work. They decided to hold a large gathering in a sweat lodge to discuss the direction they should take to end this problem. The creatures removed their outer forms before entering so that they appeared as humans. People say that this is one of the only times that this was done for a sweat lodge ceremony. The animals decided to talk to Mole, who was always burrowing underground, working in moist soil. He did not know how to contact the holy beings who controlled the water, but suggested that Frog would. The animals asked him to bring Frog a message, that they needed to speak to him. He agreed to go.

In the area where Navajo Dam (Nihwiizdzáán) is located today, there is a place called Where the Waters Crossed (Tó ahidiidlį—the junction of the Los Pinos and San Juan Rivers). Frog met the animals there and agreed to help. After holding a Blessingway ceremony, they went to a dried pond bed, removed a chip of mud from the bottom in its center, and then started digging. When the hole was about three feet deep, the animals poured water into it, gave an offering to Frog after painting him red, and watched him descend to the realms below. Using twelve rainbow ladders, he reached the home of the two rainmaking brothers (Tsoyánádleeh and Tééhoołtsódii), where he inquired why there was no water on the land above. The brothers pointed out that they had not been given proper respect and that the animals were not mindful of their prayers. If that problem was corrected, and a meaningful offering given, the water would return. The rainmakers sat there and told Frog, "We want an offering of sacred stones (ntł'iz). Then we will bring the rain back."

Upon returning to the surface, Frog told the animals what was needed and how to get it. After waiting and praying near a water hole, they saw Coyote enter in from the east, go down into a small pool of water, come out, and shake his fur, from which fell a white shell. Later Coyote approached from the south, did the same thing, but dropped a turquoise stone; another time from the west, he shook himself and deposited an abalone shell; and from the north he shook out a piece of jet. These were the ingredients of the sacred stones that the rainmaking brothers had requested. The animals made their offering with prayers and the rains came. Now, when medicine men perform the Waterway ceremony, there are twelve songs, each of which marks a level of descent into the earth, representing the twelve ladders Frog used to move below. A rainmaking ceremony discussed later follows exactly the pattern outlined in this story. Waterway and Blessingway songs and prayers about water were developed at this time as the animals danced and brought the rain back.

Participants learned the structure of this ceremony, the language to be used, and how they should pray for the needs of the people. They also learned about showing respect to the sun, thunderstorm, air, and Mother

Earth. They could no longer take these things for granted but made offerings to express appreciation. This was also the time when they understood how to work with the elements that affect weather. Their life was now back in order because of renewed spirituality so that they could live well. This story ties in with the previously discussed sacred water monsters living in the four directions at Rainbow Bridge, the meeting of the Colorado and Little Colorado Rivers, and the Gila River. These are important beings who control much of what happens with water on the earth's surface in those areas.

*Navajo Mountain, as Head of Earth Woman, is associated with Rainbow Bridge and the junction of the San Juan with the Colorado River. All of these land features bring water to the region and provide sites where people pray and leave offerings for this blessing. The result—bountiful crops like the corn and squash pictured in the foreground. (Photo by Stan Byrd)*

## *Water and Weather*

Showing proper respect to the elements is still very important. For instance, thunderstorms arrive at certain times of the year and announce their presence, but one never knows what direction they will come from. The storm will make itself known by a booming noise that bounces off the earth in an echo, so when medicine people pray, they call them The Earth and Sky Echo (seinibii'náhosiiltsá'í and yábii'nahosiilts'á'í). The sound comes down to the earth's level, then bounces back to the sky, connecting the two. The storm proclaims it is coming, bringing rain, and letting people know that spring and summer are here. Within the thunderstorm there is a leader who controls it. There is also an overall leader of all the thunderstorms on the earth; both leaders must be approached through prayer with high respect. The prayers are communicated to the main leader who controls the lesser storms. If I were to talk to an approaching storm, I would say something like: "I speak to you as the holy one that makes the noise in the sky. You are the leader of all of the thunderstorms. I pray to you this way (Nibii'nahosiiltsą'ą́ tsíłkéí naat'áanii)." The first clap of thunder in the spring awakens hibernating animals—lizards, bears, and all the others who have been dormant during the winter months. When they hear the thunderstorm, they arouse, know warmer weather is here, and feel the need to start moving about. This first echo of thunder is usually a fierce show of spring time.

Occasionally during the middle of winter, there may also be a thunderstorm. This is connected to what is called the White Rainbow, which does not show colors except for a white arch in the sky that appears at this time of year. Very few people sing or pray to the White Rainbow, who is anxious to be recognized. When it appears, people look at its white mists and begin to pay attention—the rainbow wants his song. Nobody ever sings to it except in a few different ceremonies. Once it hears its songs, it is ready to give rain, but at the outset this rainbow announces things that are not good that will take place in the near future. The accompanying rain and thunder are a visit by the gods who are part of this warning, as are the Northern Lights, which may appear unexpectedly at night. An example of this type of caution came with the influenza epidemic of 1918, disclosing that the sickness was fast approaching. In the old days, people prayed about things that were out of the ordinary, hoping that nothing bad would happen, that it would just pass. Before the flu epidemic arrived, the White Rainbow and Northern Lights appeared low in the sky. A place north of Piñon called Mountain That Crashed (Kits'iilí) had major rock slides that destroyed much of this formation. The elders viewed the mountain falling apart as a warning of what was to come and named the place The Rock That Slides. The inhabitants understood that this was a sign that a lot of people were going to die, and they did. Children and elders became very sick and passed on, and a lot of ceremonies took place as the disease continued to spread. The Northern Lights also foretold what would happen, as it and the White Rainbow sat over some of the sheep camps. This plague came in for no reason and sickened the people, the prairie dogs, and the sheep—any animal that ate grass became ill. There is always a warning like this when something bad is going to happen.

The hair on the head holds important teachings. They all connect back to the story about a rug and the woman who wove with lightning. On top where the strings are separated by the sticks, that is where the warp or rain flows down to the bottom of the loom. The rain, thunder, and lightning fall downward, just as the medicine man with a beard and mustache has that facial hair representing the same thing. He carries the rain from his chin to his chest. When he sits and prays for moisture, it comes down just like his mustache. He is the one who makes the connection of water to plants. He talks to them, they understand he is helping to grow all of this, and so their roots, which hold the medicine, go deep into the ground. That is how healing and the medicine man work together with the rain.

The same is true with a person's hair that, when it is taken down during a ceremony or at death, it represents the rain falling from the sky and also darkness. There is a story about a young man who had long hair. One day he was running away from the enemy, and even though he moved fast, they were getting closer. He started to cry, kept running, but did not know what to do, sure that his days were now numbered. His pace increased with frenzied strides, and as he did so, his hair began unraveling from his hair bun (tsiiyééł). Reaching behind, he pulled the remainder out of its coil so that it floated behind him. As the enemy approached, he tripped and fell, grabbed his leg so that he was in a crouching position, and let his hair settle over and cover him. Sure that the enemy knew where he was, he decided to quietly accept his fate and waited to die. His black hair blended into its dark surroundings so that the enemy did not detect him, only seeing what they thought was a rock against a dark background. His hair had saved this young warrior. Later, he talked and thanked it for the help. The hair spoke back: "Even though I saved you, I will not do it every time. Only in times of great stress and need, like a loss in the family, sickness that requires a special ceremony, or when nearing death, should hair not be worn in a bun. This is just one time that I'm telling you how it works." So until something drastic happens, a man or woman will keep their hair tied up. Once there is a need, they will sit in a crouched position and give prayers, just as the young man who feared for his survival. This is done only in a life or death situation. Hair, when down, also represents what is called the Black Rain and is part of the Black Thunderstorm associated with men and male rain.

# *Reflections of Personality*

During the story of the People's emergence into the White World, Coyote is said to have stolen two babies belonging to the water monster. After searching about and demanding their return, the water monsters became very angry and caused the waters to rise and flood the land in the world beneath, forcing the people and animals into this world. The water itself was filled with anger until Coyote returned the babies and the flood subsided. Today water, like the wind, maintains this attitude and is quick to punish and rage against people if provoked. The wind has the worst temper. It will blow, throw people around, knock them over, and break or destroy something around a person's home if they are not careful. There are all different types of winds and water, and each has its own beings and personalities. Some of them are good and calm, while others are testy and quick to destroy. If individuals cross their boundaries and offend, take something that belongs to them, or do something else disrespectful, then there are going to be problems. Water or wind will react. If one can talk to them, the anger may subside as they recognize the person and his or her intent. If one is in an area that is foreign, the water will respond in a different way according to the local people who live there. In the same way, if one is angry within and approaches the water in that state of mind, it is not going to be a good presentation, and the water will sense it. In other words, if someone is standing there mad, it will respond in the same way.

Water and fire are brothers. Like many things in this world, they can either help or harm, depending on how they are used. While they may have anger within, it is not until it is used in a harmful way that there is a problem. If a person is not careful with how either one is used, then it can hurt people. If someone takes water and curses everything in its path, that anger can be passed on and be destructive. Any tool or object can be used to hurt and cause problems, just as fire and water can be very ruinous, can kill or create life, or can provide comfort. In either case it can shift one's emotions. It is the individual who makes the decision as to how something is going to bless or curse. Just as Changing Woman showed in her life, change is always going to be before us, so it is up to us to make good choices or bad choices with the consequences being determined by the person making the decision. It is not the gods that are doing it, but you.

When crossing a river, a person needs to pray to the being within and excuse himself for going through or over the water. In the past, when riding through the Green, Colorado, San Juan, Gila—any river—corn pollen would be sprinkled into it and the reason for traveling explained. Prayers for protection as one journeys beyond the bounds of safety and into a "foreign land" are given to protect the traveler with the power of the holy one in the river. This ties into the story of Killer Bear (Shash Agháanii), discussed earlier, and the rivers. In that story, a water monster (tééh łį́į́') gave birth to a baby boy who also had the qualities of a bear. When a person is crossing a river, it is important that respect is shown to both the water monster and the Killer Bear, who are related, or else the traveler can be dragged into the water by the water monster and drowned. By excusing oneself before going into the water, the Killer Bear and the water monster allow the person to pass through without harm. But if not, then like the young man trying to escape, the water monster will claim the traveler for his own. Every story has teachings that tell what to do or not do, what is important to learn, and how to carry oneself. Never just sleep and cross the river. You always wake each other up and say, "Hey, we're ready to cross the river. Get up and get your corn pollen out." That is what the elders always used to say.

Water is literally a reflection of oneself. When people look into a lake or pond, they will see themselves in it. In the old days, when someone was returning home from a long trip, they would go to a water hole near their hogan, look into it, and leave an offering. As they peered into the water, their reflection told the water that they were home and that they were still part of that water. If one's tears fall into the pool, then a real connection has been made where part of that person is now in the water just as part of the water is in that person. This was almost like hugging your mother when you return home. Now that you were safely back, things would be good, and the earlier connection with this site is renewed. People say that this is a real, honest emotion that sits with this. Navajos used to do it, sit there, crying and praying for themselves. This was particularly true when they returned from Fort Sumner and were back in their land. The people were so grateful that they were home; but this was not just true about the distant past—those coming back from Vietnam also did it. When a son safely returned, a parent might go to a pond or spring and cry into the water on their behalf and say, "Thank you for returning my son. He is home now and will not be going anywhere like that again."

The same is true when a patient goes to a medicine man for help. He will ask where they are from and then will tell the person that they need to go back to a sacred water hole that is in their area. The individual returns to this "home" site and leaves an offering with prayers. He or she belongs to that water hole and their tears renew the connection that is part of them. Their reflection confirms this. This is also true no matter what water a person goes to because all water is connected, will recognize the individual, and say, "You are my son." If a person goes halfway across the United States and prays at a lake, that water will already know and accept him. All one has to do is show their face in the water, and the power will be there. It is almost like a mirror with the individual sitting in it. If it is at fast-moving water, like a river, where the image is not visible, it does not matter. People used to place their hands in the water, then put it on their face and body as a blessing. No matter how you do it, you make connection.

*Edward S. Curtis named this 1904 photo "Native Mirror," although the reality goes much deeper. Water identifies with each individual on a personal level by reflecting their mood, situation, and personality. Like a mother, it greets one after an absence and has the ability to bless lives. (Courtesy Library of Congress— Photo 100843)*

In Navajo thought, rivers are also like humans and need to be treated that way. The holy being in the water (tók'ehashíín) makes the water lively. One day it will be running fast, strong, and forceful, when at another time it is slow and sluggish. Water makes different noises and has different colors during the seasons of the year. In summer, the water appears blue-green from a distance, at other times it is brown or reddish-yellow. As a person watches the water, the tears in the eye see and reflect back to the river, and according to medicine people, connect the two. Rainbow's Children live inside the water. When I go to the river or lake to perform a ceremony, I work with the water being sitting there, who accepts the water offering. I talk to the river; I talk to the water, saying, "Tell me how you feel, what you think." Soon the water will be calm, but as you start giving the offering, it begins to move and then talks to you. It may splash water over my face, making communication between both of us, just as with a live person. I consider and treat it as a living being. Water is also viewed as a part of life itself. No matter how you look at it, they say, "If I'm going to live a good life, I'm going to drink a lot of water. It makes me live. If you do not drink water, you are going to dry up." Navajos consider water as life, so a spring, river, lake, or pond can stand for that and have its own purpose.

## *Means of Protection*

A river is either male or female—the Rio Grande to the east, female; Little Colorado, to the south, male; Colorado River to the west, female; and San Juan River to the north, male. When any one of them is crossed, it is viewed as leaving a friendly, familiar, and safe place and entering into the unknown and uncontrolled space away from the homeland. There can be enemies or new and beneficial adventures and opportunities, with the river a clear boundary between safety and danger. This is just like life—a person can stay within their accustomed space and be safe and secure, but there is often a desire to encounter new opportunities and growth, even though risk and obstacles are possibilities. All of the water, whether in a male or female river, is considered female and is addressed in prayers and songs as Mother Water (Tó asdzą́ą́), just as is a female mountain (dził yisdzáán).

I had an experience that illustrates the power of the holy being that lives in water and how it assists people. About the time I first started performing ceremonies, my twelve-week-old daughter became very sick with meningitis. I did not even know what this illness was, but I could see a large lump on top of her head and witnessed her sickness. My wife and I took her to Primary Children's Hospital in Salt Lake City and turned her over to the doctors. They said that she could not have any water because the water in her body was accumulating and could kill her. She was drowning in her own fluid, and so to add to that would only harm rather than help. She cried and tried to touch me, but she was in a cage—an incubator with metal and plastic all around—like an animal. I felt so badly and kept asking if she was going to get better, but the doctors did not know. They did not have a lot of confidence that she would live. Rarely do children walk away from this illness.

I couldn't sleep, thinking, "What would Grandfather do? What had Grandfather told me about things like this?" I remembered him talking about children coming from and the holy ones working through water. All of this was taking place around the first time I actually talked and prayed with the holy people to cure someone. I decided to try to heal her myself and so called upon my life feather (iiná—The Holy One That Never Touched the Ground), which is an eagle feather given to me by my grandfather. Next I headed into the mountains near the hospital and found a very pure, clean stream running down the south side of a slope. Taking the feather, I alerted the holy beings, saying, "I'm going to take this feather and dip it into the water" then began praying using the words and songs that were put into the water. With the life feather I brushed the water into a small glass Alka Seltzer bottle while recognizing the holy one and asking, "I want you to heal my daughter." I talked about it, cried, and meditated.

I returned to the hospital even though I knew it was against medical orders for me to give her water. The doctors told me that if I did, that I had to remove her from their care, take her home, and not bring her back. I said, "That is okay. I have the medicine for her." I took her out of the incubator, made her drink the water then rubbed it on her body saying, "You will get well with this." I put my trust in that holy being and went against medical orders. My wife and I walked away from that situation and found the next day that the baby was better; the lump diminished, then disappeared. I returned to the same spot for more water and prayed once again, but this time I took her with me so that I could put water directly on her. Within a week's time, she was back to normal without any further medication, only the water had healed her.

A week and a half after I had removed her from the hospital, I took my daughter back. The doctor who told me what was going to happen was there and so I showed her to him. I said, "Look at her. You told me what was going to happen to her if she had the holy water, but look at her." After examining her, he asked what I had done. "I am a medicine man ordained to do this, so I pray with water and this is the way it works." He really liked the idea and said, "I have another young baby over here with the same problem." This was a black infant; I did the same thing again, and sure enough, she got better, too. This is how I know that the holy ones were in the water. With my daughter's situation, the doctors told me that her brain might have damage and that she would not be able to learn as she was supposed to—she later earned a master's degree and today has a job as a social worker. Soon after this experience, we returned to Evanston, Wyoming, where I was working at the time.

## *Sacred Springs and Ponds*

Springs are highly respected. If one is close to your home, it may have been one of the sacred places marked by your clan members in the past and a place where you may go to say your prayers and make offerings. The water will not come through the earth unless there is a purpose for it. There is a reason why it comes out of nowhere, and that is why it is considered a holy place, given a sacred name, and provided offerings, making it possible for an individual to identify as belonging to this pool as her home. You are a child of this water, and Born for Water is who you are. If you are a woman, you are represented as Born for Water's child, and if a male you are Monster Slayer's child. This is how a man and woman are separated in all prayers when using the Twins for identity, and this is how one recognizes oneself, by saying, "I am Monster Slayer" or "I am Born for Water," and then "I am your child, you are my mother." The reflection of your face into the water then back to your face confirms that you are home and recognized. Every time you pray, especially after a long trip, you mention the location of the water hole then say, "My mother, I am home. This is where I put my corn pollen. Where this water hole sits is where I put my four sacred stones (ntł'iz). Through this water hole I make myself known. I am its son and there is my home." This is how you pray and make offerings.

Other tribes, like the Hopi, also view these springs as some of the holiest, most magical places that they know. Every year they leave their villages to do offerings, even if it is on Navajo land. They excuse themselves and tell the people that they are coming through, and we understand. In the old days, there was no such thing as saying, "This is my land, get off." The springs were respected as holy ones, so it did not matter what tribe or which people were making an offering. It was open to all. When I was a boy living in Piñon, there were four different sacred places/springs in the mountains nearby. The Hopis used to visit them as a group and pray at each one separately, traveling in a sunwise circuit. Before arriving, they would make themselves known, and once there, the Navajos would gather and pray with them. Later, there would be a feast at Shungopavi or whatever other village these Hopis had come from. They invited the Navajos to participate in the Harvest Day feast. This is how important these ceremonies at the water hole could be. The two different groups stuck together, prayed together, and bonded through ritual. Springs united and encouraged them to honor each other's ways.

Beginning in the 1930s, there was a lot of water resource development on the reservation. Springs, underground aquifers, and windmills began to change the face of the land. The sacred springs around Piñon became important sites for development and so were forced to pump more water, were encased in concrete, and were provided with cement catch basins. At first people continued to offer prayers and give blessings with the captured water, but as time progressed, the wells and springs became purely functional and no longer holy places of prayer. Today, Navajos leave trash

*Pools, springs, and ponds are not only a lifeline to those living in the desert, but also are places to appeal for a restoration of the land during a drought. Each spot has its own power and control, but all are viewed as one connected whole. Prayers and offerings release power in a positive relationship.*

in them and pay little attention to these traditional sites, especially now that a lot of people have running water in their homes. This bothers the earth and water and is one of the reasons that there are many droughts and problems on the land.

Artesian wells are highly respected. They are different than regularly drilled wells because water comes to the surface on its own, and some kind of dam is built to capture and store that water. In the past, people would dig a hole twenty feet deep and line it with rocks in a sunwise or clockwise circle, starting with the bottom and extending to the top as the water filled in. This was done in the early 1900s to save water, but by the 1960s and 1970s, drilled water wells with pumps were added.

Rainmaking associated with pools and ponds is a very delicate situation because it has to follow the exact details found in the story of when it was first performed. For example, if you go to a dry pond where there was once water, there will be cracks and small pieces of mud in a broken pattern of chips with raised edges. Whoever is doing the ceremony studies the empty basin, then goes to the center, where the water used to be. There he will pick up one of those crinkled chips to use as a ceremonial piece and will set it aside. Where it had been, he begins to dig into the ground with a cane or planting stick called a gish. This three-to-four-foot wooden staff is painted with the four sacred colors in five-inch sections, starting with white, blue, yellow, and then black, representing the Four Worlds. The black tip does the digging, goes down deep enough to reach moisture, and then stops. On the top of the gish is painted a footprint that has its own markings and two feathers attached. The staff is used like a digging stick in the old days to discover water. Even though it is dry, the person digging will reach subsurface water and then will use the wet soil and moisture for praying.

The origin of the digging stick goes back to the time of White Shell Woman as she traveled with the original Navajo clans. During their return to the desert from the north, there were occasions when the people needed to find water. Each clan received a holy stick to help them in their search for water, with each one taking turns on a certain day to dig. One clan found water, but it was very bitter, giving them the name of Bitter Water (Tódich'íi'nii). Another group, Big Water (Tótsohnii), also found water, as did the Tó'ahaní (Near the Water) Clan. These names are based on the types of water they found as they dug with their stick. This is the same kind of staff or digging stick used for planting and is connected with water in both instances.

After the hole is dug the same length as the staff and widened at the bottom, a frog is found, painted red, and placed in it. Corn pollen is put all around its mouth and then sprinkled on top as prayers are said. The medicine person also places the four crushed sacred stones in the hole with him as an offering and then pours water on top, filling the small opening made for the frog. This water is collected from an old sacred water hole, spring, or creek, which is given an offering of sacred stones, a mud chip from the dried pond bottom, and prayers. The medicine man has brought this water to assist the frog by pouring it into this hole, where it seeps down to the bottom. This gives the frog the moisture he needs to descend to the levels beneath. The more help he receives, the better he will do. One of the dry flakes of mud from the empty pond is put on top of him, and then the freshly dug dirt is placed back in the hole with another mud chip placed on top. The frog has been asked to go deep down, find the rainmakers, and request that they send water back to the surface of the ground. The amphibian knows what to do and starts his journey, digging his way to the underworld. This is just as in the story I told before.

The medicine man next takes a flake of mud that he had initially removed from the dry pond and brings it to the top of a mountain with more sacred stones. He tells the mountain that he is making an offering to it through the highest point that reaches into the sky. This is often the tallest tree and is called the First Tree (Ni' Yiyah Niizíní Yá Yiyah Niizíní) and the closest place in contact with the heavens. It is a type of sky supporter (Yá Yiyah Niizíní) just as is Shiprock and El Capitan—volcanic necks that keep the sky above and the earth beneath as they act as large support columns. This is as close as the sky can get to the earth and provides the next level at which birds can fly. The tree that touches the heavens is the highest point that also maintains gravity to keep things on the ground and not in the air so that everything sits in its correct place. The earth's surface includes as far as the eye can see into the sky until the air gets too thin and then stops. The air pushes water and other things down so that they do not fly off, while the tree holds the sky in place.

When a medicine man goes to the mountain, he prays at that tree, leaving the offerings beneath and the songs at that place. This is called "painting the mountain." After the medicine man sings his songs for rain, the next evening he holds a Blessingway ceremony, where he and others chant all night. The songs of this ceremony are connected with the earth, the mountains, the morning dawn, and evening sunset—all of the holy beings in the different directions have their songs sung at that time. Everything becomes connected through it. In the middle of the ceremony, there is a prayer that says, "This is the reason we are giving these prayers. This is why we want the rain here. There are new crops in the ground, and so we are asking for an abundant harvest in the future. The grass needs to be green again, the earth needs to be green again, and the mountains will be happy. We all want to be happy together." This is why the Blessingway is used. Soon a storm will approach. This is how I was told that ceremony is performed. I do not think many people practice it anymore, but that is the old way it was done.

My grandmother told a story about how she obtained water. She spent one quiet summer day weaving but eventually grew tired and wanted to rest, so she took an afternoon nap. Grandmother unrolled the blanket that she had been sitting on, spread it out on the floor, and lay down. Everything was so quiet, she quickly dozed off but soon awoke to an unfamiliar noise. She wondered what it was, looked about, cleaned her ears, then lay back down, only to hear it again. The noise seemed to be coming from the ground. It started to bother her, but as she listened, she realized it was running water. She asked my grandfather to listen, saying, "There is something down there.

I want you to dig it out. I want you to dig down there and see what it is. There's something moving in the earth beneath the hogan." Grandfather placed his ear on the ground and agreed that he could hear it, too. He took his digging stick and began burrowing into the soil. Three to four feet down he found a frog sitting in mud and water, spinning around and around. He removed the frog and noticed a lot more water. Grandfather mentioned how dry the summer had been and felt that his new friend was there for a reason. He took him to a dry pond nearby, dug a hole with a sacred stick, put him into it, gave him corn pollen, poured water on top, and placed a crusted flake in the hole. He commanded, "Give us some rain. Go tell your people we need rain." Taking the staff that he had used to dig, he marked a level on the side of the pond that he wanted the water to rise to, but then decided to play with the request a little bit. He said, "Why just fill up the pond? Let's have this thing run over." So he scratched it over the top with his digging stick, and then marked beyond the edge all the way around, saying, "This is how much water I want."

By evening he saw clouds forming, and that night it started raining. At noon the following day he returned to the pond and found it overflowing on the markings he had made. Eventually the retaining wall of the pond burst, channeling water into the valley below and taking all of his corn crop with it. My grandmother was furious. She scolded, "You are only supposed to mark a little way inside the pond, not so far over. Look what you have done. Now our whole crop is washed away." That sacred staff is holy, and when you make the marking in four different directions, that indicates how deep the water is going to be in that pond. He wanted to clown around and did more than that.

# CHAPTER THREE

# Up in the Air

## Wind, Moon, Stars, and Weather

While this chapter is concerned with different aspects of things found in the sky and the heavens above, there is nothing "up-in-the-air" about the extensive Navajo teachings that exist on this topic. The sun, moon, stars, winds, and weather have distinct inner personalities that tie directly to ceremonial and daily life. Entire books discuss these aspects; here, this introduction provides a broad overview of each element, points to sources that offer more depth, and enhances some of the teachings Perry mentions below. Starting with the loftiest and descending to those directly moving about Mother Earth, these phenomena form a bonded relationship with the Navajo who worship and depend upon their availability. There is nothing distant about their impact.

The sun, moon, and stars have already been introduced in chapter 5 concerning divination, and so that aspect is not repeated here. In addition to the sources mentioned below, there is an extensive literature on Navajo astronomy and starlore, and its connection to ceremonial practices.[1] The sun and moon are the two most prominent celestial orbs. The sun, a fiery disk made of turquoise and other elements, should not be confused with Sun Bearer, the deity who carries the object across the sky on 102 different trails lying between the solstices. Sun Bearer is a handsome deity, noted for his strength and amorous ability, who figures frequently in the mythology.[2] He was said to have a turquoise mask and was the giver of life and heat, while Moon Bearer had a white shell mask and controlled female rain, mist, fog, and dew. During the latter part of May, Navajos held ceremonies to bless the tender shoots of corn and other plants. This was the only time when the sun and moon communicated with or "saw" each other (one rising, the other setting) to discuss the seed blessing ceremonies and night prayers offered previously by the Diné. With a good report, the two deities continued to favor man.[3]

The concept of celestial blessings also occurred on an individual daily basis for the Navajo. If the sun rose in the sky at dawn to find a person still sleeping, he said, "This is not my child." The sleeper was obviously lazy and not worthy to receive the blessings and riches from the holy people. Metaphorically, sleep is said to be dressed in "torn clothing," and so will the people who lie in bed with it.[4] The moon also blesses or curses an individual. For example, if a person prays to it while holding a fire poker and invokes its warmth for a newborn child, the baby will not get cold easily.[5]

These heavenly bodies may assume a vengeful attitude. Sun Bearer, when speaking of his daily travels, said, "Every time I make the journey east and west, one of the Earth People shall die. That is my pay." Moon Bearer agreed to the same price. Now, the sun or moon will stop at their zenith if they have not received their compensation, but fortunately, someone has died every day, and so this has not happened. Interestingly enough, the sun demands the life of a Navajo, while the moon accepts a death from a foreign race. Because the moon is "the sign of the Anglo," there are no formal prayers to him as there are to the sun, the sign for the Navajo.[6]

The most dangerous and prophetic time is during a solar or lunar eclipse. Although Navajos refer to the sun or moon as "dying," they still believe that Sun Bearer and Moon Bearer are immortal and that only the "fire" is going out. When the moon is eclipsed, everyone is awakened until it recovers, and if it is the sun, then all work or travel ceases, people sit quietly, and only the singers of the Blessingway are heard chanting. If a pregnant mother looks upon an eclipse, the unborn child will "take on its image." Other ills inflicted during this time include: if people are eating, they will have stomach troubles; if sleeping, their eyes will not open; and if they look at the eclipse, they will become blind.[7] The Windway ceremony (Chíshíjí) is used to cure problems created by either a lunar or solar eclipse.

Stars, like the sun and moon, also warn and guide man into the future. Although accounts vary as to detail, First Man and First Woman are often credited with placement of constellations and patterns, eight of which are most significant. These are Ursa Major (Revolving Male) and Cassiopeia (Revolving Female), the Pleiades (seven boys who run and dodge as they practice shooting arrows), Orion (First Slim One), Corvus (Man with Legs Ajar), Scorpius (divided into two parts—First Big One and Rabbit Tracks), and the Milky Way (Sitting for the Dawn). Navajos also recognize individual stars or other small groupings such as Antares (Coyote Star), Hydra (the Horned Rattlesnake), and Polaris (the fire around which Revolving Male and Revolving Female circle).[8] Those stars not in recognizable patterns or of special significance are there because Coyote, the trickster, impatiently flung star material into the heavens.[9]

Stars and humans are closely related. Navajos tell of how the stars serve as a calendar and clock because of their movements. Many commented, "That is how we know our time from day to day, month to month, season to season, and year to year. These stars follow a special pattern every day of the year."[10] They are named in prayers, each has a Blessingway song, and each has a special power to benefit people. The holy beings established these powers, saying, "We are creating the stars to help the Earth Surface People to find their way, so that they can regain their faith and reestablish their balance and their direction."[11]

Navajos tell of how the "laws" are written in the stars. First Woman wanted to have a constant, unchanging reminder of proper behavior for mankind. She could not write it in the water because it always changed, nor in the sand because it just blew away, but in the stars there was permanence. So she chose Rabbit Tracks, whose ends point upward as a sign that in the spring and summer, people should not hunt, but in the fall and winter, when the tips point downward, it is appropriate to kill game. Another set of stars called Horns shines brighter in the autumn, signaling the time for hunting mountain sheep.

One should not plant crops until Pleiades disappears, around May 15. Once it is over the horizon, the planting starts—seven seeds to a hole, the same number as the stars found in the constellation. Man with Legs Ajar assumes a stooping stance because he is carrying a heavy load from the harvest. The brighter his stars shine, the better the crop yield. This reminds the Navajos to work hard during this season so that they will have enough food for the winter. The Horned Rattlesnake controls underground water that gives life to springs and streams. Most of the animals are given a star or constellation to remind them of their responsibilities, whether it is the meadowlark who sings to the sun in the morning or the porcupine who checks the growth of trees in the mountains.[12]

Stars also prescribe important principles in human relations. Just as astrologers use the horoscope in Anglo society today to align stars and planets with the lives of individuals, so too do the Navajo have traditions concerning the same heavenly body. For instance, Revolving Male and Revolving Female circle around their fire (Polaris) in the summer and winter patterns, teaching that "only one couple may live by one hogan fire." Coyote placed two identical stars (Gemini—Pollux and Castor) in the wrong place, and so now there is contention and strife on earth as they try to get to their correct positions. Black Star was never "lit" and so wanders about, bringing bad luck and painful pricks on the shoulder and back with the little arrows it shoots. Big Star is not to see the Pleiades; they are in-laws and are there to remind people that a husband should never see his mother-in-law. And the Milky Way is a trail for the spirits of the deceased, each star being a footprint for those who travel between earth and heaven.[13]

Weather, from a purely practical standpoint, is critical to understand and predict. Broiling heat, freezing cold, powerful dust storms, intense winds, soaking rains, and deep snows are of great concern to Navajo shepherds with their flocks, not to mention to the farmer dependent upon moisture. Medicine man John Holiday explained why some of the twelve months are named for these conditions.

> January is called Cook the Snow [Yas niłt'ees—among other names]. A story tells how long ago, snow, having the consistency of dry flour, fell from the sky. The people gathered, cooked, and ate it. Coyote came walking by and said, "My, my—my feet are frozen; the snow is cold," so the dry snow turned into frozen water, the way it has been ever since. . . . In the fall we had snow-capped mountains, and that is why October is called Upper Portion, or Back to Back, or Parting of the Seasons. This is when all of the corn turns white, the mountaintops are covered with snow, and the vegetation turns red and yellow. During Slender Winds [November], the wind starts to blow, and Big Winds [December] is when they strengthen. There are twelve months total, and they all have sacred songs and prayers.[14]

Taking John's lead, we'll conclude by looking at snow and winds before going to Perry's teachings.

There are many different types of snow, which are often categorized by how it falls, the strength of the wind that blows it in, the way it freezes, and the time of year it arrives. Jim Dandy laughed when he talked about the early winter snowstorm called an "in-law chaser."

> When the first snow (ałtsé yidzasígíí) comes in as a blizzard with sleet and hail, it is the start of the winter season. Accompanying hail drives in hard and fast, encouraging a person to move quickly and get all of the chores done before it is too late. This storm is an in-law chaser, as the little hailstones encourage the in-law to carry the water, chop wood, and get livestock fed to obtain approval. A person might come into the house and say, "The in-law chaser storm (Ayéhé née dinó yódí) chased me all over." When you talk about this everyone laughs at the situation it describes, bringing families together.
>
> People don't usually use the first snow for water. I do not know why but it is not melted for cooking, washing, and drinking like the snow from later storms, but instead is left alone. Families do not let the snow from these later storms sit in the sun to melt, but bring it inside to heat on the stove because the sunrays are so powerful with radiation. For this same

reason, people should not lie in the sun or sunbathe. Snowballs are not thrown, because they belong to the wind. When snow falls slowly and gently it is female and when it comes with a strong wind it is male. Anything that is soft is female; clouds that are white and fluffy are female, dark, threatening storm clouds are male; hail that is driven and hurts or damages, male, little, light balls, female.[15]

Rhoda Kascoli, raised with traditional teachings, mentions three other types of snow. "On the branch snow or one-sided-snow (bíziigaii) only sticks to tree branches, telephone poles, fences, and highway signs, so does not stay very long, melting in a matter of hours." And "Horse tracks snow" (łį́į' habikéé') is so thin that when a horse walks on it, the hooves expose the bare ground. A third type is called chííl nááḍǫ́ǫ́s, a heavy blizzard.[16] The Franciscan Fathers at Saint Michaels categorized dozens of other types of snow according to its qualities.[17]

Winds, like snow, have their own personalities. When Navajos talk about winds, there are two types. Níyol is strong, the one felt blowing against one's face, while nítch'ih is the Holy Wind or spirit guide that gives life to things and helps direct and protect against evil. It whispers, teaches, and brings help to people. Níyol is controlled through nítch'ih and its supernatural power. For instance, a tornado can be stopped by leaving an offering and saying a prayer. It is through nítch'ih that the destructive force is commanded. When the winds blow, some will be soft (female) while others, like tornadoes, are hard (male). Those winds that pick up objects are always male, as are strong whirlwinds that turn and tip over trees. If one of these winds breaks a pole or rips branches off a tree, just as with lightning, they are not used, for they belong to the wind. When a strong wind visits a home, it is not by chance but may have been sent by a person involved in witchcraft who wishes to destroy something at that place. If destructive winds like tornadoes strike a community, scheduled ceremonies should be postponed. Winds can also cause cancer, swelling, and other illness.

Round objects belong to the wind. Smooth, circular stones are called Wind's Rocks (níyol bitsé) and when picked up, cause it to blow; these should not be brought home because they are the wind's babies, just as sticks that have been carried and piled up by a river belong to the water. In either case, proper respect must be shown, or else wind or water becomes angry. Do not lie down where the wind has left a trail or build a home where a concave impression is found in a rock because they are the wind's home. Do not place a finger in a sheep's eye socket when butchering since its shape is that of the wind's home. Playing ball inside a house and whistling causes the wind to wake up and blow; leaving a window cracked causes it to whistle, creating hearing loss. When a whirlwind approaches, everybody says "naadaaní, naadaaní, naadaaní," meaning "your son-in-law, your son-in-law, your son-in-law." It will then change its direction.

The winds from the four directions have prayers, songs, precious materials, and qualities associated with their personification. One of the best studies concerning the ceremonial qualities of winds and their abilities is found in Leland C. Wyman's *The Windways of the Navaho*.[18] Complex knowledge exists about how they function and interact with humans, but only an overview is provided here to outline their qualities. There are four different colored Big Winds, similar to tornadoes, each associated with its own cardinal direction. They warn of bad events that will take place in the future; when one blows through a camp and tosses about possessions, it is a portent of bad luck. As the world becomes increasingly profane and wicked, these Big Winds wait poised, ready to take lives, just as they did with the Anasazi in the past.[19] As long as Navajos continue to perform the Blessingway, asking in humility that they not be destroyed, the Big Winds will constrain their power.[20]

Small whirlwinds gather bad gossip and conversation and report it to the holy people. Some Navajos believe that if they spiral in a clockwise direction they have a good spirit in them, counterclockwise an evil one. Ghosts travel in the winds and can affect breathing, requiring a ceremonial cure. If a whirlwind takes a person's possession, he should let the object go, offer corn pollen to the wind, tell it that the item no longer has any value, and declare that if the wind placed a curse on that person, it was no longer in effect. This counters the belief that the wind, by taking sweat and dirt from a victim's body, stole his thinking so that he would not know what he was doing.[21]

Briefly, one story from the Windway tells of a whirlwind that approached a man, Older Brother, who unsuccessfully tried to dodge it. He became angry, shot the counterclockwise-moving twister, and watched the dead body of a person materialize. Then he realized he had killed the son of Big Wind and that soon the father would come to reap vengeance. Older Brother built a hogan; covered it with cactus, yucca, and other plants having sharp protrusions; drew zigzag marks in the path of the approaching cyclone; burned a crescent-shaped design on his breast; then waited. Big Wind approached in the form of a man, but could not cross the line. He promised to help rather than harm Older Brother if he restored his son. Older Brother ceremonially revived Whirlwind, and, as agreed, Big Wind taught three sacred songs of protection to him.[22] Holy people should not be taken lightly. They provide warnings and help a person to learn. Claus Chee Sonny believes the gods want humans to know the songs and prayers, but this can only be done if the "Wind people want to communicate them to you."[23] He explains that this is the reason that some people fail to learn them even though they try very hard. The gods simply do not want some individuals to have this power.

## *Stars, Stories, and Power*

The heavens and the holy ones who live there have a lot of power and influence with the people residing on earth. Stars are referred to as The Ancient Ones Who Left this World (Iizází) and display themselves during certain seasons. When these beings departed earth, they became stars who still cared for humans and now watch over them when they are sleeping or having ceremonies. The stars come out at night and need to be shown respect, even by wild animals who lie down and rest, because the stars are aware of their activities and attitudes. This is the best time to practice medicine because the holy ones are out and about, listening to see how they can help. When they identify a sickness taking place, they can heal that person by making connection with all of the winds, lightning, storms, and creatures who have the ability to help. The stars are like the middle people between the gods in the heavens and the medicine people on earth who are conducting ceremonies. They are listening to find out what needs to be done. Let's say that there is a person who had lightning strike close by. That individual is going to be sick. A medicine man will talk to the lightning and the stars, asking if the Lightningway ceremony (Na'at'oyee) should be performed and if Starway (Sǫ'tsohjí) ceremonial prayers should be connected in with the Lightningway.

When a person performs star gazing, stars associated with different directions are referred to as the Black Stars, Blue Stars, and Yellow Stars and are asked for guidance from their direction. As a human I cannot foresee things the way stars do, but they can give me the power so that my eyes and mind can visualize what needs to be done and what will happen. They tell me how things will work. When I am meditating, suddenly I will receive a lot of information that answers my questions and gives direction to my efforts. The stars guide me as to what ceremony is needed. They also work with the moon; a lot of times when a star and moon appear together, they indicate a child is going to be born into this world. Even the position the Milky Way (Yikáísdáhá—That Which Awaits Dawn) sits from north to

*Buffalo skin (preferred) rattles are used in the Blessingway, Antway, and Shootingway ceremonies, among others. The buffalo tail gives life and its hair offers power, while the life feathers tied to the corners also provide energy and carry the prayers and songs to the heavens. The zigzag lightning etched into the hide produces strength and protection; the rattle is painted black to represent the dark sky upon which were painted short rainbows. This instrument calls to the holy people, encouraging them to bring their powers and be in attendance. (Photo by Kay Shumway)*

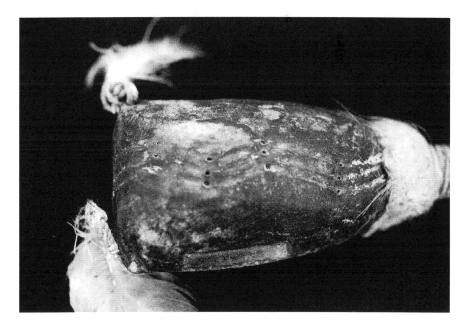

south as it trails across the sky can indicate how bad the winter is going to be. The constellation has strips in it, and if there is a light portion there will not be a lot of snow, but if it appears really bright white with lots of stars in between, then the snow will come.

There is also a story about the Milky Way. It is said to be bread that was to be given to the gods. Jack Rabbit (in some versions Coyote) grabbed it and ran away, with the holy people chasing after. His strong back legs proved to be too much for them, as he jumped high into the air and bounded off. While running, he left a trail of bread behind, which became the Milky Way. Another constellation added to the night sky because of this incident is called Rabbit Tracks (Gah heet'e'ii), which is the lower part of Scorpius. It was created from the footprints left by the bounding animal. Jack Rabbit also changed as he ran toward the north. He became one of the medicine people, so his ears developed into two feathers. This is also when the practice of giving a medicine man a loaf of bread baked underground started, symbolizing an offering made by the people. When this underground bread is given, the healing is very quick and good, and the medicine strong. This was how the elders spoke of these teachings, tied in to part of the Evilway and Windway ceremonies.

Another story about the Milky Way includes three gods—First Slender One (Átsé Ets'ózí) or Orion, brother to First Big One (Átsé Etsoh) or the upper part of Scorpius, who are following the leader, Man with a Solid Stance (Hastiin Sik'ai'í) or Corvus, on a trail across the night sky. They all carry medicine and are called the three Wise Men because of their knowledge in healing. Prayers that use this constellation in ceremonies are addressed to these three individuals, just as Talking God (Haashch'ééyáłti'í), Dawn God (Hayoołkááł), and White Shell Boy (Yoołgai Ashkii') are mentioned in prayers to the east. The ceremony that uses these and other stars is the Gila Monsterway.

The Big Dipper or Ursa Major (Náhookǫs Biką'ii—Male One Who Revolves), Little Dipper or Cassiopeia (Náhookǫs Ba'áadii—Female One Who Revolves), and the North Star or Polaris (Náhookǫs Bikǫ—Revolving Ones Fire) are all related. From a medicine perspective, the Little Dipper is associated with small short rituals and the Big Dipper with longer—five or more night—ceremonies. Revolving Male and Revolving Female are both healers as they move around the central fire. They discuss medicine and how to help people; if their "tails" or the handle of the dipper points up or down during a certain time of year, that will determine the type of ceremonies, whether they will be male or female, and what healing will take place. Offerings are made to these stars according to the position they hold in the sky at that time and indicate when a ceremony should be held. This is similar to the moon, which has its phases. You do not want to perform any ceremony

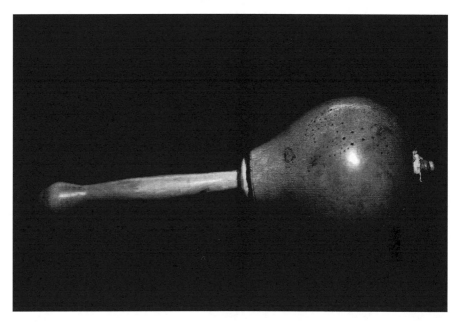

*This gourd rattle with a juniper wood handle creates the sound that connects the heavens with the earth during the Windway, Nightway, and Featherway ceremonies. The punctured holes in the gourd represent the sun, moon, and constellations as portrayed on different sides of the rattle. (Photo by Kay Shumway)*

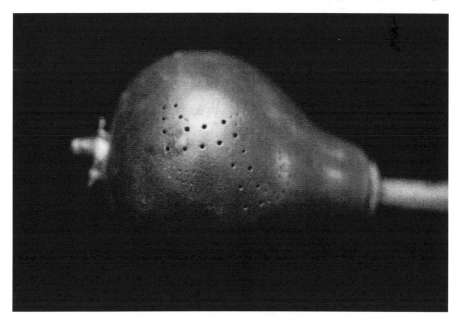

when there is a full moon, but instead you should wait until the new moon arrives. [Note: The new moon to the Navajo is when the beginning crescent first appears in the sky, not when it is totally dark.] That is when the healing begins to take place, coming together more each day until complete. The dipper is the same way. If the tail is down, a ceremony should not start until it begins to stick up in the air before it slowly starts back down. That is when the healing takes place according to the stories.

The Lifeway mentions that there are four holy beings that sit in the cardinal directions in the heavens, controlling the tails during different seasons. They are the ones who receive offerings and represent some of the ceremonies. If a sick person is going to live, the ceremony in the center of those four holy people has to become the main focus of prayers and offerings. Big Star (Sǫ Tsoh, also known as Venus or the Morning Star) is visible before the break of dawn and controls the four holy people associated with the dippers. Big Star is involved with divination, is able to tell what is causing an illness and which ceremony to use to heal it, and is the one prayed to.

## *String Games and the Heavens*

During the winter, young and old amuse themselves with string games (na'atł'o'), which reproduce constellation patterns in the sky. They are practiced only during this time and belong to Spider Woman, who taught the different star formations to the People. She knows a lot about the constellations and how they operate. She is the one who put the string games together, identifying the North Star, Big Star, and many others according to their names, characteristics, how they travel back and forth in the heavens, and their relationships. Her web has the four sacred colors; she is also the one who invented weaving for the Navajo people. Spider Woman is important to Navajo females because she set the pace or timing for womanhood with its practices and ceremonies and taught how to be thrifty, be patient, accomplish tasks, and do things right. Spiders are always the keeper of anything put together with string and weaving.

There are a couple of reasons that string games are done only in the winter. At this time of year, spiders are not really out and about, but rather sit back in their nests. They look out from their homes at the fire and smoke in a hogan or remain underground, knowing it is not yet time to be outside and involved in warm weather activities. Their timing is similar to Navajo ceremonies; some are performed in the summer and others only in the winter, some only at night and others during the day. For example, the Yé'ii

Bicheii and fire dance belong to the fall and winter group, the Enemyway to the spring and summer group. They are separated just as the animals and insects are. String games played only in the winter show respect toward Grandmother Spider Woman. If people do them during the summer time, they will be crippled with rheumatism in their fingers, hands, joints, and other places so that body parts will not be straight. Spiders hold that kind of power. A second reason is that winter is when people have more time on their hands and may become sick or sore.

String games help pass the time and assist in storytelling. Navajos call it stringing. My grandfather used to do that. He played with string, making all kinds of patterns, and then he would gently whip the person with it to chase evil away from them. The People respect spiders, who have their own songs, stories, and ways of doing things. If one is abused, however, that spider can make a person sick. If a person burns the spider's house, they will bring sores to the culprit's body. A lot of times my grandfather would take a string that was long enough to make the desired form and create a design. He would then let go with one hand and hit a patient suffering from sores with the loose end of the string. This chased away the sores and cured the person.

Through the string games, the spider and the constellations work together. Both are aware of human activity and are involved. Stars and the constellations place themselves in visual patterns to make people aware of what medicine and powers are available. For instance, the Big Dipper is the first to show itself, allowing for the other formations to follow. They talk to you through divination, declaring who they are and answering questions. Songs are made the same way, and so when medicine people sing to Black Star, "Yoo oyana éí yéí yóda éí naa yóó ó'oo ąą nada ąą ąą shei nei sǫǫ sodiłhił ąą bee hadishee ąą," they are talking about how it is dressed with horns of power. That is why Spider Woman placed those horns with the string pattern that represents this star. Thus the things of the earth are tied into the things of heaven—"on earth as it is in heaven." When performed with respect, it is a good thing.

## Spiders, Cloth, and Homes

There are many other teachings about spiders in addition to string games and marking the times that winter stories can and cannot be told. The spider is recognized as the weaver. Spider Woman was the first one who taught the people how to make clothes, blankets, and anything that covers a person and has different designs on it. She was also the one, living underground, who

*String games, performed only in winter, came from the Spider People when they challenged the Twins passing through their land. They wished to ensure that these strangers had proper knowledge and so dared them to picture four different constellations using their web material. The two men easily succeeded. Although there are dozens of different patterns, they all require only four basic moves. (Drawing by Kelly Pugh)*

was visited by the Twins on their journey to meet their father. She gave them their life feathers and instructed them on how to avoid being hurt by the monsters they would encounter on their trip. She taught them with wisdom. The Navajo term for spider is na'ashjé'ii, which means Wise One with Long Legs. Her knowledge has been important to a number of different Native American groups. For instance, she is the one who taught us how to build four different types of houses in our region. Even when spiders live in the dirt, they spin a web in a cone shape that moves from the outer edge of the hole to the center. This is where the idea of a tepee came from, and the webs are sung about in the morning songs. They call it naak'ạ'áłgai, meaning there is material that was made into a house, that is, the cotton-like web that was woven into a home. It is called the Morning House (yikai hooghan). This is what some of the Apaches adopted when they separated from the Navajo a long time ago, just as they also wanted a somewhat different language. They traveled a lot and needed help with some type of home that was different than ours, and so they went to Spider for assistance. The Mescalero, Chiricahua, and Jicarilla were told, "There's a place you can find cotton that can be spun. Make it into a web, into clothing, and into a home just like mine. You can build a fire inside, and smoke will come through the top, and there will be wisdom there." So the Apache copied the spider's design, spun material, and put sticks together to provide a frame, which soon became a tepee that was open at the top with a bottom where people could enter. The Spider People formed their own stories about how the spider put things together with different colors and in different ways. They say that those Indians who live in the western United States learned from the spiders living in their area how to build their homes and make designs on different objects.

When Navajos sing about the morning dawn house, it is made from this material. My father was both a road man and a traditional medicine man. He was often asked where tepees came from, with everyone expecting him to answer the Plains Indian tribes like the Cheyenne or Sioux. He would say that they came from here, thanks to the spider. Actually, there were three other houses in addition to the tepee. One was made out of wood, which was the hogan; another, made out of dirt, was the sweat lodge; and another, like that of the Havasupai, is made out of plants or brush with skins that allow the air to circulate and keep people cool. The spider is the one who designed and shared all four of these different kinds of homes.

When living in a hogan, it is important to show respect to spiders. They may reside in the corner of the house, but they are aware that people are living in the structure and so will not put up big webs across the open space, staying in their own little area. They are allowed to stay there, and so people and spiders are thoughtful of each other. These creatures are very smart. If somebody leaves a house unattended and there is no fire or smoke, no songs or children, and the house is abandoned, then they will decide to take it over and create large webs. Spiders start to place designs all over and claim the space for themselves. Whatever comes through will know that they are there. When people move back into their winter home, they will cut some long stemmed brush to use as a broom, tie it together, and sweep through the webs to clean them out. Once they start walking and talking and living in this space, the spiders will know that the humans are home, and so it is time to pack up and leave. Whoever stays behind will respect the people, but should also be respected themselves. The way my father talked about the spider was that their chief is designated with red markings on the bottom of his belly and should not be fooled with. This is the black widow spider and should be left alone. It has its purpose. If for some reason it bites you and the wound starts to swell, then the medicine person will find some of the yellow flowers and small green leaves below them for the medicine, then will grind, boil, and chew them. Next he will spit the juice and pulp on the wound, just as I explained earlier about healing the young girl in Page, Arizona. This is a good cure for any kind of spider bite or bee sting. The taste, however, is very bitter. If the pain turns into a sore, then add sunflower to it, but that is even worse and tastes even more bitter. It has its own juice that works with the rabbit brush, and when used together, they are very powerful.

A tarantula is considered a different kind of spider. He was told to not be like the other spiders that we live with. He inhabits the mountains or hills. That is why he has a fur coat that he sheds and why he is more of a visitor. His body structure was designed for this kind of life and is similar to that of the animals that live in that type of habitat. The tarantula was told not to come around until all the flowers and leaves had turned colors and the piñon nuts started to fall. These are the first days that he is allowed to come back to the native people. Even though he is scary looking, he really does not have any powers to speak of. His job is to show that fall is here. He is not a designer like the other spiders, but is pictured as a lazy person who wants to be at certain places at a certain time. My father used to tell me, "Don't be like a tarantula. Don't act like him. He walks too slowly. People don't like to talk to him or bother with him." He is just to be left alone.

## Sun and Moon, Night and Day

The moon (ooljéé'), a shiny disk of white shell, is carried across the sky by Moon Bearer (Tł'éhonaa'éí') who has a lot of power and influence in activities on the earth. He is the father of the sun, and like humans, is half male and half female. In ceremonies he is referred to as "Grandfather," but in some instances the female side is portrayed, since the sun always represents the male side. That is why it can be referred to as both "Grandfather" and "Grandmother," depending upon which of his powers or forces he is using at that time. Like a grandmother, he sits in his place as a child is being born and oversees the activities of birth between the new moon up to the full moon. The monthly "growth" of the moon or waxing is the best time to have births and perform ceremonies because once it becomes a full moon and starts to wane, its powers on earth decline. Life is given and life is taken on the new moon. Even when a person dies of old age with a new moon in progress, as the cycle moves toward maturity, people who are grieving will be healed slowly over time until the full moon is reached. The grandmotherly comforting side is there with you throughout the process. The same is true with a newborn who matures within the stages of the moon under the guiding, caring spirit of the moon's grandmotherly presence. Even before birth, the moon is the main keeper of the fetus and is responsible for its protection. Every birth that takes place is a new moon, and every new ceremony belongs to the new moon. Compared to the sun, the moon is mellow, does not have as harsh a light, is a good healer, and follows a monthly cycle just as women do. So when the ceremony demands it, he comfortably fits into a female role. All of this is communicated by its changing appearance in the night sky.

Unlike the moon, Sun Bearer (Jóhonaa'éí) is a powerful warrior, father to the Navajo, and the embodiment of a total male force. At the time of emergence, when Moon Bearer and Sun Bearer entered this world as two young men—a father with his son—the holy beings gave Sun Bearer the task of carrying the sun (shá), a large turquoise disk, on his back every day through the sky. After thinking about it, he demanded as his payment a human life. He said, "One of the most precious things that I know you like about this new creation concerns human beings. I will be given one man or woman each day as I complete this task." So the agreement was made that he could take one human life with him every day as pay, but this was not the case with the moon. Still, the moon became the keeper of both life in the fetus and death for old people. The sun, on the other hand, selects people during the day who are not old, then takes their lives. That is his choice, but the moon is in charge of the new ones and the old ones; the sun takes care of those in between.

The father works at night and the son during the day. If there is going to be travel at night, then that person sings songs that make reference to the moon. But if traveling during the day, then the songs referring to the sun are used. The same is true of ceremonies, with some being held during the day and others at night. In general, the primary part of a ceremony is held either in the day or the night. There are specific holy people who are awake, observant, and waiting for their songs and prayers during the day, while other ones are available mainly during the night. This goes back to the time of creation, when the animals held a shoe game to determine how much day and night would be on this earth. Since neither side won nor dominated, the day creatures and other holy people have their times, and the night creatures have their own. The Evilway and Mountainway ceremonies are held at night, while the Enemyway and Kinaaldá are performed mostly in the day. But each will have elements, such as a Blessingway, that are tied on and accomplished during the other part of the day or night. Still some ceremonies are more evenly split, half and half, such as the Windway and the Yé'ii Bicheii, which have important parts in both the day and night.

Healing by the moon in these ceremonies is slow and undramatic but steady. As an elderly person, the moon is far gentler than his son, who can quickly take life and harm people. His light is softer when compared to the harshness of sunlight, and he follows twenty-nine distinct stages. He was also the first one to move in the night sky before sun brought in daylight. Once the moon has become full, healing and growth slows down and ends until the next lunar cycle begins. The moon is moving toward the dark. As the new moon appears, it is very thin but grows larger until it becomes a full moon, when the healing is complete. As the moon gets brighter and brighter, there is more and more of it. Every day or night is new, so if a person is in an accident and is harmed, he or she will have a Lifeway ceremony (Iináájí) started on the new moon, and will drink the medicine from this ceremony until a full moon is reached. The moon serves as a measure for that person to determine how much healing has taken place. The medicine man might tell the patient in terms of how many new moons it will take, pointing out that using this type of medicine for this illness is slow but steady. There is no quick fix for some sicknesses.

Weather forecasting is also part of the moon's responsibility. If the moon has a crescent shape in the sky, the orientation of its points can indicate future weather. For instance, if the tips are pointing down, it is called Water Coming Off (Bąąh náálį), and it is going to rain or snow. Think of it like a cup turned upside down, emptying its contents. When the points of the moon are facing up—the cup is upright—this is called Held in a Container (Dahyook'áál) and means there will not be precipitation and the weather will be steady. If the moon has colors like a rainbow encircling it, it is called biná'áztłéé', meaning that the next day is going to be cold and indicating change.

The moon also serves as a ceremonial safety valve when a certain ceremony is needed but is out of season. Let's say there is a real necessity for a particular Lifeway ceremony that is usually held only in the summer but is needed, because of an accident or sudden illness, in the winter. The emergency has to be handled at that time and cannot wait. Also, the patient might not be able to endure a full-blown ceremony and so needs to have an abbreviated one. For example, a Nightway ceremony, usually held in the winter, must be held in the summer in a shortened form because of a person's physical situation. In both instances, there is a way to provide this service when necessary.

The medicine man performing the ceremony will determine when the new moon begins. The ceremony starts on that night. The growing crescent will appear right side up or halfway up to the right or the left, which indicates how the moon will work to heal that person. The more complete the crescent, the greater the healing. As the moon moves through its cycle, there is always a star that goes with that person and sits behind the edge of the top of the moon to guide the process of healing. The stars start to move around the moon so that by the time it is full, the stars will have surrounded it. This is over a three-week period when the healing is taking place. Once the moon is full, the healing stops. Remember that this is not just about curing physical ailments, but also mental issues. Medicine men aid not only sick bodies but also mental and emotional problems. The patient's thoughts may have been traumatized. As the new moon makes its tracks toward the full moon again, this is also the time when thinking, thoughts, and trust—whatever the patient has lost emotionally—will be replenished. Perhaps the patient will also drink herbs during this time until the full moon.

It does not matter which month this may be performed as long as the correct pattern and respect are shown. The holy beings involved in the ceremony and who control the power have to be pleased so that there is no problem as they work with the healer. They will understand when the regular pattern cannot be followed. Lifeway ceremonies are often the ones most affected by this where drastic measures are taken to heal trauma and save a life. The patient needs services right away. This can actually be done with any ceremony.

## *Winds: Friends and Foes*

The winds are also part of the heavens, and they affect man on earth. They have four different colors and thicknesses. There are four types of wind stacked on top of each other, the heaviest or thickest is on the bottom resting on top of the earth, a thinner wind rests upon the bottom one with another one on top of that, and the fourth or thinnest one on the highest level. The higher one goes, the thinner each one gets. If you watch a film of a person climbing a high mountain, eventually he will need a breathing apparatus when he gets to the top. The lower the winds, the more powerful they are. Remember that there are two different types of wind. The one that blows across the ground is níyol, but there is also the Holy Wind (Nííłch'ih), which is a spiritual presence. It gives the physical wind its temperament. The winds can be kind as in normal situations, but when the force and speed pick up and they start buffeting things about, their personality has changed. Sometimes the wind starts to blow before a storm and then increases when it arrives. It looks to me like its temperament has changed. I think the wind on the outside has its own attitude, but it is the Holy Wind on the inside that communicates to it. Just as a human body has its own mind and attitude but can hear the promptings of the Holy Wind, so too are the winds that we feel

*The four winds, each associated with one of the cardinal directions, are summoned by the prayersticks to participate in this Windway sandpainting, photographed by Curtis at the turn of the twentieth century. The ceremony heals people affected by whirlwinds, who have used wood torn from a tree by the wind, or who have stayed in a place created or inhabited by the wind. (Library of Congress—Photo 59799)*

on our face or that move the leaves on a tree. The same is true with every other living thing. It is part of that being's spirit—The Holy One That Sits Within.

Each of the cardinal directions has its own wind with the same colors as other things coming from that direction. They have their own responsibilities, healing powers, and specific illnesses that they can cure. For example, the White Wind is a holy being who lives in the east and is part of what is called the White Face ceremony, which helps with problems of the eyes and restoring vision. The ceremony is male and is called Male Wind (Na'at'o' biką'). The Blue Wind from the south has its own ceremony called Navajo Windway (Diné Binílch'ijí); it is female and helps to heal injured feelings. The Blue Wind sits in a neutral area so that it can be attached to either the Yellow or the White Wind ceremonies. The Yellow Wind from the west is called Chiricahua Windway (Chíshí Binílch'ijí), which is used to heal migraines or general headaches. This one is considered Female Windway (Nílch'ijí Biką'jí) and is associated with the Cactus ceremony, which concerns anxiety, paranoia, or fearing an unknown factor, and also works to heal problems with headaches. The Black Wind from the north is male and deals with harm from big winds like hurricanes, tornadoes, and twisters where chaos has resulted or some large problem needs to be overcome. Thus, the Black or Dark Wind and the White Wind are paired together as males, and the Yellow and Blue are females, but each acts separately, has a ceremony that is performed differently, and controls its own blessings. No single ceremony handles all.

Asking these winds for help is done in a particular way. Take the Black or Dark Wind for example. Perhaps a person is blacking out, their head is spinning, and they are disoriented. The holy people told each of the winds that when they are addressed in a respectful way, they need to assist the person calling upon them. The medicine man might say something like, "Dark Wind (Níłch'ih Diłhił), I am asking for your blessing in this way. Something bad has happened when a tornado came here and disrupted my life. I am now sick because of it—I am always dizzy and falling down, and things are not going well. I am asking for your assistance to come and fix that. I am calling upon you so that where your feet go, mine will follow; my legs and my body will be like yours. The place that you stand is where I am going to stand and will walk behind you. You go in front of me as my protector. I will be your child standing behind you. In this way we will work together—you as my god standing before me to protect. This tornado harmed me, and now I am sick because of it. Take that illness away from me. Stand before me, and become my parent, and I will be your child standing behind you." This is how you actually talk to it.

The old people have teachings about whirlwinds or dust devils. It does not matter if it is spinning clockwise or counterclockwise, a person should avoid being touched by it. An individual can sense the change—they might feel nauseous, dizzy, disoriented, or forgetful; they may experience unclear thinking or faintness. Even going into an area where a whirlwind has been can affect a person. These winds have evil in them. Today, people are blessed in a different way than in the past with different rules of behavior, according to the medicine that determines what they can or cannot do. In the old days, if a person was walking along and a twister moved over them and blew off a hat, that person was affected by it and left the hat alone. It now belonged to the wind. He might have headaches or blurred vision. A medicine man would say, "Okay, there's a spinner that came around, the twirler took your head and spun it off, and that's why you're sick this way." If you had already had a ceremony for this performed, you might have to go back and have it redone to chase the evil away to the north. Then the person was cured.

Sometimes when people see a whirlwind approaching, they will take a fire poker (honeeshgish) and stick it in the ashes of a fire and wait for the advancing column of air to get close enough so that they can throw it at the wind. The wind knows when somebody has got a fire poker waiting for them, and so it will leave in another direction and avoid that person. People say there is a bad spirit inside that is moving around looking to create problems. Whirlwinds are considered bad and may have been directed by someone who wishes to harm a person. Somebody may be praying against them, and that prayer turns into the whirlwind making its way toward the cursed being. The old people taught that it was pushed in a certain direction by somebody telling that spirit where to go and whom to bother. The fire poker is always a protector and is feared by the wind. Once the twister gets hit, it will leave because it knows that something is working against it. The old people would start swearing at the wind saying, "Evil thing get away! Get away from me!" It was kind of funny to see this.

There are other types of winds that affect the Navajo. In the fall there is One That Steals You Away (Neest'įįgo Níłk'aaz). It appears at the end of fall and the beginning of winter as the seasons shift from warm to cold. This wind sneaks up on people from any direction. It is called this because people are moving from a comfortable climate and will now have chills and colds. Sometimes the sun will be out warming the land and it feels good, but suddenly the cold wind will be waiting for you. It comes in and takes all of that away and "captures" you. You catch cold, and when you go back into your house, you know that it has affected you. Chills, fever, and feeling miserable—this wind will get you sick quicker than anything else. The reason that this wind acts like this is that it lives between seasons. There were some winds that were hot and others that were cold and were well known, but this wind is in between, and not many people paid much attention to it. This wind was a composite of the summer and winter winds, and it was unsure of its position. To make itself known and to have a clear identity, it formed its own personality so that people would take notice that winter is coming. It is said that just before this wind arrives, there is a small bird with a pointed head who comes to warn people. This small dark bird, called The Change is Coming (Dilt'óshii—Baeolophus ridgwayi—Juniper titmouse), tells that the frost is now going to cover the land.

Another wind that is a relative to One That Steals You Away is called The Frost or Day Freeze (Jį atin); it sits on top of the mountain, and like its relation, it comes to do damage. In January or February it descends below with a bone-chilling cold for a few days, and during that time it freezes everything solid before going back to its home on top of the mountain. It is very cold and can freeze things instantaneously even during the daytime. This wind is trying to capture all of those things that usually are flowing or moving during sunlight hours because they have broken away from the frost and cold that comes at night. It stops the running water and anything else that is moving, including human life, by freezing them. Plants are killed by putting frost into them and laying them down. The animals cannot drink water. This is a bad wind that sits there, trying to destroy anything that can bear fruit by not letting it grow again. Even human beings are damaged by this wind as it brings frostbite to their legs and fingers and causes their toes to fall off. The Day Freeze is awful because it comes around to stop everything. It only visits for a few days and then goes back to the top of the mountain, where all of the snow is piled high.

Winds are important to understand during the lambing season. The wrong kind will kill the newborn with a sharp frost that can wipe out a herd's yearly growth. Navajos communicate with the birds. There is a type of bird with a yellow throat and black markings that is called Sheep Face (Dibé'nii'í—*Sayornis saya*—Say's phoebe). This is the one that is supposed to bring back all of the warm air and springtime weather. He also lets people know it is time to plant corn and perform summertime ceremonies again like the Enemyway. That is what the medicine people used to say: "We're going to wait for that bird to come back." Once it did, the bird would sit up in the trees and chirp in a different tone, and you would hear people say, "Hey, Sheep Face came home. Now we can do our thing." These birds taught the winds and told them when they could arrive.

The warmer winds come in from either the south or the west. Navajos would also watch the position of the Big Dipper to know when to plant and also to navigate on the ground. Summer winds sit in the four different directions in a circle. They can come in from the east, south, west, and north and also the northwest. A lot of these winds talk about dryness and removing different pollens that are in the air. Spring brings lots of allergies from buds and flowers as they pollinate. The summer winds blow that all away, dry out the plants, and nourish them with sunlight, warm weather, and summer rain. These winds are considered to bring growth and fruit to the plants as they foster positive change. They are caregivers that help young plants grow. My mother was a medicine woman, and she talked about how the spring winds, because of pollination, took place on top of the plant. They are concentrating on creation at the top with flowers and leaves, but when the summer winds arrive with all of their heat, the plants get dried out. Now the plants have to think about their root system in the ground, where moisture provides growth and allows for survival. It is time for the bottom of the plant to prosper. That is what mother talked about.

# CHAPTER FOUR

# *Between Heaven and Earth*

## *The Role of Trees in Traditional Teachings*

The Navajo have long had a relationship with various types of trees found in their homeland. Literally. Many Anglos may struggle with the concept of communicating, seeking assistance, and forming a lifetime partnership with something as close to inanimate as a tree, but as Perry points out, it is perfectly natural. The depth of the relationship can be profound as the inner being of the tree and human interact and bless each other. Perry stresses this aspect of the relationship in his teachings, and so this introduction provides a more mundane view of trees in Navajo culture. Most species have a specialized use, teaching, or way to help man either spiritually, physically, or both. Navajos raised close to the land realize that beyond food, medicine, material, and fuel, there also exists assistance in less tangible necessities of life. A brief look at the variety of trees that grow from the sands of the desert to the height of the mountains will illustrate the far-reaching knowledge Navajos hold of their environment. The next chapter provides a similar overview of smaller types of plants.

Beginning in the higher altitudes of Navajo land, one finds ponderosa or western yellow pine (*Pinus ponderosa*; in Navajo: nídíshchíí'—the pine). This tree has a variety of uses such as medicine and as equipment found in at least six different major ceremonies. For example, a piece of lightning-struck pine can be used by a medicine man to fashion a bullroarer to frighten away evil from a patient. Once the wood is carved into an elliptical shape about eight inches long, it is covered with lightning-struck pitch mixed with charcoal, three turquoise beads are emplaced for eyes and a mouth, and an abalone shell is secured on its backside as a pillow. A sacred buckskin thong two to four feet long is attached to the back end so that the bullroarer can be twirled above the head to make the sound of thunder or voice of Flint Man, the first holy person to use this object in a ceremony.[1]

Ponderosa was often preferred when fashioning cradleboards, but other wood such as juniper (frequently referred to as cedar), cottonwood, willow, weeping willow, piñon, and slats from boxes were also used. The wood was cut from the east side of a tree that is typically secluded; it provides either the split-back or single piece for the backboard, while a protective bow over the head may be made from oak, cedar or some other type of wood that can be molded and bent into shape. This, the footboard and backboard, and the baby, once placed in the cradle, are secured by leather thongs. The creation of the cradleboard did not start until after the baby's birth and the infant's ability to survive was ensured, the time varying from a few days to a month.[2]

There were other external as well as internal uses of ponderosa products. The cones from these pines were burned and the ashes placed on sores. Its pitch, like that of piñon, is mixed with grease and put on infected sores or chapped skin. When given on a spoon, the resin fought pneumonia and whooping cough as it opened the breathing passage. For those who desired long hair, ponderosa pine needles soaked in water then rubbed on the scalp helped its growth.[3] This tree also provided food. Between the outer bark and the dense wood lies a thin layer of soft cell material called phloem that conducts water and nutrients to the living parts of the tree. In the spring especially, the phloem is rich in nutritional substance and easily scraped from the outer bark once removed. A pound of this material provides 595 calories containing five grams of protein, 139 grams of carbohydrates, three grams of fat, and fifty-six grams of crude fiber. High in calcium—equivalent to nine glasses of milk (2740 milligrams or 342 percent of the Recommended Daily Dietary Allowance—RDA)—as well as phosphorus, magnesium, and ten other trace elements, this sweet food was used both in times of plenty as well as famine.[4]

Growing in the same area as ponderosa pines are Gambel or Rocky Mountain white oaks (*Quercus*). This tough tree, known to the Navajo as "rock plant" (tsé'ch'il), provided a brown tan dye for wool, a ceremonial emetic, medicine to lessen afterbirth pain, and wood for digging sticks and other objects that require resilient material such as handles, fire drills, weaving tools, and stirrups. Its acorns, also considered a starvation food, were eaten raw, roasted, dried, boiled like beans, or ground into a meal. Oak wood is best known and frequently used in making bows, which when sinew-backed could shoot an arrow a hundred yards. Once the bow had been heated and bent into shape, the sinew, which came from the back of a deer or horse, was soaked in water to soften it, then applied with glue and reinforced in layers. There was both a male "black bow," given its color by rubbing it with burned piñon boughs and tallow, and a female bow (tseiskáán) colored with scorched juniper ashes also mixed in tallow producing a yellow finish. The only distinction between the two bows was made during ritual discussion; Perry elsewhere shares teachings about the "black bow." Arrows came from oak, currant stems, flowering ash, or greasewood, and were smoothly polished, straightened, and then marked with designs of zigzag and straight lightning, reminiscent of those elements used by Monster Slayer and Born for Water.[5]

From these examples, one can see the depth of knowledge Navajos have about trees and their multiple uses. A few shorter examples will round out the variety and bring us to the two mainstays of traditional culture—piñon and cedar. Alder and mountain mahogany grow at higher altitudes. They provide red, tan, and brown dyes used to color parts of baskets made of sumac, wool for weaving, and leather products. White dust from straight quaking aspen is rubbed on a kinaaldá's face to prevent wrinkling and from being bent over with old age. Cottonwood, in addition to having a sugary phloem used as a food extender and sweetener, is a favorite material for carving ceremonial objects, household utensils, games, and toys. This wood has opposite qualities compared to fir trees (*Abies*—white Douglas fir) associated with strong, violent winds. This kind of wood is not used in or around the home. Willows (*Salix*) have leaves that serve as an emetic, medicine, or tobacco.[6] All of these and other types of wood have defined uses found in specific ceremonies.

A wide variety of wood can also be burned for heat and cooking in the home, capitalizing on some of their unique characteristics. Cottonwood, for instance, makes a good summer fuel since it gives off a lot of light but not much heat; it is used outside during warm weather because of its acrid smoke. The opposite is true of greasewood, which burns intensely hot, is relatively smokeless, and does not require large amounts for a cooking fire. Like oak, it burns for a long time. Piñon and juniper (cedar), because they are prevalent throughout the lower elevations of Navajo land, were the most frequently used firewood, the former being preferred for heating, the latter for cooking because it does not give off pitchy smoke. These were the only kinds of fuel used in ceremonies. Yet none of this wood can be utilized if it is from a lightning-struck tree or a "death hogan" in which someone has died. The same is true when a person finds a partly burned piece of wood in an old campfire. Without knowing the "history" of the wood—where it came from, who built the fire, and if it has been touched by lightning—the charred piece is discarded.[7]

There are other concerns or teachings about firewood—some of which are more folktale while others are of deep significance. For instance, if a burning piece of wood "sings" to a person by emitting a small hissing sound, the noise is viewed as coming from a small friendly being to whom one can make a wish after tossing an offering into the fire. Another less religious belief is that if a newly wed couple moves into a hogan and builds a fire that smokes and sputters, they will have quarrels; if the fire quickly dies out, divorce is in their future. Of much greater significance is the use of the fire poker (honeeshgish), the importance of which will be discussed elsewhere. To stir the fire with the wrong end of the stick is socially and ceremonially inept. "The growing end of the poker is used to stir the fire and when not in use, the end should always be pointed toward the fire so that the next person to pick it up will not be confused and use the wrong end. Anyone who reversed the ends of the poker when stirring the fire would be called ignorant or simple minded, a common remark being 'even a child would know better.' In passing a poker from one person to another, it is never held so that the end points toward either individual. This would foretell that the one it is pointed at would later suffer from severe burns."[8]

The piñon pine (*Pinus edulis*—chá'oł) is brother to the female juniper. Since it is a male tree, it has a more pungent odor, when used in some forms of medicine (emetic) it can create a strong reaction, and its branches and needles are often associated with male activities such as building temporary hunting lodges, are used as materials in the Mountainway, or are carved to create a male fire poker. Its pitch is melted into a liquid that seals and waterproofs woven baskets, when added to tallow it can pull out the poison in an infected area, and, along with juniper, it is a preferred wood for weaving looms and building hogans. Their needles can be boiled and the liquid used as an antiseptic, and when prepared as a tea, they help combat coughs and colds.[9]

One of the best known uses for this tree is the nuts it provides in the fall. Rich in protein, potassium, magnesium, iron, and zinc, these nuts, either cooked or raw, provide a distinctive but subtle flavor. They became an important source of income for Navajos, who harvested them by knocking them off branches or picking them from the ground. Placed in sacks that could hold up to eighty pounds, they were brought to trading posts, then shipped from coast to coast. For the Navajo, they provided a welcomed income as well as a food that could be added to stews and breads, turned into piñon butter, or mixed with parched corn as a snack. Whether selling them for cash or eating them for food, the people relished and respected the piñon tree and its products.[10]

As Perry discusses below, Navajos have a strong dependence upon and relationship with the juniper (*Juniperus*) tree. From birth to death and many events in between, this plant played a significant role. Starting from the time of creation, as the holy people were determining what type of house the

Navajo should inhabit, trees as a building material entered into the discussion. Juniper became the mainstay. A story tells of how the people visited various creatures to examine their homes to learn what they were made from and how they would work for them. Animals opened their homes for scrutiny: Eagle with its nest constructed of branches from the spruce tree, Oriole living in a cottonwood tree, Woodpecker inhabiting a hollow stump, Cliff Swallow with its abode of plastered mud, Beaver exhibiting his beautifully constructed dome ceiling with interlocking sticks, and others provided examples. From all of them came ideas that helped shape the hogan. The first Navajos agreed, "Our homes will be round as all of the homes we have visited have been that shape. We will build the walls of logs and make them higher than our heads, as do the eagles and the beaver. We will have a dome-shaped roof with an opening to the sky, and we will have a doorway facing east so the sun can waken us in the morning. Our floors and walls will be plastered with adobe mud like the homes of the swallows. When it is finished we will cover the house with earth to resemble the land all about us, and we will hang a woven blanket over the doorway."[11] Juniper was the ideal wood to do much of this. Its logs resist rot, the peeled wood inside reflects sunlight during the day and firelight by night, and the bark is placed between the logs to keep dirt out and serve as insulation, while even the short pieces of wood are used in its cribbed roof. Cedar bark is also an excellent fire-starter and absorbs moisture in the bottom of a food storage pit. Its berries and leaves serve as an emetic, provide a headache and stomachache medicine, relieve body pains, and cure spider bites.[12]

For desert dwellers, it is also a good source of food. The tree's berries in the fall, although at times bitter, can be eaten alone or mixed with piñon nuts and ground into a meal that is formed into patties and grilled. The berries can also be boiled and made into a juice or tea. But its most important contribution in the kitchen is as an ash. Preparing it is fairly simple. Green branches are collected from a tree and placed on a grill over a fire with a pan beneath to catch the falling ash from the burned leaves, which is then sifted to remove stems and berries. This product stores easily, and when needed, is added to food recipes—especially those made with corn products like mush, bread, and meal. It can also be used to seal a frying pan when grease is not available, to prevent foods like tortillas, paper bread, and other "baked" goods from sticking. Cedar ash's distinctive flavor adds to blue cornmeal mush and other traditional foods.[13] There are also dietary benefits. Nutrition experts determined that "eight teaspoons of juniper ash per serving of corn bread increases the calcium content from 69% to 317% of the Recommended Daily Allowance, the carbohydrate content from 31% to 38% of the RDA, and the iron content from 95% to 316%."[14]

There are also ritual and medicinal uses for juniper ash. Evil influences fear and are repelled by it, so it is applied over a patient's body for protection or is scattered at night to keep ghosts at bay. In some ceremonies, blowing ashes pushes the evil away.[15] Traditionalist Jim Dandy recalled his family members using ashes for a variety of purposes, all based on this same theme of protection and well-being. Jim's grandmother, when he was born, took some soot from a spent fire and patted it on his bottom to prepare him for his new beginning and provide protection from evil. Later she bathed him in a solution of yucca root and juniper leaves to make him strong. Juniper leaves on branches were warmed in a heated firepit and applied to an expectant mother's stomach as a means to relieve pain and to act as a lubricant for ease of delivery. Every morning when his grandmother awoke, she started the daily household routine by praying with ashes, and when she finished cooking and had put the food away, she would again "pray through the ashes." Grandmother taught that after the fire had died down and it was time to remove the remains, that those performing the task had to be very careful not to leave a trail of residue as they brought the ashes north of the hogan. "Ashes are a very sacred thing. You have cooked your food on them and so you do not leave them lying around your home." They were also used for relief from an upset stomach, prayed to for assistance, placed on a gun before shooting at a skinwalker, thus overcoming its supernatural power, and when at a funeral, placing juniper leaves in water so that people could wash away the influences of death and burial. Literally, from birth to death, juniper was an integral part of Navajo life.[16]

## *The Power of Piñon*

The first night of the Enemyway (Anaa'jí) was over, and many of the participants had gone home to rest. Family and community members had spent the previous day preparing large amounts of fry bread and stews to feed the guests and participants the next morning. All through the night the cooking fires had burned, but now they had died down to a smolder. After a full evening and then early morning of ceremonial activity, it was time to slow down and begin preparing for the next night's events. Quiet filled the dance area. The children had not gotten the message. A group of them were in the midst of a game of tag, when one of them jumped over a pit of ashes, followed by my grandson. The first child cleared the obstacle easily, but not the second. He missed the far edge. His feet landed in the gray ashes on top and sank into the red hot coals at the bottom, instantly melting then igniting his plastic sandals.

Screaming with pain, my grandson stood there stunned until a relative grabbed his back and yanked him from the pit to quickly extinguish his flaming shoes. But the fire had done its damage. Both of the boy's feet were badly seared with the imprint of burned plastic deeply etched into his flesh. Blood covered them, but what was visible looked like it had been deep fried and sorely injured. When I saw what was happening, I picked the child up and plunged his feet into a bucket still filled with water and ice for cooling sodas. The boy, wracked with pain, found calming relief in the cold water, but any attempt to remove his feet renewed intense, instant, and agonizing torture. My mother, who had been a medicine woman all of her life, specializing in the Windway, ran out of the house not far behind me. Assessing the situation with a glance, she did not hesitate; she turned to me and commanded: "Go get your auntie. She is the only one who can fix this."

I went to her home in a nearby camp, told her what had happened, and listened to her answer. "Take me to the piñon tree. The one that has little tips on the end. That's what we need to pick." I quickly found one that had light green tips of new growth that would eventually turn into a cone on the end of a branch. That is what we began to pick. After she felt she had a sufficient amount, we returned to my mother's home to see how my grandchild was faring. As long as his feet remained in the water, the pain was controlled. When my aunt (At'ééd Begay—Girl Begay) removed the burned sandals from his feet, an inch and a half of skin and flesh peeled off, causing more bleeding and painful screams that turned the child's face purple. Putting the tips of the piñon needles in her mouth, she chewed them into a thin paste, as a lot of the green compound seeped from the corners of her lips. When ready, she sprayed the mixture on the burned area then chanted a song, singing: "The pain is going down. Béé yoh yoh yoh." She continued to spread the mixture on the burned area, applying a thick coat before finally wrapping the feet in bandages, while intoning her song (doo áyóó): "You sing and dance; you set foot on the water." ("Sa sǫ diłhił dził diłhił yikááji' hanádááhgoo keet'ą́ą́ yáti' dayooléélgo bee bináhadził bee bináhadził bee haahot'éégo bee haahot'éégo"—from a Mountainway song about Black healing from the north.) Suddenly, the child quieted down.

These words and songs are not normally used in Navajo language because they came from the holy people and are appropriate only for special healing occasions. The person using them is actually pushing the medicine forward as the pain goes down. That is what is being said. This song was made by the fire gods and is used, along with their sounds, during the fire dance in the Mountainway ceremony. These holy words are to be said when someone gets burned; they cool the person down. My aunt used these powerful phrases for that purpose. In the Mountainway, the dancers put hot coals in their mouth and on themselves, as they say béé yoh yoh yoh, and dance around. They do not get burned and can use their medicine obtained through this power to heal those who have big sores on their body. The medicine person puts coals and fire on the open wound, then pours water on it, chanting these words. The sore heals the next day, providing one more reason why people gather for the fire dance ceremony to be blessed. These powers are holy.

These magically powerful medicine words and songs are only given to people who have themselves been touched by fire with second or third degree burns. If they have at some time had this happen, a medicine man may perform a ceremony that passes on the right and power to heal burns. This is provided as a gift for someone who has had that relationship with fire. It becomes their right to help others. In my aunt's case, there had been a house blaze that had caught her hair and the clothes on her back on fire as

*Trees provide many teachings about life, growing old, withstanding the severe storms of conflict, connecting to the heavens, and obtaining healing powers. There is also serenity.*

she fled the structure. Her back had third degree burns, and so a medicine man performed the ceremony for her, she got well, and she could then use the power to cure others. Now, speaking of my grandson, she said, "Don't worry about this. It will be okay. There will be no scars from the fire." I could not believe her, thinking there would be massive tissue damage on his feet and legs. It scared me.

By 10 o'clock that morning, we had wrapped the burns, and for four to five hours he rested quietly, then started to walk on his two injured feet. I said, "Son, please don't walk on them. You are going to break your skin and start bleeding again," but it did not happen. By the end of the day as the sun set, we began the second night of the Enemyway while waiting for the food and people to arrive. My grandson was now up and running around as me, my wife, and brothers watched him and said, "Look at that. He's running with it." My aunt said, "Don't bother him. Let him go. Leave him alone. Don't unwrap the burned area for four days," and so we waited. Everything that was scorched eventually turned pale, but there was no sign of bleeding or red marks to indicate a serious burn. Within two months, all of the dead skin had sloughed off, the sores disappeared, and his brown skin returned to normal. Today, he is a grown man, and there are no scars on his feet and no white skin.

## *Establishing a Relationship*

This whole experience is a fundamental example of the principle behind which traditional Navajo religion and medicine operate in this physical world with spiritual roots. It is all a matter of establishing a relationship (k'é) with what you are working. One may pray to the spirit in a rock, leave an offering in the river, talk to a tree, address a plant that will be picked for medicine, and so many other things. In all of this there is a relationship between the medicine person or the individual who is praying and that plant or rock or river that is going to be crossed or used. This is the best way to understand Navajo interaction with the entire world—looking through the glasses of k'é by establishing a relationship with that object. It responds to that person if done in the right way. It can assist because the person has had a positive interaction. If the rules of correct behavior are not followed, if the prayers are not said properly or an offering is not given, then that relationship can turn negative and may produce the opposite of what is wanted. In other words, it turns against you. You haven't shown the proper respect, and so the good relationship that should be there is not.

Only one individual with his or her thoughts and interpersonal action is the one who will determine the outcome of the relationship with that object. One starts by introducing oneself to the plants and to the holy ones. Say, "This is who I am. I am your grandson. And my name is so and so, by the sacred name given and recognized by the holy ones. We are here today and my name is The Warrior That Brings Back (Hashkénéyoo'ááł); the people have asked us, me and you, to come and make them better; they have given us their thoughts and trust us today that you and I will come together and heal this person. This is who I am, and I'm going to ask you to heal this person. Here is the problem that we have and this is why I am asking you for help. I am going to be making offerings to you. I am going to put my offerings down. I'm going to be doing this in a good manner, in a good way, how it was set, and then you will give me your medicine and I will take it back to the person." This is how I talk to the plant in Navajo. It is a matter of me coming to it—working with it, and not with other people. This is between the two of us. "When we make this medicine, we are doing it to heal that person, but how he eats it, how he takes it, how it affects him, that is another story."

I make it holy, then take it to the patient and sit down with him and say, "I give you the medicine that will work for you if you want it to. You are going to have to put in effort because you are going to have to be holy and believe in being healed. You have to stand with it if it is going to totally help you. If you just let it go and dump the rest of the medicine and walk away, we are wasting our time." One has to have that type of respect. By talking to the plant and the person, you help form a relationship between them where trust is built. Every time you go back to the place where the medicine plant is found, you say, "It's me again. The Warrior That Brings Back has returned to talk to you again." The plant already knows you and says, "Okay. Here comes my grandson." The relationship is already set.

Understanding the power and nature of trees is important. The piñon is considered a male tree, while the juniper or cedar is female. The brown tip on the end of a piñon branch is referred to as its penis and cannot be used for healing burns—it has to be green, and so this medicine is only available during certain times of the year. Juniper trees are viewed as females and its berries as food and decoration, while it heals in a gentle way. They have always worked with the people as an important mild medicine, the opposite of the piñon, a male tree with a strong, pungent scent that works with strength in painful, desperate situations. Young junipers are patient and bend, no matter how difficult circumstances become. They also remember— a tree may have been born before an individual and lived after that person died—but it will "know the story after we leave," and record in its own way the history of the people and community it is near. That is why they are also "teachers" that help us to become the type of person we should be. Once its life is through, it will have given back to the people and to the Creator. Humans can learn from the tree that weathers difficult times and sometimes receives bruises and broken branches in its life. We should be as our companion tree and say, "I have had a lot of burdens placed on me and have been hard on myself, and so I need to forgive myself, give everything back to the Creator, and then walk a little lighter." That is how the tree thinks and what it stands for.

This leads to the teaching about how a tree can be selected to be a guide and helper throughout one's life. In picking one to have a special lasting relationship, an elder might take a child and find a young sapling, shorter than the intended companion, that has no broken branches, is fully developed with well-formed limbs and plentiful scale-like leaves, and is pleasingly proportioned. It should also have no lightning marks or reddish hue or different colors on it—only green. This baby juniper (gadyáázh) presents itself as a young person that is very clean, just as one's mind and body should be. The tree should also be no taller than the person choosing it and very young with the ability to grow, so that it can mature just like the boy or girl who will become its brother or sister. Regardless of sex—it must be a juniper, because everyone comes from a female.

No chosen tree is shared with another person; it stands for a single individual. The juniper represents the person being reborn or renewed, so time is taken to find just the right one. The child is replenished, calling upon Mother Earth (Nohozdzáán shimá) with the Baby One or tree, representing the earth's relationship with the child who represents him or herself. The person choosing tells the plant, "You are young. You are so full of life and green that even when storms come and the greatest heat suffocates you, the greatest cold chills your branches, you never change your colors. You always remain the same. This is why I select you, so that my life will always be green. I will grow with you, my life is going to be evergreen also, and that is how I see it." These trees also live a long time. In this prayer, the candidate mentions that there are countless numbers of trees on this earth and that this one is being chosen from all of the others to be a caretaker; likewise, the tree recognizes that of all the people living on this earth, this person is now committed to it as a friend. The adoption goes both ways, and they become brothers or sisters after that.

Once the youth selects a juniper, an offering of ntł'iz (sacred stones) is placed at its base. A prayer such as "Heal me and help me to come back to you as a stronger person, having accomplished my purpose" is given. The offering speaks to the ground, and this young tree unites itself and earth to the patient as a relative. As the tree grows, so does the person, able to withstand the heat of summer, the cold of winter, and the trials of life. In a

*Far beyond the functional use of juniper, there is a spiritual bonding that a person can initiate by leaving sacred stones and prayers as offerings. The tree, like that individual, grows in experience and wisdom in a lifetime relationship. The site becomes a place of holiness and peace. (Drawing by Charles Yanito)*

sense, the person and tree walk together as their existence parallels their intertwined lives. This single tree—out of all those that are on the earth—has now been chosen to be a caretaker for the person who prayed at its base. The individual accepting this two-way adoption, like a family member, may return many times to pray, think, and draw upon its powers.

Accidents occur often in a lifetime, and so a juniper tree can also serve as a healing force for those harmed. By using the earth offering (sacred stones) to petition for help, an individual can receive aid for injuries, uniting tree, soil, and patient in an important relationship. One way or another, everything returns to Mother Earth, who is there to help and accept an offering for health. Either a mineral offering to the tree or a water offering (river or pond, etc.) needs to be made, depending on the type of accident. Navajos are taught that as human beings, they live by the sun every day; that they live by the storm and its water that they drink every day; that the air in its different seasons, whether hot or cold, is necessary for life; and that those who live on this earth make tracks and walk on top of it every day. These four elements are the holy ones a person interacts with—the sun is represented through white shell, water by turquoise, wind by abalone shell, and the ground by black jet.

When an accident happens or an injury takes place, for instance if a man gets bucked off a horse, he should return to the spot it transpired and leave an offering. A medicine man may walk back with him and put corn pollen at the site and offer a prayer. Some people bring water to "cool" the ground at the point of impact, where blood was shed and pain occurred. Pouring the water at this place is called the Cooling Time. The four elements—wind, fire, water, and earth—represented in the stones are addressed. These four gods we live by, and so they are called in from the four directions to help heal. They must work together at the same time, not individually. The water is there to cool things down; the earth has been hit by the falling body that now aches with pain; the voice crying out in agony and the trembling of the body was transmitted through the air; and the pain and swelling reddens and aches like burning fire. All four of the basic elements represented in the sacred stones play a part in healing and cooling the body down and are used in the first part of every ceremony as an offering and invitation to the holy ones for help, even when a person is just gathering herbs. They are the four gods that allow any living thing or object to heal.

Following the prayers and the cooling, the medicine man and the patient leave for a mountain to select a small tree, sit down, and make another offering beneath it. The four precious stones are asked to walk with this person so that there may be better ways from this day forward. "Forgive us for what happened, and allow us to heal so we can come back and be stronger people again." That is how we talk to it and make offerings. We also explain what we were trying to accomplish, that there was a purpose that got interrupted, but that we would like to continue in a successful life. The four minerals talk to the earth, the young tree, and the air. They are very sacred.

The healing process begins to work as both tree and person grow straight and stronger, walking in a better life. Every time a serious problem arises, that individual returns to the tree where the medicine was put down and talks to the tree saying, "Brother, I have a situation, a problem. Help me with it." Prayers are given again, knowing full well that things will change for the better. The person fosters this relationship over many years, walking in this way. Some time ago there was an old medicine man lying on his death bed. Relatives asked him what his last wish was before he went. The elder replied, "Take me back to the mountains. There's a small tree that I have dealt with. I need to say my good-byes to that tree," so they took him. He directed them precisely to the spot; they found the tree that had grown halfway through its life and was still young and beautiful. The medicine man sat and talked to it saying, "From this day, we are going to part, but I will see you again in the spirit world, in this way. Thank you for standing by me; thank you for standing with me on this earth. Now I can go." He had made peace with his companion and soon died. But it was understood that he released all of the commitments between him and the tree, which they had both upheld, and was being fair and true to his helper. He was nice about it. Stories like this are very sacred. This is why we select a tree that will never forget us and we will not forget it.

Navajos in the past talked about these things like this. Before they started getting medicine from western society, they had to have these prayers and songs performed to be healed. Medication and hospital care have replaced a lot of these practices, but even today, when the two are combined, they are very effective. Doctors may prescribe physical therapy or pain killers or muscle relaxers. These are good, and a person needs to abide by them. But another part is talking about what has happened and the problems that are being faced. The tree listens and knows, and so as one speaks about issues, the more the situation improves. The same is true with herbs. Once a mineral offering, prayers, and songs are given to the plant, there is a relationship that raises the patient to a higher spiritual level. After this, the medication from the doctor will be very effective. There may be medicine and procedures, which are good and have their own rules for use. Sometimes I talk to Anglo people who want to adopt Navajo practices like this, but I tell them that they will not be successful with a lot of them. They are trying to inherit someone else's story in a symbolic way, but it is not there. They are not part of our clan people. We don't acknowledge them.

# *The Patient Teaching of Trees*

Juniper trees have always worked with the people as far as medicine is concerned. The holy people selected them for that purpose. Compared to the piñon tree, it is almost opposite, because the piñon goes with the Lightningway, has a strong scent that makes itself known, and can work violently during the healing process. It has to do with lightning patterns, and its qualities are harsh, boastful, and manly. Even the needles of a piñon tree, when used as a medicine for painful burns, heal in a male way unlike the calm, slower juniper. This tree has a lot of patience, is not brittle, and does not fracture like piñons, but bends and is more agile.

Another way that the juniper tree helps and heals is during the Enemyway ceremony when someone says, "Let's go find and cut the staff." A man will locate a young tree with a full, well-shaped body, from which he cuts a nice straight branch. After doing this, he makes an offering of sacred stones, placing it on the cut end where the bough had been. He says, "I'll take part of you and make it into my staff as a healer." The same thing is done when making the drumstick, cutting another branch from the same tree. The drumstick has to be green and not an old dry piece of wood. After the ceremony, the staff and drumstick are put back on the earth and left with a lot of offerings, and a "Thank you for helping us today. You have healed the people with this."

Communities as well as individuals can have a relationship with a specific tree. They say trees have long lives, much longer than humans. Sometimes they were saplings well before we were born, and so they know the stories from a certain place and remember them long after we are gone. They will still be there as a teacher for the next generation and the next, recording all of the stories that take place. They will carry them—that is how the people talked about it. There was, in Black Mesa, a tree that was so sacred that people really respected it and called it Big Tree. This landmark had a five-foot diameter, was big and round, and was the tallest tree in the area as it sat next to a road. That tree stood there for the longest, longest time until somebody chopped it down. Cutting it devastated the people. They cried and wanted to know who had done such a thing and were terribly upset. All that was left was the stump, but residents continued to visit it, leaving offerings on top. I never thought Navajos would be that concerned about a common juniper tree. I watched an old man sit there praying to it; he had walked a mile on crutches to reach the site. It meant a lot to him. For two or three generations, it had served as a place of meditation, and now it was gone. The same is true for certain rock formations. There is one in Rock Point called Two People Sitting and Talking Together. One day the formation collapsed, so the people held many Blessingway ceremonies because they believed there would soon be some type of catastrophic change that would harm the community.

Trees have always been teachers; my grandfather talked about how they stood their ground with only the branches moving. People say a tree has a left and right branch—one side belongs to the people that you live with, but another branch on the opposite side belongs to you. The main stem of the tree is your mind that you think and reason with. If you put too much weight on either one of those branches, it will strain, crack, and break. To lessen that load, part of it is given back to the Creator through prayer. On one side of our life, we have the demands of people insisting on change. At the same time, the other tree branch sticking out represents a person wanting to forgive himself for thinking and burdening his mind. "Perhaps I have been too hard on myself, and so I need to forget what I have done by giving these problems back to the Creator. Then I can walk a little lighter." This is what the old people said the tree stood for.

Trees teach people and animals in another way through the shifting of seasons. Humans change over a long period of time, for years the process is

*"Just as a man gives his wife beautiful things to wear, so our Father Sky does the same. He sends rain down on Mother Earth, and because of the rain, the plants grow, and flowers of many colors appear. The plants with colored blossoms are her dress. It wears out. The plants ripen and fade away in the fall. Then in the spring, when the rains come again, Mother Earth once again puts on her finery. This is what the elders say." —Anonymous. (Photo by Stan Byrd)*

underway as skin and hair color and body structures mature with age. Trees do the same thing but on an annual basis. They follow the seasons—the frigidness of winter, the warmth of spring, the heat of summer, the coolness of fall, the strong and light winds, and seasonal moisture—all affect trees in their lifecycle. Colors change, leaves bud and later shrivel and fall, bark becomes harder, and sugar flows then slows, while the elements determine degree. Change is constant. The mountain holds the wardrobe to all of this, the trees and plants are its clothing that change throughout the year. Fall with its golden leaves, spring dressed in bright green, summer with its dark green leaves and multicolored plants, and the bareness of winter until new life starts over again—all follow a seasonal round. Animals watch these things. The mothers tell their young, "Look at the trees. They're changing. That means cold weather is coming. We've got to prepare." All the teachings of humans also belong to animals is what I was told. They are looking at things, and this is how they see, as visual learners.

## *Juniper: The Tree of the People*

At the time of creation, the holy people separated the trees between those that were to live on the mountains and those in the desert. Earlier, there were a lot more mountain-type trees in the desert that the gods used, but before departing, they decided to assign certain ones to specific areas. In their standards, they decreed that all different kinds of pines and spruces were to live in the mountains, but in the desert region of the Four Sacred Mountains there would be only two main types left behind—piñon and juniper. These became the main focus for the Navajo people after the gods left. That is why there are so many teachings and so much use of these two types of wood for shelters, tools, and ceremonial functions. Take the hogan for instance. Juniper trees are selected from among other trees and told, "You will be the doorway with life, and you will be the helper of the people, and you will keep us safe, and you will make for us a home." After hauling the logs to the site, the bark is peeled off to later put in the cracks between the logs, which are laid one on top of the other with the growth end following a clockwise direction. The logs overlap each other so that they will fit together and meet at the top. At the end of construction, the builder offers a hogan prayer for all the logs that were used. Each one has to have corn pollen sprinkled on it while the Hogan Song is sung, since these holy ones were built into the home that day. The logs used for this home are holy people and must be treated that way, to maintain their sacredness. In this home, people should only say kind words and avoid speaking evil because this is a holy house. The builders selected these logs from among the tree people, and so this wood should be treated as holy ones are. Every four years the structure needs to be reblessed to show it respect. Sweat lodges are also made from juniper logs in the same shape as a male hogan.

Another temporary structure is built for the Mountainway ceremony held in the late fall and winter, when the Yé'ii Bicheii begin dancing. The grasses are down, many animals start hibernating, lizards and snakes are gone, and most of the birds have flown south. As part of the Mountainway, a large open corral-like structure called Trees Put in a Circle (iłnáshjin) is fashioned from juniper branches. It follows the pattern of a roofless half hogan with the limbs laid down to form an enclosure for the participants in the fire dance and other activities. People who are not involved in the ceremony stand on the outside and look over the wall to see what is happening inside. This structure is also holy with its design given by the gods.

Today juniper wood is also used to make the traditional Navajo cradleboard, but in the past, when the first one was made by the holy people, it was made from spruce. First Man found White Shell Woman as a baby tied into a cradleboard placed at the top of Gobernador Knob (Ch'ool'į'í— Fir or Spruce Mountain). This formation is in the heart of the reservation and has a variety of high altitude plants like pines and spruce on its heights. The cradleboard that held the baby was first carved from two kinds of spruce— blue (cho' deenínii) and white (ch'óshgai). There are four types of spruce— white, blue, yellow, and black—each associated with one of the cardinal directions. The blue spruce has sharp pointed leaves that are tough and poke into a hand when touched. This is a male plant and associated with turquoise, while the white pine is female and its needles are soft, connected with white shell, and can be used in ceremonial dress. When the two types of wood were used in the first cradleboard, they represented the male and female side of the baby, and so they were always found together. The pieces of wood are cut from a tree, noting which end came from the lower part. When the backboard is carved, the bottom part is kept down because, like a baby, growth is always from the bottom to the top. This helps the child to be tall and continue to grow. The footrest at the bottom represents the earth, and the hoop above the baby's head a rainbow of protection. Remember also that the spruce, because it grows tall, sits in the ground deeper than many other trees, reaches to the heavens, and may communicate with the holy beings. It may also serve as a sky supporter, as previously discussed. Today, however, many cradleboards are made from juniper and have a beautiful grain and design.

*Curtis named this photograph "Yeibichai—The Beggar," but it is more likely the Water Sprinkler god who comes at the end of the line of Yé'ii Bicheii dancers. His collar is of spruce, a neck covering material that is also used by Talking God and House God. In each instance it stands for long life, "ever-green." (Courtesy Library of Congress—Photo 39004)*

# Aspen, Sacrifice, and Tragedy

The aspen (t'iisbái) is another mountain tree that has been used in religious rituals. In 2001 shortly before the 9/11 attack on the Twin Towers in New York City, a large group of tribal people representing many areas of the United States and different nationalities came to Big Mountain, part of Black Mountain, for a ceremony. The Sioux and Crow came in from their country and joined the Navajos and members of other tribes, working for a resolution to the Joint Use Area controversy. The issue was about relocating Navajo people off of lands that had been determined by the courts to belong to the Hopi. This was the last of a number of sun dances that had been held around this time, and so it was very sacred. My family joined in with other families to observe, along with a lot of our community leaders as well as many of the Lakota chiefs who traveled for the event. The religious leaders conducting the ceremony went into the San Francisco Peaks to select a tree from a female mountain. They drove to Flagstaff, Arizona, and cut one of the biggest aspen trees they could find. It was the tallest one I had ever seen and was so long that the leaders had a special escort back to the site where the ceremony was to be held.

The people called it Tree Day and brought their medicine offerings to tie to the pole. They prayed as they fastened their tobacco to it and spoke about how their world was troubled, they needed help, and they were struggling with life. For two days the tree lay there, accepting more medicine offerings, but on the third day, people raised the large pole and set it upright not far from a second sun dance pole used the previous year. Many, many, colored ribbons—red, yellow, black, and white—fluttered in the breeze, holding the medicine and carrying the prayers to the four directions, each with its own sacred color. As the wind began to pick up, the flying ribbons looked very beautiful. Next came the piercing of the dancers and offerings in cut flesh. Ropes tied to the top of the pole were attached to the men, who had an incision made in each breast with a wooden stick inserted in each. A rope attached to the top of the tree was fastened to the skewer so that the dancer could move in toward the pole and then go out to the rope's limit and pull against it. For four days they danced. On the last day, the men started dancing but were then hoisted up by their pierced flesh while other people cut themselves. This whole ceremony was about sacrifice, and once those who had been lifted up tore loose from the ropes, they fell to the ground and were removed to another area to begin healing.

Following these events, there was feasting and more sweat lodge ceremonies. I have never seen so many medicine people from different countries attend an occasion like this. There were men and women from Japan, New Zealanders came with their medicine, aborigines from Australia showed their medicine and danced with it wrapped around their feet—all kinds of people participated to celebrate life. They all wanted to be a part of this last ceremony that needed to be held on the land being taken by the federal government and given to the Hopi. This tribe wanted the area and the Navajos off of it, and so the Navajos held this last dance to protest. A few days later, some federal employees visited the site and did not like what they saw. They ordered a bulldozer to knock over the two poles, level the ground, and remove any trace of the ritual. The plow destroyed everything, driving in a circle until the whole area was totally flattened. The people who had conducted the ceremony were really upset after returning to see the devastation. Many of them cried, insisting that this should never have happened. Why would anybody want to destroy a celebration of life?

Nature has a way of knowing what happens. The wind will come, the rain will come, and they talk. They viewed the remnants at the site and reacted, just as humans do about the wrongs committed against those people who held the ceremony. The enemy has spoken and the elements let it be known in their own way that they were displeased. Within seven days, terrorists from another land flew aircraft into the Twin Trade Towers in New York City, taking both buildings down. Just like the two poles that were bulldozed at Black'Mesa, a national tragedy occurred, and these two huge buildings were destroyed with massive loss of life. The two sacred poles came down, the two towers came down. That is how holy and sacred the ceremony connected to trees can be. Medicine people say that through their medicine, this is what they learned and saw. Trees are sacred; perhaps this is a coincidence with things happening at the same time, but in the medicine world, this is what was said.

These types of events and practices cannot be played around with. Someone is going to get hurt; there are repercussions. Sometimes we just have to respect the tree because the holy people have put them here for a purpose. We have to allow it and keep it sacred. There is another point that should be made about this incident. The entire ceremony performed on Navajo land was very opposite to many of our beliefs, but they still have power and are connected to the spirit world. The whole idea of piercing, cutting flesh, allowing blood to flow, and dancing in this manner is very un-Navajo. In fact, it is wrong. In the Navajo way, there is nothing like this. No such ceremony was ever practiced with blood or used in any kind of similar situation. Even the Enemyway ceremony that uses part of an enemy's scalp, bone, or related object is done with the idea of cleansing a person from blood.

In this case, I think the Navajo people were in such a desperate situation with their loss of land, that as a last resort, members from AIM (American Indian Movement) were allowed to move in. They were the ones who brought in this sun dance. They felt that they could defeat the federal government and hold on to the land by performing this ceremony. I think that because of the small number of Navajos living in the Big Mountain area, they saw this as an opportunity and jumped on board to see if it would help. There was so much hatred toward the federal government, so many discussions, and a lot of disappointment that they decided to ally with these other groups and became friends, feeling that they should do whatever was necessary to defeat the removal.

This is the only way that I can explain what happened. Much of the land where this incident took place was at my father's sister's place. I know that if my father had been alive, he would not have allowed anything like that to occur. My grandfather would never have allowed anything like that, so even in the same family there were big differences in holding or preventing a ceremony like this. The small group of Navajos defending their land at Big Mountain had lost confidence in their own tribe and its government. The Navajo Nation backed off on a lot of things and allowed the federal government to come in and do what it needed to do to remove the Navajo and give the land to the Hopi. But the Navajos living there said, "No, we're going to fight back. We are called resistors and we will resist," so they stood their ground. The Navajo Nation never backed them up or provided help and so they were alone, bringing in anybody who could assist in their cause. That is why this sun dance took place on the reservation.

Those people never understood the purpose of that medicine. They were told that Sitting Bull used it to defeat the cavalry at the Battle of the Little Big Horn, when the Sioux were fighting their own war. They knew the story to that and so believed if it worked for the Sioux at that time, it would work for them here on the Navajo Reservation. They were ready to oppose the same people again through religion. I believe this was what they were thinking, but my family just tried to stay out of it and away from the conflict. When I listen to accounts of those who were there, I know there was a lot of sacredness. It was very holy. The Sioux defeated their enemy using this medicine, and the Navajo wanted to hold on to their land and stop outsiders from taking theirs. My family and a lot of other Navajos just stepped back and watched, not knowing what to say. Many of my family members on my father's side were doing it, but we did not agree. I decided the best thing to do was to say nothing, back off, and let them do what they thought best. They were the ones losing the land, not us. Our land was safe, but theirs was not.

# CHAPTER FIVE

# Plants and Herbs as Food and Medicine

## Harvesting the Earth's Surface

raditional Navajo herbalists and medicine people—whether women
or men—often have an encyclopedic understanding of wild and
domestic plants. A number of excellent studies have attempted to
preserve this knowledge, but the topic is vast and is, at times, kept between
practitioners or relatives.[1] Here, Perry shares some of the medicines he has
found effective as well as information about corn, beans and squash, the use
of pollen, the origin of peyote, and healing with wild plants. In this
introduction, supplementary information is provided to give more detail to
topics mentioned and to present origin stories that illustrate just how
connected the Navajo are to plants.

As the holy people climbed into this world, with raging flood waters
chasing the creatures out of the hollow reed, Turkey was the last to emerge.
Each of the animals escaping this disaster brought something from the
previous world to use in this one. First Woman, one of the holy beings,
ordered everyone to empty their containers so that all could take stock of
what the refugees now had. Dutifully, each of the holy people laid out their
goods except for Turkey who had no basket, pottery jar, or object in his
grasp. First Woman was furious, scolding, "Perhaps you think it is enough
that you bring nothing but feathers on your back when everyone else brings
something that will be of use in the new world! You are fat and lazy and you
kept all of us waiting until the angry waters almost caught you and us too!
You are all speckled with muddy water, and just look at that dirty foam on
your tail feathers!"[2]

Franc Newcomb, careful student of Navajo culture and raconteur of the story, continued:

> Hosteen [Hastiin] Turkey grew very red in the face when he heard First Woman say this, but he did not answer in words. First, he stretched out his wings and flapped them up and down, up and down. Out fell all kinds of corn—white corn, red corn, blue corn, yellow corn, and variegated corn; then he spread the feathers of his long tail and out fell all kinds of beans and sunflower seeds. When he shook the feathers on his back and legs, out fell the seeds of squash, melon, gourd, onion, and pumpkin which made a pile on the floor. Finally, he stretched out his head and ruffled the feathers on his neck so that a shower of small seeds flew in every direction—seeds of wild millet, wild rice, barley grass, tobacco, and cane grass, also mustard and sage. These were the last of the seeds, and Turkey folded his wings over his back and walked away.

All of the creatures were embarrassed and regretted what had been said by First Woman, who, at this point, was particularly ashamed. They realized that if the seeds had been left below, starvation would stalk the people. After apologizing for her tasteless comments, First Woman pronounced,

> When we reap our harvests we shall thank him for providing the seeds for our farms so we may have food for the winter months. From now on we shall call Turkey the "Farm Bird," and his feathers will be used on our prayer wands, while his beard—because it is dotted with water from the flood—will be a charm with which to bring the rain. He shall be called a "rain maker" because of the marks of foam on his tail. . . . From now on, Turkey shall be a very important person in our community for we will use his feathers in all of our important ceremonies.

The holy people then decorated his breast feathers with the color of corn seeds and the brown of tobacco seeds, his legs with melon seeds, then hung a bean vine around his forehead. They colored his feathers with sunflower pollen, his beak with wild barley, and the scales on his legs with squash and gourd seeds. The animals declared, "Now whenever anyone looks at Hosteen Turkey, he will be reminded of the seeds Turkey saved from the flood, and of his importance in the community. He will always be permitted to live near the homes of the First People, and no one shall do him harm." Navajos today still respect and use parts of this large bird, who made the seeds of both wild and domesticated plants available.

At the very time of creation, when the holy people charged Mother Earth and Father Sky with future responsibilities, the female side received the primary task of caring for plants. Black God spoke of the many beautiful things that both Mother Earth and Father Sky had been blessed with so that each could be helpful, then saying to the woman, "That is the purpose for which it was done [given vegetation and other materials] to you, not to enable you to help just a few! See then, you the woman have been made to be placed in charge of various kinds of plants, therefore for all future time, food has been placed in your hands. Thereby you will be useful. You too, who are the man [Father Sky], into your hands dark clouds, male rain, and dark mist, female rain especially have been given. Thereby you also will be useful."[3] Ever since, women have been responsible for much of the care of livestock, food preparation, cooking, and other related tasks. By extension, human mothers, like Mother Earth, care for, provide, and nurture their family members. This is made evident through the Navajo language, where, "Earth Woman, human mothers, the sheep herd, corn fields, and the mountain soil bundle are all called shimá [mother]. It is not adequate or accurate, however, to say simply that some are mothers and some are not mothers but are a metaphorical extension of the concept of motherhood. They are all mothers, but each one is a mother in a way that in part resembles the others but in part is distinct from the others."[4]

Medicine man George Blueyes explains further the relationship of humans to plants and nature as follows.

The Plant People were put here for us. The sky is the one who does the planting. He moves clouds over the plants. He moves clouds of male rain. He moves the female rain and dark mists over the plants, and they grow. We live by the plants. They are our food and our medicine and the medicine for our livestock. . . . There were more plants long ago. It seemed as if there was no bare ground. Sunflowers covered the earth with yellow, and among them were flowers of red and blue. There were so many different plants. But the plant people move wherever they please. If they choose to go back to the land, they will. You cannot plant these kinds of plants. If they choose to move somewhere else, it is up to them.[5]

As with most things in the Navajo universe, plants are either male or female. The qualities that separate the sexes are sometimes unclear, ranging from descriptions of bark to size, shape, and leaf type. For example, mountain mahogany is used for a male sacrificial cigarette and cliffrose for a female because the male plant is larger and coarser. Cliffrose is also used as baby material, associated with the female task of changing diapers. Cottonwood trees with "beaded earrings," or seeds, are female; those without are male. Some practitioners believe that female plants or parts need to come from female mountains like Black Mesa, and male plants and parts from male mountains like the Chuska. This may be one reason that travel is prevalent, one medicine woman from Aneth going to Blue Mountain, Mesa Verde, Ute Mountain, the Carrizo Mountains, Navajo Mountain, and the La

Sals in search of plants—an area with a diameter of approximately 150 miles.[6]

A brief look at wild plants, just as with trees in the previous chapter, will show how Mother Nature is both a cornucopia and pharmacopeia for the Navajo people. Red Indian paintbrush is put in water, then given to stop nosebleeds. Bottle plant is used for someone who is having problems with urination. For an animal with a cut, snakeweed is pounded with a stone, swished in water, and given orally to encourage healing and prevent infection. When sheep get an eye disease, the stem that protrudes from a yucca plant is burned, the ashes are crushed and mixed with salt, and the ingredients are put on the eye. Narrowleaf yucca root is also crushed and used for shampoo; its tender stalks can be placed under a fire; when cooked they taste like corn, if fried they taste like squash. Broadleaf yucca is a remedy for vomiting and heartburn. Mint removes a child's fever when mixed with water and given orally and then applied externally as a bath. Rock lichens cure mouth sores.[7] This glimpse into a vast knowledge of wild plant foods and medicines is the product of what the Navajo have accumulated over the centuries.

Domesticated plants have blossomed into significance to the point that corn is attributed to be intertwined with life from birth to death. Medicine man John Holiday believes,

> Life was given to us from the tips of the white and yellow corn stalks, where pollen is found. People say there is a corn seed that exists somewhere as another world. The Holy Wind comes from there to give us life, entering our bodies when we are born. We use this Holy Wind as we live on this earth until we die from old age; then we go back into the tips of the corn stalk that produces pollen. This is why Navajos use corn pollen to pray. As children of the Holy Wind, we are given life through it, so when we die, this life will return to the corn pollen stalk. Songs and prayers change us into people.[8]

To sustain that life, corn is the most important of all of the traditional foods. A quick survey of Charlotte Frisbie's *Navajo Food Sovereignty* reveals dozens and dozens of recipes about how to use it. Perry's anger at corn bread being made incorrectly underscores the high value placed on preparing traditional foods correctly. The same was true of planting, caring, and harvesting, each phase being surrounded by religious proscription as well as wise field management. Separating certain strains of corn so that there was no cross-pollination; planting in the center of the field and then expanding outward in a sunwise direction or planting in rows; putting a dozen seeds in a hill so that the corn grows in bunches, thus protecting the inner stalks from desert winds; and adding beans between the rows so that the plant can grow upward around the stalk while also replacing nitrogen removed from the soil by the corn—all were good practices. There were also religious teachings such as keeping pregnant women away from the field to prevent the corn from becoming unhealthy, barring menstruating women from entering to avoid stunted seed growth, and tempering active forces like lightning and destructive winds through songs and prayers.[9] Navajos cared for their crops both physically and spiritually.

One of the most important aspects of corn production is the gathering of pollen. While there are many different types of pollen collected from a variety of plants and used by medicine men in a number of ceremonies, corn pollen (tádídíín) is the most common one carried by many people in a personal pollen pouch (tádídíín bizis) on a daily basis. It is gathered during a two-week period (if planted in early June, the corn may not tassel and silk until early August), by shaking the pollen into a bowl, sifting it a number of times to remove foreign matter, and then drying it for a week or more before storing. The task is performed by women who often sing Blessingway songs and maintain positive thoughts as they obtain the pollen that will be used for daily prayer, blessing the home, giving an offering, assisting in a ceremony, protecting oneself, and summoning the holy people.

The meaning and power of pollen is expressed in a number of forms. After Talking God built the first hogan, he blessed it by strewing cornmeal around the circumference of the structure before inviting the other holy people to enter. Hogans today are blessed in similar fashion. Next, he encouraged all present, "You may address your petitions [prayers] to all things, none excepted. When you plead with this wind [soul] that stands within you, you will make a pollen application to it. And you may petition your hogans, you will make a pollen application to them. And you may petition your fire, your utensils of every description that serve you for meals. Petition your food woman, your food man . . . say to them while you rub yourselves with them, 'Keep me in your care to the end of my days, may I continue life with your aid.'"[10]

John Holiday, to illustrate the power of pollen and the purifying influence it has on speech, tells of how an apprentice, before receiving his instruction, kisses five times the medicine man's tongue covered with pollen, after which the teacher applies sacred corn pollen all over his student, making him holy and receptive to learning.[11] To Leland Wyman, "The pure, immaculate product of the corn tassel is food eaten by the gods and man. Pollen, the beautiful, is a fit gift for the gods. Their paths should be strewn with it. When put in the mouth it really is a gift to the person [inner form] within the petitioner who should accompany his action with a prayer to that person. It enables the user to go on in life, to say kind and pleasant things. Pollen guards against abuse."[12] Of all of the plants that symbolize the

Navajos' religious commitment to the holy people, corn and pollen say the most about the Diné.

## *Food is Life*

There are four sacred plants of the Navajo Nation—corn, beans, squash, and tobacco. They were first brought to the people at the time of emergence, when Turkey, the last of the creatures to enter into the White World, cleared the reed through which he had traveled, and shook his tail feathers and body, dropping all types of seeds from various plants. Now there was food in this new world. Today, on many of the prayersticks, small grains of corn, beans, squash, and tobacco are tied on to the handle, along with a turkey feather, as part of the healing and blessing power. It would be difficult to overstate the importance of corn, which is considered divine in nature, is used in some form in almost all ceremonies, is thought to have been with the Navajo since the beginning of time, and is an integral part of daily prayers. It is the basis from which the first humans were formed, serves as the staff of life in traditional culture, and is the connecting link between man and the holy people. In a religious sense, it is considered a "magic" or spiritually powerful food.

In Navajo thought, food is spoken of as life. If a person can produce and prepare it, then they are prepared for life, since just the act of obtaining, fixing, cooking, and serving food takes a lot of effort. From growing or hunting it to placing it on the table requires many different steps. The word for food, "ch'iyáán," means "abundancy of something to eat," which we have today, but in the past, everything arrived slowly with a lot of effort. People planted corn, beans, and squash, but none of it came immediately. My grandfather always talked about food and the work it took to get it. Even something as simple as obtaining piñon nuts takes time to find and pick, while also ensuring that it is done in the proper way before preparing them. People have to know what they are doing in order to survive in this world. Today it is so different that we do not talk about food in the same way anymore. Now a person does not even have to move before someone will bring it to them. There are all kinds of government programs that guarantee everyone is fed.

In the past, Navajos really considered the whole food cycle as life connected to the holy ones. Food has its own prayers. People used to sing a lot of songs to bring the rain, good growing weather, and abundant crops.

*Corn is the single most important food in traditional Navajo culture. This gift of life was the basic element from which the Navajo people were initially created, the food that sustained them in a desert environment, and the single most important plant to connect them to the holy people through pollen. Corn, like sheep, is life.*

Food had its own sacred words that were used in thanksgiving to the holy people for what they had provided and for the life sustained by it. Water was usually the first thing to be mentioned because everything living depends upon it. Prayers talk about its flow and how it is the main stem of food whether plant or animal. Water is always the main prayer. Especially for the Hopi, who live on high desert mesas, and who depended on the holy people sending water so that crops would survive. They formed relationships with the Navajo around exchanging food, praying for weather, and storing surplus for later use. Navajos traded meat for apricots, peaches, and other things the Hopi grew. Food created relationships and fostered respect between people. But it all took work and communication.

## *Bread and Relationships*

One important aspect when exchanging with the Hopi and also just between Navajos is bread. This symbolizes a sharing of friendship as part of a gift— it was always about the bread. When the holy people created the first men and women, they were made from corn (naadą́ą́'), which was cooked in the ground. This was one of the first foods ever made out of corn. The bread represents the fire, earth, plant, and everything that goes into the water and falls with it from the sky. Medicine people say that bread cooked underground is one of the most complete foods and is one of the holy ones. It must be made of blue corn—no processed flour—starting with the ear that is picked off the stalk, the kernels ground with a mano and metate, and the batter that is baked in a pit at least four or five inches deep and covered with a layer of dirt with a fire built on top. The blessing comes from the ground. If you want to hire a medicine man, he will say, "Cook the bread in the ground (łeehyilzhoozh), and I will accept it." Once it is baked, the loaf may have ashes on it which are brushed off before giving it to him. The bread is considered of high value and a very fitting payment when requesting a ceremony. Once the medicine man accepts the "ash cake," or "ash bread," there is agreement as to what needs to be done.

Another kind of bread that is baked in a similar way is kneel-down bread. This is made by putting the dough in corn husks and again, baking it underground. I had an embarrassing experience with this when I was working in the Shiprock area for the Department of Human Health Services. Another man and I were invited by some people to eat with them. They said that they were going to have kneel-down bread and knew how to prepare it. My companion and I watched for a while. This type, like the other bread, is never cooked on top of a fire—the ground does the baking. All these people had put together was a fire and so we helped by digging a square pit five or six inches deep, built a fire in the hole so that it would get really hot, and eventually shoveled out the ashes and coals that filled it. It was all ready and looking good, when one of them asked, "What are you doing? Aren't you going to do the kneel-down bread? This is not ready now. We don't cook it like that. We'll show you how." Instead of using the heated pit lined with corn husks, they placed a wire screen with aluminum foil over the coals and put the corn husks on top, occasionally turning them. I was shocked: "Is this how you guys do it? Who taught you to cook like this?" Then it really hit me. "Your wife is the one who taught us how to do it this way." I was stunned and could only get out, "This is not cooked that way. Not where I come from. People are going to laugh in your face with this. You are supposed to do it like this," and then I showed them how to use the hole, put the husks in order, cover it with aluminum foil, shovel dirt on top, then add the coals and fire. The cook occasionally checked inside the husk to see when the batter had turned firm like a cake. The way they were cooking, the kneel-down bread would be totally raw inside and burned on the outside. Sure enough, after they baked a lot of them, the raw bread just fell apart.

This bothered me so much, I had to go home. I told my wife, "I want you to go over there now!" She asked what was so important but all I could say was, "I want you there now." We returned to the cooks around the fire and I told her, "This is your teaching," but she denied it and said she had taught the people differently. When she saw the mess they were in, she explained again and got things in the right order, the way it is supposed to be. I finally straightened the whole thing out and told my wife, "From Black Mountain to Shiprock, this is the way we teach cooking. You better start really teaching things well, in a good manner because somebody misunderstood you. Ash bread and kneel-down bread are always baked in the ground because it is the earth that does the cooking, the fire just sits on top. This is how the first foods were cooked."

When baking for a medicine man, a person removes the bread from the fire, brushes any ashes or dirt off, and hands it to him nice and hot. This is the first step in requesting that he perform a ceremony. There are four possible offerings that can be made, but only one is necessary. If an individual chooses to present more than one, that is also acceptable. Giving bread shows some of the highest respect when making a request. The thinking behind it is, "If you have done this for me, then I will do things well for you." This is how it used to be when the people had nothing. Another kind of offering is blue bread made from blue cornmeal batter and cooked on a hot stone or steel plate. When the bread is finished, it is something like thin bread made by the Hopi called piki, but it is thicker like a tortilla. This and the kneel-down bread are two types of offerings given to a medicine

*Cultural food specialties communicate important traditional values, the status of an individual, the inclusion of the holy people, and a society's identity. Kneel-down bread performs all of these roles, the reason that Perry insisted that it be cooked in the proper manner.*

man, with tobacco being the third and corn pollen the fourth. Any one of these four offerings is highly important because of the sincerity it shows by following traditional practices. Once the medicine man accepts it, he starts preparing. Following the ceremony, the patient and family will make a payment with livestock, silver jewelry, money, or other valuable goods. But these first four "down payments" are called "bee ajooką̄ąh" or "hired by payment," which is the sincere way to approach medicine people about a request. This is done on the highest level of mutual respect.

## Beans, Squash, Gourds, and Tobacco

Beans (naa'ółí) are another food that is used in ceremonies. In the Enemyway, they are referred to as "the food that never ran from hunger." The reason for this title is that, like corn, they store very well, are rich in nutrients, and when ground, can be used in a variety of ways. There are four colors of beans—yellow (pinto), black, red (kidney), and white (navy).

When planted with corn, beans provide a nutritious diet. If a person has mistakenly killed or injured a cat, who is a holy person with strong protective supernatural powers, that individual may suffer from stomach bloating and gas. As an offering to the cat and as a cure for the patient, beans are mixed with sheep fat and foxtail grass into a batter that is placed in a corn husk and put under a rock. Which type of beans to use for this is determined by the color of the cat. Its spirit must be returned, and so through prayers that go to Wildcat Peak (Náshdoíts'ǫ'í—Wildcat Guts) located north of Tuba City, Arizona, the spirit accepts the offering and the individual is healed.

Squash (naayízí) is called "One That Grows in Many Directions" and is found in a number of clan names such as the Squash People Red Running into the Water (Naayízí Diné'é Táchii'nii). This vegetable is appreciated as a food by the Navajo, but its brother, the gourd, is used only for external purposes. There is a story that tells how this came to be. Sister Squash and brother Gourd sat in a garden one day when an argument erupted between them. One of the holy people had put some markings on the squash that angered her jealous brother. The two had grown up together, shared the same patterns, and had hoped to be used as edible food. But now Gourd was angry, swearing that he would leave the garden and not provide food to those who grew him. "I'm leaving," he said, "but when I am grown, I will be used in a different manner and not eaten." Squash replied, "Okay. If you're going to do that, then we're going to take some of your insides away from you. You will have nothing but seeds internally and not be edible; you will not be able to nourish people and will be a bad person. Your only use will be in a sacred manner, but you will always have a bad pattern on you." The bad pattern referred to is skin inflammation and skin cancer, which gives hardship to people. "You will be left apart from us. Perhaps someday, somebody will use you for something else, but it will always be as an external medicine. If two people do not like each other, are arguing, and want to separate, you will be used in this way. You're not going to be a good person." [Perry described the gourd plant as having dark green leaves, with spirals coming off the vine.]

Because of this disagreement, medicine people use the gourd accordingly. They split it in half with only a little attachment left on each side. They will paint female markings (a dress, stirring sticks, or long hair) on one side and male symbols (hair bun and bow) on the other side, then sing a song and hold the gourd behind the medicine man's back. He then separates the two partly cut pieces, and hands the male part to the man and the female side to the woman. The medicine man will make an offering to each and soon the couple will separate. That is how medicine using a gourd was practiced. This way is not good and results in divorce. True, gourds are used as rattles in the medicine way or as a cup, but they will never provide nourishment or anything concerning growth. People are told, "Don't touch it. Leave it alone. Stay away from that," especially if you are a young person. "Stay away from the gourd." Squash, on the other hand, has many colors, but on the back of a gourd rattle, medicine people put stars. Squash decorates itself and may have all the formations in the heavens and the mountains in its design, plus there is a lot of nourishment. That is how the story goes.

Tobacco, the fourth sacred plant, has a long and involved story that tells how a number of different medicine practices came about. The narrative starts during the time when White Shell Woman traveled with the people as they encountered many new and strange things. The Navajos had four fire pokers, each representing a cardinal direction, who had experienced a lot, and so the people turned to them and said, "Tell us a story about some of these things we are seeing." The fire pokers began to teach. The one in the east explained that there was a holy person, Talking God, who lived in that direction. He sat there to give answers and guide, but the people would have to travel there to receive them and had to take that fire poker with them. White Shell Woman, the fire poker, and the people walked together to the east. There they climbed a high mountain made from white shell. On top there was a big stone of white shell, which she sat on and prayed for answers. Suddenly, two white doves descended, singing their songs. The birds said, "We'll give you directions to a sacred plant, white-tipped tobacco, which sits ready to help you." Each time White Shell Woman went in another direction—south, west, and north—with her people, she found birds of different colors—blue (mountain bluebird), yellow (lesser goldfinch), and black (redwing blackbird who has a yellow and red patch on its shoulder, signifying it is the keeper of dawn where darkness meets daytime). Each told her of a tobacco plant that had the same color, while each bird had its own song that tied in with their direction. This is how the four sacred tobaccos were gathered.

As the group returned to the center of Navajo lands, White Shell Woman found a pond of water. The Holy Wind whispered to her to sit by the edge and look into it. "The sky is going to open up to you and the clouds reflect behind you, and together they will capture your eyes and you will see something special." As she did this, there was suddenly a vision, with a light coming in from the east that shone into the water. Someone was about to enter the pond and then come out and shake itself, revealing something important. She waited there until a coyote came in from the east, bathed in the water, came out, and shook, releasing a piece of white shell. Three more times a coyote came in from one of the remaining directions and shook turquoise, abalone shell, and jet onto the ground, completing their donation to what now became the sacred stone offering. White from the east represents light, turquoise is water, yellow is air, and black Mother Earth and the things that grow from it. The gods were present and had shown how to make an earth or mountain offering.

White Shell Woman learned a lot of songs and prayers at this time, so she taught the people in the hogan framed by the Four Sacred Mountains. At one point, she introduced two men who had assumed the role of women (nádleeh) and were very knowledgeable about how to make and do things. White Shell Woman asked one of them, "How do we do this? There's tobacco here, and we need to use it as medicine." The two nádleeh sat down, discussed the problem, and then went to the river, where they fashioned a clay pot and a tobacco pipe, then baked them. The pot and pipe assumed the colors of the fire, proving once again that this holy being was sacred. This is when the people learned that fire was very powerful when used to create an object for medicine or a tool. The fire made a lot of patterns on the pipe, leaving blue, yellow, red, black, and white markings. Even today when people light their kilns to bake pottery, the colors come from the light, water, air, and earth. The two nádleeh had taught about the four elements, how they listened to them, and how their songs started. One of them said, "Today I will sing a song for you and you will listen," sitting there until everyone was quiet. He sang, "Hei ei yąą ąą nei yaa nei haa'ánádei haa'ánádei hei yee ya ei yináh ei yik'eh ánádei hei yee ya haa'ánádei haa'ánádei hei yee ya ei yináh ei yik'eh haa'ánádei hei yee ya ei naa ha'ii'ashii hei yęę biyázhii ęę ęę na dzil bikflk." It was all about the white shell house to the east that sat upon a white shell clay basket, which held a white pipe that burned white tip tobacco. The smoke from it, when blown out, turned into white dawn. Through that white dawn flew two white birds, singing their songs, later to become husband and wife. Now there is always a couple who teaches about parenting as a father and mother using this knowledge that belongs to the east. The same pattern, with directional differences, came from the south, west, and north, each with their own sacred pipe, tobacco, and teachings.

This is all part of how a person is healed. The smoke that a patient receives is itself a healer, while the medicine man is like the bird who sings and helps the person to find their way through the "smoke" of depression and sadness. Smoke, like these feelings, cannot be measured; it comes and goes, spreads, and then disappears, just like depression. Using tobacco in ceremonies such as the man's smoke ceremony (diné k'ehgo diihnályé) goes back to the first time an offering was made to the earth when these ceremonies began and the problem of depression was first addressed. Tobacco works on the mind, thoughts, and feelings. When the four different types of tobacco are mixed together, it becomes the main tobacco of the Navajo people.

There are other types of tobacco used for special purposes. When these are made, at least one of the four main tobaccos just mentioned have to be included in them. For instance, if a medicine person makes water tobacco, they would always have to add one of these to make it complete—even though there might be eighteen different ingredients in addition to it. There are water tobaccos, plain tobaccos, mountain tobaccos, deer tobaccos, and others that have different names and are used for specific occasions in certain ways. Take for instance a person who needs to use a Deerway or Mountainway tobacco. The medicine man has to go to a mountain and locate a plant called "deer ears" (Frasera speciosa—bįįh yiljaa'í—mullen), then find a place where a deer has urinated on the ground with its little plants, then obtain plant material that the deer has eaten and regurgitated (biih háá'iis'aalígíí), blend in other ingredients, and add one of the four sacred tobaccos. That is what this ceremonial tobacco for the Deerway or Mountainway requires. Waterway tobacco (tóó yee k'ehgo nát'oh) is made the same way with plants that come from the water and are used in the Waterway ceremony (Na'at'oyee). There are a lot of different tobaccos that can be found locally and do not require going to the mountains or distant places.

## *Wild Plants for Healing*

The entire natural world is filled with plants that serve the Navajo people for food and medicine. A few examples of medicine follow. Diarrhea (átsą́ hodinih—aching stomach) is a common problem. A medicine called Daisy Rock That Breathes (tsé gháníłch'ih—*Pectis angustifolia*—lemon-scented cinchweed) looks like a blooming yellow daisy that has a strong smell and is available from July to October. It has small crowns that grow on its stem; that is what is picked for the medicine that serves as my main cure for diarrhea. I pay top dollar for anybody who picks it for me. There was a little girl who lived in an area where these flowers just covered the neighboring hills. I told her mother that if she let her daughter pick and put them in jars, I would pay forty dollars for each. Her mother couldn't believe me but went to work with her daughter. They earned $160. I use this for three different ceremonies, one of which is the Windway, in part of a mixture of herbs that one drinks. It is really good for relaxation, calms anxiety disorders, and aids in sleep.

As a medicine man, sometimes I do not know what is causing the sickness, and so I explore through prayer to find an answer. For instance, there was a young girl living near Page, Arizona, who was herding sheep when suddenly a spider, probably a black widow, bit her. Relatives put hot packs and cold packs on the bite, but nothing seemed to work, and within

*Wild plants provide many types of food and medicine for the Navajo people. Bee plant (waa) is being harvested here. It serves as a food after being boiled several times. It may be eaten like cooked spinach, used in making bread, boiled in water for a yellow-green dye for wool, and placed in moccasins to remove foot odor.*

minutes her leg swelled so badly that they took her to the emergency room at the local hospital. She received shots, but the swelling did not go down, and the skin puffed up so that it looked like plastic. Eight hours passed without improvement. The leg appeared to be blown up with air, which badly stretched the skin, the girl suffered in pain, while the doctor feared she might go into a coma. After reaching the hospital, I performed a small ceremony in which I asked the Creator what was going on, how I could counteract this spider bite, and what medicine to use. He told me, "Go down and find a certain plant for medicine. This is what it is called; just pick the tip. Chew some of it and spit the mixture on the wound. That is all it is going to take." I went to where she was living and found everything I needed was right there—common rabbit brush (*Chrysothamnus nauseosus*—k'iiłtsoi' nitsaágíí—big yellow on top). Below the yellow top there is a greenish leafy section on the bottom near where the stem comes out of a branch. I picked a lot of those leaves but left the roots and yellow flowers alone. Once back with the patient, I sang a particular song, chewed those leaves, and then spit the mixture on the large, black-marked opening around the wound. Within thirty minutes, the swelling began going down, so I added more mixture and wrapped the wound. In an hour, the leg had returned to its normal size. The doctor, who monitored the situation, was stunned and asked how this whole process worked. I responded, "The Indian way. The Navajo way. This is how it happens." The next day the little girl was running around again. That is the way one works with medicine and herbs. It really does happen like this.

Snakeweed (*Gutierrezia sarothrae*—ch'ildiilyésiitsoh—big dodge weed) is another plant quite similar to rabbit brush that cures snake bites. It grows just like a regular bush, but if you have any of it embedded in your hand, it will swell like poison ivy. It only works on a bite when using the Snakeway (Hoozhónee) prayers. This herb is left alone unless it is to be used in a ceremony or as medicine when an occasion requires it. You don't play with this plant. Both with a snake or black widow bite, this medicine causes the swelling to quickly go down. When medicine people talk about these types of cures, they usually do not tell a story about its origin, but only show what it is and explain how it works. There are just too many plants.

## *Peyote: The Outsider*

Peyote, a cactus button used by the Native American Church (NAC) as a sacrament, is one of the most frequently ingested natural plants used by Navajos for religious purposes. It does not grow locally but comes from Texas and Mexico, and can only be transported by Indians who have a license because it has hallucinogenic properties and is classified as a drug. My father was a road man who presided over the all-night ceremony and the use of peyote. He liked the idea of attending these meetings, singing the songs that go with them, and helping people to overcome their problems through its use. My grandfather was on the other side and had no part of it. He would counsel that it was not our medicine, but had come to the Navajo Reservation in the 1930s and 1940s brought in mostly by non-Navajos. So my father and grandfather—both medicine men—disagreed, my grandfather insisting, "That's not for us. That's for different people. The real medicine men, the real medicine is here." Even though they talked and debated about it, my father never really argued, but he just liked the way it worked with him and could see things with it.

In order to use peyote, a person has to be a member in good standing with the Native American Church. A membership card is issued based on the chapter that a person votes in. If the police raid a ceremony and find people who do not have cards, they will be arrested, and if they have NAC paraphernalia in their hands, they will be charged for that violation, too. For the road man who travels to other places on the reservation to perform a ritual, he must have his license with him. A lot of Navajos go to North and

South Dakota to hold ceremonies, but they have to have their NAC card, showing that person holds North American Native American Church membership that is good for all over this country. The card can be obtained in a lot of places, but the individual has to be certified. I am often asked by people going to Texas if they can borrow my card, but I refuse. There is a police station where one has to check in and show his card to let them know they will be purchasing peyote. The police also inspect what is bought, take a picture of it, and perform a background check before sending the purchaser on his way. I have seen people sit in jail for months and months because they did not have a card, waiting for the Navajo Nation to arrive and pick them up.

One time I asked my grandfather how peyote came to be, what was its story? This is what he said. After White Shell Woman left the people for the last time, Talking God ordered all the medicines in the White World to come together at a place called the Holy Mountain Hogan (Táálee Hooghan), a large medicine house [rock formation] on Black Mesa, northeast of Dilkon, Arizona. Everybody came, even the little plants. If any of them were useful, they were told to be there. They all sat in their ranked order in a circle, where they introduced themselves, told where they came from, what medicine they held, and how it could heal others. Just as the meeting started, one plant entered late. Everybody looked over to see Peyote trying to find a spot. He was a young man who stood by the doorway as he surveyed the filled-to-capacity hogan, searching for a seat. Talking God, sitting in the place of honor to the west, commanded, "Make room for him. Let him sit by the doorway." Peyote looked, then said, "I want to sit in the west and be the main person." The twelve primary medicine people in charge did not think this was right and felt he would be sitting out of order based on the type of plant he was, so denied his request. "You can't make your way to there. You're not part of that group but belong to a different one. Go ahead and sit down."

"No," he said, then began arguing with everyone. He became very angry, demanding, "If I'm not part of this group, I'm not going to be part of any group. If I can't sit over there, I'm not going to stay." The other plants begged him not to go, not to talk like that, but he just turned around and walked away. Sage sat in the north and was urged by the other plants, "Go get him. Bring him back. Put your arms around him. Talk to him. Have him return." The messenger caught up to the young man and grabbed him, saying, "Hey, brother, come on, friend. Let's go back in there. We are all in the same group here. We are all medicine people." Sage, because of his size and shape, was the only one of those plants that could put his arms around Peyote without being hurt. This is why sage is the only medicine plant that has a relationship with peyote and is now part of the Native American Church ceremony.

Peyote refused. He turned to the medicine plants watching him and said, "All of you, you think you're high medicine people, but one day people will forget about you. One day most of you will be forgotten and become extinct. When that happens, I will return. That will be when traditional teachings and medicine will end. People are going to lose their way of doing things, their hair buns, their moccasin, how they used to dress. Next will be their language, and they will forget how to speak Navajo. Then they will become like western [Anglo] people, and that is when I will come back as the only medicine." He turned and walked away to the east. Although everyone encouraged him to stay, he would not, so they left him alone. Still, the people insisted on giving him a name and so bestowed "The One That Came with the Earth" (Ni' bił hodeezliní ni' bił hodoolkǫ' tsíłkę́ę́h naat'áánii) and even though he said all of these things, he will still be part of the cactus people. His name indicates where he lives now—in little humps in the ground, visible at dawn and located in Mexico. That is where he was headed, and so that is the name he received. It is also the reason why peyote never became part of the regular Navajo medicine group.

## *The Buffalo and Lifeway Medicine*

Following the council, all of the plants dispersed. The next night, however, after the meeting ended, the people heard a rumbling sound coming from the south. Dust and dirt flew high in the air as a large herd of buffalo ran past the medicine house doorway and continued to the north. They slowed to a walk, grazing, urinating, and defecating as they continued on their route. Wherever they peed or pooped it sprouted medicine on the trail that led to the north. This is now called the Medicine Trail that goes from Dilkon to Chinle and Many Farms, Arizona, where a path of red stone was made, then to the area around Hite, Utah, where they crossed the Colorado River to the Henry Mountains and now reside. The buffalo were told not to return to reservation lands because the medicine had been planted and should not be disturbed.

On the second night there was another rumble that appeared in a dream about a white buffalo coming to the people. In it, this buffalo ran alone; the people learned that they should follow him—he had the main medicine. Where he went, there would be major healing sites filled with power, and where his droppings and urine fell, potent medicine plants would grow. The people started after him as he pursued the rest of the herd that roamed to the

*From Dilkon, Arizona, to the Henry Mountains, Utah, buffalo—powerfully spiritual
animals—created a medicine path through their droppings left during their travels.
The plants and herbs in Monument Valley and in Valley of the Gods hold special
powers for Lifeway ceremonies.*

north. One of those medicine sites was Valley of the Gods. Some of the
sacred plants located there are said to cure difficult diseases like cancer. This
is why the Valley of the Gods is the only place where the holy plants like
that are found. When he left, all of the gods created from the red dust started
singing and later turned into rocks as they settled into their place on the
ground. These holy people stretch all the way into Monument Valley and
remain there with their songs to heal people. From the Valley of the Gods to
Monument Valley this area is known as White Valley (Tsé Bii'nidzisgai—
The Rock That Had White Going through It or The Rock That Has White
Shadows) and is where the white buffalo traveled, leaving medicine that is
still used today. The frozen gods with their songs are also present. This red
dust, once stirred into the air, then became gods in human form who sang
and prayed before turning into stone and are there to help the medicine
people today.

Now, a person can go there to communicate with these holy ones. When
a medicine man performs a Lifeway ceremony, he makes offerings at many
of these places. Not many people know about the sacred areas and where
one really needs to go, but there is a place near the turnoff into Valley of the
Gods and also a big corner in the back of the park where the ridge bends that

serve as offering sites. People conducting the Lifeway ceremony are the only ones allowed to leave offerings there. We call them the Lifeway Ceremonial People (Iináájí dahataałígíí). They are given the authority to do that, which includes both Valley of the Gods and part of Monument Valley. This is also how the old men used to talk about the way the medicine worked itself into human form and then turned into rocks. When a medicine man went there and sat among the rocks, they would join in with him, singing and giving instructions.

This is what I learned from my grandfather, but I never asked a lot of questions about it because my dad was always saying, "Don't ask too many questions. Some of this is sacred. You don't want to know that. It could be harmful. Some things you can't talk about." But that never stopped me. Every time Grandpa and I were together and alone, I would ask him to talk to me and tell what he knew. At first he would say, "Don't ask about that. You can't talk about that," but I would say, "Why not? Since you know about it, why can't I? What happens if you die and have never told me? It will all be lost." He would answer, "Don't talk like that," but would eventually share what he knew. I received a lot of information from him and am glad I did, because otherwise he probably would have told me nothing.

There are other medicine teachings about buffalo to consider. The hide is highly prized for its healing values, suggesting that all of the knowledge and wisdom that the animal has will accompany the person who uses it. If a medicine man sees a brown or white buffalo when star gazing or feels an impression of one when hand trembling, then he has to go behind the buffalo to the story where the clouds were formed, the medicine droppings left behind the footprints in the dirt, and the sprouting plants of medicine, and connect these to the Lifeway ceremony that he will use. There are buffalo sounds and specific medicines that go with those teachings, and so as the medicine man sings the buffalo songs, an image of the medicine comes and says, "This is the one that you're looking for." Now the healing can start.

Navajos have always considered buffalo as one of the great holy ones that came from the south. They appeared one day as four people with buffalo heads and human bodies. These creatures came from the pueblos like sacred gods and began dancing in a circle, kicking up dust. As they performed, they turned into animals, but through the dust, the people began seeing spiritual things and visions that spoke of the holy people and the powers of the buffalo. Even the hair on the animal represented medicine. They finished transforming and moved away; the dust settled and left a lot of medicine herbs, which are now called the "Fur of Buffalo Medicine." At this time there was a lot of sickness and disease, but with this medicine, people were healed. Now this is known as buffalo hair medicine (ayání yilghaa'). Occasionally people would sleep in that same place and buffalo would appear, teaching them about the use of their hooves for a rattle, meat for medicine, horns for a drinking cup for sacred water, and the beard/goatee on the handle of a rattle. These were not to be items for everyday use, but available for offerings and as part of the Lifeway medicine.

The Hoof/Claw (Akéshgaanjí) ceremony is one of the Lifeway (Iináájí K'ehgo) rituals and gets its name from the buffalo hoof rattle. The accompanying ceremony was first performed when a group of Navajos were hunting buffalo. One of the horses became skittish and threw a young man who was badly trampled by the stampeding herd. He bled from his mouth, ears, waist, and other parts of his body from the hooves of the animals. The man was all but dead. The hunters asked the medicine people how to heal something like this. They used a buffalo hide for a stretcher, brought the injured warrior to a shelter, and began singing Lifeway songs, buffalo medicine, and using an akéshgaan rattle made of buffalo hooves. The young man recovered, then began employing the rattle and songs to heal others who had been in very serious accidents and were suffering from deep cuts, broken bones, bruises, and trauma. Medicine people who have such a rattle are considered to be very powerful and experienced practitioners who know sacred words of healing. There are also four words that when spoken to an enemy, can defeat him. By saying the words and then walking away, the person will die.

This happened in the old days at the time of the Long Walk. There was an aged man living in the Black Mesa area when the U.S. soldiers came through to capture Navajos. The white men wanted to speak to him, so they arranged a meeting before taking him to Fort Sumner. He attended the conference, spoke the four words, and left. The next day, Kit Carson at Fort Sumner had a heart attack and soon died. This shows the power of the buffalo medicine. The rattle with its hooves is part of this sacred power, and so people who do not understand how to care for it should not touch it. There is a certain way to carry it and a way to care for the songs and prayers that go with the ceremony. If the rattle is inherited, the new owner has to either be initiated in how to use it through learning at least five big ceremonies or pass it on to someone who already knows. A person who carries a hoof rattle is very powerful and may be feared by some people, regardless of how mild and kind he may be.

Although the buffalo and some of the medicine people left our lands long ago, they still return to help with healing. We sing and pray to them and summon them with the rattle. When it is shaken, you can hear the hooves in the ground and feel it tremble. When the person initiated does the dances and uses the words and rattle, everything starts to move around, and even other medicines are enlivened. If a person has been struck by lightning and

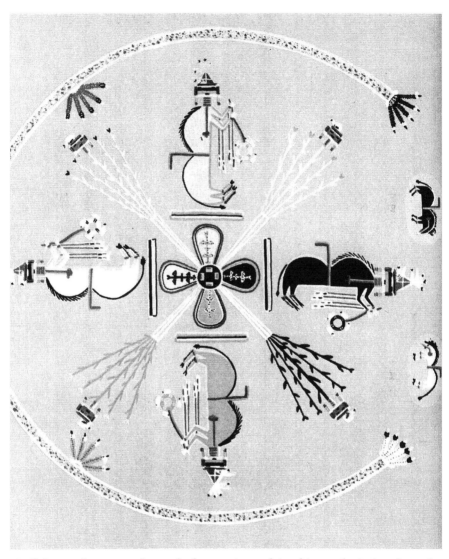

*Buffalo, medicine people, and plants, pictured in this sandpainting from the Shootingway, illustrate the close connectedness among the three. The line that bisects and constricts the center of the animal, as well as the life line extending from the heart to the neck, are symbols of life restoration. The hoop each carries is the magical means by which they travel; in the other hand are strings of lightning.*

is considered dead, a medicine person can bring them back to life. I have seen it happen. Lightning hit a young girl about thirteen years old and threw her about fifty feet from a shade house she had been sitting in. Everybody had been seated and motionless, but still the lightning came in and moved her. The downpour continued with water gushing four inches deep where the girl lay face-first in the mud. Her mother was screaming and wanted to run and pick her up, but her sister warned not to touch her and just wait. Eventually the rain decreased, and someone fetched a medicine man. He sang over her until she began to revive. First her feet started moving, then arms, until pretty soon she raised herself off the ground and began screaming and crying. Her mother ran over and hugged the girl, then helped her into the shelter, where the ceremony continued.

I have also helped an individual in Phoenix with this power. She was in a coma caused by an aneurism in her broken and bleeding skull. All she did was breathe, but the rest of her body and brain were not functioning—needles in her toes, nothing; her arms, nothing. The family called the hospital in Shiprock and requested I come as soon as possible. When I entered her room, I began singing, and eventually placed my rattle with an arrowhead on one side of her foot and pushed, then did the same to the other side. She kicked that foot into the air. I repeated this on the other foot with the same result. Next each arm, her mouth, and forehead—then she woke up.

The doctor observed all of this, but I told him not to say a word. "After I leave, you guys can talk, but don't say anything now. Just be quiet." Later, he asked to know more, but I declined to discuss what had happened. The reason for the rattle and arrowhead is that they represent both ends of the story and situation—life and death. The buffalo had his life taken by the flint arrowhead. He gave it to the people, as well as the meat for medicine and nourishment. In this manner, what I did represented going from a lifeless state (arrow) and reversing it to bring back life (rattle). Life came back to order again by the arrowhead and rattle working together.

## CHAPTER SIX

# Antlers of Power, Food from the Gods

## Holiness on the Hoof

In 1975 Karl Luckert, religious scholar and avid student of Navajo ceremonial beliefs, published *The Navajo Hunter Tradition*.[1] This in-depth study provides information that parallels and expands upon that which Perry presents below. A number of versions of this story and its main personality Black God—also referred to as Game Keeper, Deer Raiser/Deer Farmer/Deer Owner—describe him as a selfish individual interested in maintaining control of his domain. The accompanying cast of personalities found in this story such as a dog, crow, and a hero who tricks Black God into releasing the deer and other associated animals, fits well with what Perry offers, in spite of the differences in versions provided by Washington Matthews, Franc Johnson Newcomb, Berard Haile, and Luckert's informants.[2] Rather than analyze the narrative variations, here we will examine the importance of deer as a sacred animal and how this holiness manifests itself in the daily use of what it provides. Many of those practices and teachings that apply to deer are true of other antlered/horned creatures—elk, moose, caribou, and antelope—as well.

A rich body of lore teaches about this special animal and how it is hunted. Each practice has its own rituals, songs, prayers, and story that explain how and why a particular technique is used. Anthropologist W. W. Hill in *The Agricultural and Hunting Methods of the Navaho Indians* provides a list of these practices with their descriptive names: Wolfway; Big Snakeway; Mountain Lion, Tiptoe, or Deerway; Talking Godway; Encircling by Fire; Stalkingway; Arroyoway; Witchway; and Sacred

Buckskinway.[3] Two are discussed here—the Sacred Buckskinway because the products from it are foundational to ceremonialism, and the Mountain Lionway as a representative sample of the intense ritualized behavior characteristic of many of these hunting techniques. Both examples are abbreviated.

To obtain sacred or unwounded buckskin for the creation of masks, pouches, and numerous other ritual articles, the animal could not be shot but had to be chased down, either on foot or horse, then smothered. Participants practiced running long distances or training a special horse during the spring and summer in preparation for the hunt in the fall. The hunters worked in relays, singing as they gave chase, often as far as eight miles, until the buck or doe was so tired that it could be lassoed or seized by hand and brought to ground. The men then put water and pollen in its mouth, tied its nose, and strangled it with a rope or placed a bag with pollen over its face to smother it. They then marked places for incision and the pattern for cutting on the hide before removing it, the organs, certain bones, and the head—with or without antlers—according to prescribed procedure. The meat was divided among participants, the hide tanned, sinew removed, and all was shared. Other deer considered unwounded and whose hide was eligible for ritual use included those whose antlers became entangled in trees or in fighting, those gored by other deer and died, or those who accidentally ran off a cliff. In most instances, as long as it was not a man-inflicted death, the skin qualified.[4]

The Mountain Lionway required more ceremonial procedure. Starting with the food—cornmeal and meat—the hunters had to cook and eat it in a certain fashion. To blow on the mush to cool it scattered the deer, to get ashes on the meat meant that the person cooking was sloppy and not fit to obtain more. The east-facing hunting camp shelter had to have the ends of the cut branches pointed toward the back of the enclosure, the woodpile outside needed to have the tips and butts of the wood oriented east-west, the hunters had to keep the same sleeping area throughout and remain on their side; if a man needed to shift position, he had to stand erect and then make the change to the other side. Paying particular attention to elements in dreams could indicate success, failure, or the direction of game. When urinating, one needed to face toward home. The list goes on. Primary attention was on killing deer—songs, prayers, and discussion focused on this end. Before starting, rifles were prayed over, the hunters covered their bodies with "medicine," departed in different directions, each one tiptoeing and investigating possible locations. Once the hunter spotted his prey, he gave a wolf call, summoning others to move in the deer's direction. When the animal was killed, there were strict procedures followed in skinning it, cutting the meat, disposing of the bones, handling the head and antlers, giving the remains an offering, and dividing the proceeds among participants. At the conclusion of the hunt, there were still four days of restrictions as the men traveled home singing Blessingway songs, taking a sweat bath, washing their clothes, abstaining from sex, and participating in a Blessingway ceremony. Failure to follow these procedures endangered future success and the health of the participants.[5]

The powerful influence of deer and related animals does not stop after the hunt but continues in the domestic environment of the home. In Navajo thought there are those things associated with the home, female responsibilities tied to birth, children, life, tranquility, nurturing, and peace that are in direct opposition to the male side of hunting, warfare, political strife, protection, and the untamed wild. Deer, an undomesticated animal, is found in the male domain. Navajo Jim Dandy, a man raised with many medicine people in his family, explains what type of influence the elements of the deer can have.

Deer meat is particularly powerful as a medicine. When a person is internally ill or has some form of cancer, they should not eat deer meat because of its power. My mother told my wife not to eat deer meat because she had kidney disease. The same thing is true of piñon nuts. One can eat them before becoming sick and deer meat as a medicine, will prevent that kind of a disease. This is because deer are in the mountains eating medicinal plants, which are usually bitter. This is good medicine, but once a person has internal illness they should not eat deer meat because it is too strong. Before getting sick it is fine to do this, after it is too late. With a sore already started inside, it is just too powerful.

When cooking deer meat, it is not to be mixed with mutton; it must be kept separate, and the deer fur is always kept from the sheep or else they will go wild. Men hunt deer and women herd sheep; one is associated with what is wild and hunting in the mountains while the other is with the home, the woman's place. If something from the deer comes in contact with the sheep, the animals get sick and skinny and become wild. If we have some part of a deer, a hide near the corral or even just loose hair in our yard, it serves as a curse. Nothing can be left lying around. The same is true of the livestock, because deer are such powerful supernatural animals.

People as well as animals must also be careful when exposed to deer hides, hair, and antlers. For example, if I had some hides or fur in my yard, I do not want my children urinating on them. Deer hair affects them with problems in urinating. Also, it is a very powerful way to negatively affect thinking. Medicine men who do not have good intentions can use deer hair to attract women, getting them involved in excessive sexual relations, or can generally curse an individual. If there are antlers or a hide lying around the house, this person can pick it up and use it to work against someone. If the hair comes off while tanning a hide then it needs to be taken care of. The hide is okay but the hair is the thing that can be used against a person to make him crazy. These are powerful things because of the deer's supernatural nature. The deer also has strong powers to positively affect the psychological well-being of a person. The hide is used in the Enemyway ceremony for those who need to be cleansed of evil experiences. Sheep cannot be used to curse people, but they too can be affected by a spell placed on deer hair. The power, once it is opened, hurts the animals. They begin to have poor thoughts then become sick or wild.[6]

On a more positive note, deer can use their association with the mountains to bless the land. Both deer and rabbits are said to have the marks of rain—and in particular, lightning associated with rain—in their legs. This is what allows them to bound. Deer also have lightning marks on their antlers, where lightning strikes during a storm, which allows them to remain unharmed. Clouds and cloud cover are also associated with these animals, and that is why the holy beings direct that mating take place when clouds are present in the mountains during the fall and when storms are prevalent.[7] Today, one of the most common uses for deer hide is in making traditional Navajo moccasins. Cowhide, because of its thickness, is formed as the sole with the upper part made of deerskin tanned using the animal's brains then dyed to a rusty red obtained from the crushed roots of the mountain mahogany plant. Interestingly, the word for foot (ké) and moccasin are the same.[8]

In Perry's opening story as well as the other accounts referenced with it, Crow (Gáagii), a bird often associated with deer, is portrayed as a deceptive soul who knows more than he wants to tell and at other times says too much. He is an ally and spy for Black God, he is often embroiled in controversy, his beak is used in the Enemyway against the evil spirit, and his feathers brush off evil by blowing away ashes in Evilway ceremonies. Crow eats spoiled flesh, is tricky, is associated with wrongdoing, and gossips to get others in trouble. If a hunter sees crows flying about and chasing each other, it is a sign that his wife was being unfaithful during his absence. These are some of the reasons his sacred name for ceremonial use is "Turned on His Side by the Dark Wind."[9]

Navajo Oshley provides an excellent illustration of the personality and type of problems this black spy can create. He shared this story:

While hunting is going on, someone still had to cook. The person who was taking care of meals was directed not to go outside [the brush corral] while the hunters had a ceremony going on. When it was midafternoon, this person ate, even after he had been warned not to do so while the hunting party was out. No one was to eat until everybody came back together. A crow flying overhead cawed, "Ga ga—he ate, he ate." The hunting party heard this and conjectured that the person at camp had eaten. The men returned to the camp, and the man in charge asked the person who had remained if he had eaten. The cook learned that the crow had told the hunters so admitted that he had. The men had to perform another ceremony before going back to hunt. Hunting is very sacred, and it is real.[10]

Oshley's use of the words "sacred" and "real" capsulize the meaning of the traditional Navajo hunting experience. The sacred is real. Both the visible and the unseen reality join together; the two are inseparable.

## *Bringing Back the Game*

Deer are a very sacred animal to the Navajo people. There are many traditional teachings related to them that tie in to different practices concerning hunting, weather, food preparation, and curing illness. Stories and teachings go back to the time of creation, as the animals learned about the workings of the earth and the importance of the holy people. One narrative tells of a time of drought, when the rain refused to come and the deer disappeared. The grass stopped growing, withered, and died; even the birds stopped flying, sitting down because it was too hot and dry. Shade is what they wanted. The creatures wondered, "What is going on? What's happening? There's no meat any more. There's no deer anymore. There's no rain. Surely something is wrong and must be fixed. What should be done?" As they talked more and more about the problem, all agreed that there must be a council to discuss how to bring the rains back. Many of the animals turned to the Bird People because they could fly in the air to see what was happening at long distances. Yet they had been silent. "You birds fly high and go into the mountains, but you don't say a thing. There's no help for our problem or explanation as to why the rains have disappeared, the land dried out, and there are no more deer. Let's have a meeting in a sweat lodge, bring all of you in for a discussion, and talk about what is happening."

The birds and other animals met at Holy Hogan (Táálee Hooghan), a sacred rock formation on Black Mesa between Dilkon (Tsézhin Dilkǫǫh—Smooth Lava Rock) and Keams Canyon, Arizona. They built a large sweat lodge, then placed heated stones inside that made it very hot. The animals removed their fur or feathers and began to enter, looking just like naked human beings. Outside, someone noticed a strange smell that seemed a lot like deer meat. A quick search through the outer forms hung on branches led to the discovery of some jerky. "Whose feathers are these?" All of the birds turned to Hummingbird, who not only had hidden the dried meat under his wing feathers, but smelled of it on his breath. Crow, too, had that smell. Everyone knew that Crow was cunning, sneaky, avoided blame, and was hard to talk with, and so even though they interrogated him, he never admitted knowing anything. Next the animals turned to Hummingbird for the answers. Crow wasted no time, leaving immediately after his release, explaining, "I have to go and take care of some things," but the animals knew he was just as guilty. "Keep looking at him. See where he's going to go," the animals advised. One of them, a small beagle puppy, had keen eyes, so he followed Crow's flight. Eagle and Hawk also watched the fleeing bird. "You both have got good eyes and can see things from a long way before your tears run down. Keep watching where the crow is going."

*This mesa, known as the Holy Hogan (Táálee Hooghan), is featured as a meeting place for the animals, plants, and other creatures in some of the stories about the creation. Inside, the holy people planned for their responsibilities to the earth surface beings. (Photo by Perry Robinson)*

From Holy Hogan to Fish Point (Łóó'háálí) southwest of Chinle is a long distance. The dog and the raptors faithfully tracked the escaping bird, but halfway through its flight, Eagle almost lost sight of him as the figure became smaller and smaller. But not so for the dog, who announced that he could still see him. The watchers moved to the top of a ridge, and the birds finally admitted they had lost track of Crow, yet the beagle followed him all the way to the end. He reported, "I see where he's going. He's going to the mountain called Fish Spring, where he is sitting down on a ridge to talk and counsel with someone." Now the animals and birds knew the direction they must travel to find the deer, but they still had to deal with Hummingbird. They turned and confronted the bird, sensing that he knew something about the cause of the trouble. He cried, insisting, "No, I don't know anything," but there was that piece of jerky found underneath his wing that proved otherwise. Where had that come from? He insisted that he had just found it, but everyone knew better, plus his breath smelled of it. "Your whole breath and body smell of it and tell us that you are eating meat from somewhere." They continued to interrogate him, but he insisted he knew nothing. The people grew angry at his stubbornness and decided to force an answer. They threatened, "We'll make you talk by taking you to the sweat lodge and will change it so that it will no longer be a dry heat, but will be steam when we pour water over the hot rocks." This is the time when the animals remade the old sweat lodge and turned it into a sauna by making a willow frame and using deer and buffalo hides as a covering to contain the wet heat.

One way or another, they would learn where the deer were hidden and how they could obtain meat. They seized Hummingbird, put him in the freshly built structure, and began adding water to the hot stones. The steam arose in large clouds, making the small bird squeal and cry for mercy. He was ready to talk. "This is the situation. You people don't make offerings anymore, and so the Black Body holy people who live on this mountain (Black Mesa) talked to the Water People, who agreed to hold back the rain and the deer. For us to find them, we will have to outwit Black God and go to the place he is keeping them." This spot is called Bidáá' Hoodzohó, meaning The Edge or Marking of a sacred place that is forbidden to outsiders and where only he lives [located four miles south of Rough Rock]; people do not go there today. "This is the cave where he is keeping the deer and where someone now has to go and talk to him as keeper of the game. When that person reaches there, he will not find anything, so smoke some tobacco on the east side of the formation, then the south, west, and north. Black God is a mountain deity and loves the smell of mountain tobacco. Whenever you visit him, you bring that with you, and he will be happy, come out of his home, locate you, and ask to borrow some. Insist that you go to his house to smoke it." This is where all of the deer were located along with other animals that have antlers—caribou, moose, antelope, and elk. He had invited all of them to a ceremony, but once they came into his home, a large spacious cave, they were trapped. The keeper of the game had them all there.

The puppy volunteered to free the captive animals. To fool Black God, the beagle decided to dress as a poor wandering creature in need of help. He removed all of his nice clothes and jewelry and put on worn apparel that made him appear as if he had been traveling for a long time. After reaching Fish Point, he smoked in the four directions, then sat down, puffing on his mountain tobacco. Suddenly Black God appeared and complimented him on the fine smelling smoke he had and inquired as to where he had gotten it. The disguised traveler answered, "I'm a wandering person and go all over the earth to pick up my medicine. My tobacco comes from many different areas, but this one is very special. We can't smoke it here, but wherever your home is, we could go there and light it up in your fireplace." Black God was tempted. "Oh, yes. I have a place over here, but it is forbidden to allow people to go there because it is very sacred. But if you give me the tobacco, I'll let you in so that we can sit and smoke together." The two agreed this would work, as the traveler lit up some water tobacco, which he had just rolled. This really tempted Black God, who commented that it smelled so good and inquired about its taste. The traveler promised, "Well, let's get to your place first, light up with your fire, and then it will have an even better aroma."

They began walking and talking until they reached Black God's cave. Inside he brought out a stone he used to scrape mountain stones called a tł'ish. It serves like a flint that is made of sulfur and when struck against certain rocks, gives off sparks and the odor of a struck match. It has a sharp, awful odor. This is what Black God used to light his fire. Even though his guest hated the scent, Black God explained, "This is my sacred way of opening the door to this mountain. When I scratch this stone, most people settle down because they don't like the smell. This is how I quiet my deer, have them come to me, and then capture them. Every time I strike this rock, they don't like it, but it subdues them to the point where they become very mellow and stay in one place, almost hypnotized."

The traveler inquired, "Do you keep animals in here?"

"Oh, yes. I have meat here, too. Do you want some? I'll put it on the fire. It's good to trade." As the two sat there exchanging tobacco for meat, they talked and smoked. The traveler took the stone and striker, examined it carefully, and then laid it to his side within easy reach. He next arose and opened a curtain that had been drawn across a second entryway in the cave; there grazed quietly a large herd of deer and other antlered animals. He turned to his host and offered, "I'll put my tobacco by the doorway. You can have the mountain, water, and other types of tobacco while I go for a little walk. There are ten different ones in that pouch. Take your time to sit and smoke all of it. I'll leave my bag right here."

Black God was delighted and continued lighting and puffing on his rolled tobacco, becoming more and more relaxed and forgetting about his visitor. Sensing the time was right, the traveler picked up the stone and striker and showed it to the deer. He explained, "I am going to use this to remove its influence and then open the door that is keeping you inside so that you can run out and go to the lands you used to inhabit. As you exit, run over Black God, stampede through his home, and make your way to the outside. Do not stop for anything." He talked to the main leaders in the herd, one of whom was Caribou, and pointed out that when regular deer run in a large group, their antlers that protrude to the sides of their head often get tangled and slow their speed. Caribou, on the other hand, have antlers that point to the front and can cut things that are ahead of them and in their way. Caribou agreed and accepted leadership of the stampede—the one who would create a path out of the cave. For this, he received the name that day of White Deer. "If you can cut a way through and lead the others, you will be one of the holy ones." And that is what he did. He led the entire escape and opened the door while Black God sat there smoking and lost all of his captives. Caribou was the first to run over Black God and stomp him with his large hooves. Still Black God caught the caribou by his throat and cut him from there down to his chest, but the animal kept running, pushing his way forward. He remembered the words, "Don't stop. Keep running. Every time he does something to you, it will heal and grow back; it will get wider and sway in your front, but it will also lead you into a new direction and eventually turn white." Even with a cut chest, it healed just fine and now caribou have a floppy neck area in front. He had made it possible for all of the other antlered animals to escape and return to their previous areas.

Black God was furious that he had been tricked and trampled and had lost all of his captives. He had been so involved in smoking tobacco that everything else became unimportant until it was too late. His home was ruined and uninhabitable, so he left and took up residence on a different mountain called Naahsilá (Something Crossing Over the Other One—Butterfly Mountain—also called Suanee) to the south. This is now a sacred place where people who are helping with a Blessingway ceremony gather white clay to mark the pubescent girl's face with dots during a four-day ceremony (Kinaaldá). Black God tried to control other things, but it did not work out for him. Other holy people had earlier warned him not to get addicted to smoking. Because he had not listened, he lost everything. This is where some of the teachings about how smoking addiction can push a person to the point that they concentrate on only one thing, like smoking, and forget about other important responsibilities until they get trampled.

The animals were not yet through with Hummingbird. They scolded that he had been part of the problem and now he needed to be helpful and would have to change. The animals charged him with having to quickly fly about to learn what was happening in different places and then return and report. He would have the ability to move swiftly so that he could accomplish his tasks. His first assignment was to determine what needed to be done to bring the rains back to Mother Earth. He started by talking to the Flower People, who still maintained a little moisture in their blossoms. Next he spoke to the bees and other small creatures, who insisted that the real

*Black God is one of the primary keepers of game and is the holy being in charge of fire. He is associated with hunting and works closely with Talking God. His black mask has a crescent new moon at the top of the nose-line, while on his left temple (covered) is the Pleiades. The kit fox skin worn around the neck may be substituted with spruce foliage. (Courtesy Library of Congress—Curtis Photo 101843)*

answer would be found with the frogs. Hummingbird reported this to the animals who accompanied him to a dry pond whose mud bed was now cracked, flaking, and curling up.

In the middle of this dried earth bottom was one chip that had been turned over—that was Frog's shade where he was sitting. The animals approached him about how he might be able to bring the rains back, but he was adamant: "I can't make connection with you people because you have no respect for the rain or what is happening. But I will talk to my brother." So the blue frog talked to the red one, and the red one to the yellow frog, and the yellow one to the white one until he sent a message beneath the earth to the water monster, explaining what people were saying. Water Monster confirmed that the creatures on the earth's surface had shown disrespect by forgetting to make offerings, and that until they did, he would not release the rain or underground water into the rivers and lakes. "Wait four days and go to the Holy Hogan (Tááʼlee Hooghan) to prepare for a ceremony. Send one person to a holy place where I will cause some water to seep into it. There that person will receive a vision and watch from a distance what needs to happen with the coyote." This is when the coyote entered the water and came out and shook a white shell onto the ground, and later turquoise, abalone shell, and jet, as discussed previously. All of these things were part of an offering to the water monster.

The Blessingway ceremony came from this with its songs about the mountains, the water, deer, and all the good things happening—as symbolized by this offering. Now Water Monster was ready to help but needed assistance. The first seven rainbows went down twelve steps and into the water, bringing the offering of the people with them. Water Monster received it along with the prayers and songs and was pleased. He told them, "Now, when you walk back with the rainbow, there's going to be a prayer called Hááyátééh [defined: the offering of a sacred prayer as one reenters the physical world]. You will have come back from the bottom of the Black World through the Blue and Yellow Worlds to the White World. Four times your prayers are going to be said like this as the rainbow guides you all the way out. By the time you get back to the surface, there will be a cloud arising in the east, and one from the south, the west, and the north. All of them will be different storms coming in, and each will have its own sounds. When the noises from these thunderstorms stretch out before you, your eyes will open with the first strike of lightning, and you will have arrived at the surface. You will no longer be able to recall what you did when at the bottom of this world with Water Monster. You will not talk about me and say 'Remember how I lived, what it looked like, and how things worked.' It will be as a dream that happened when the thunderstorm struck and you entered a new reality. The storms have now returned."

This is the story of the return of the deer and moisture to the surface of the earth. Both are connected and are taught in the Mountainway ceremony. It tells how new laws and rules of behavior were established. They are all about respect. At first the rain, the deer, and their meat were just taken for granted. The people ignored the holy ones, and so they were removed. Even the rain was to be distributed in a different way with an offering every year and a specific ceremony. When storms come in and rainbows with their seven colors appear, they must be treated with respect. There are also seven joints of the body, starting with the ankles to knees, hips, shoulders, elbows, wrists, and neck that determine how one's life will be lived because water is already inside of you just as are the four sacred colors. For instance, white is found in the teeth, yellow or abalone in the nails, blue in water, and black in the hair and eyes. A person's mind, thoughts, and personality will also have nice colors to them. Even when giving birth to a child, there are really beautiful ways of looking at it. This is made possible because of the rainbows that are in the water that started to guide the people in the medicine way. When you follow these colors, they will take you to good places if you do the right thing.

The teachings about tobacco show how people need to be careful and not become addicted. It should be used only for sacred purposes at certain times to collect one's thoughts. Otherwise, when people use too much of it, the animals and enemy will smell that person, and he will be quickly defeated. The smoke that should have been a helping friend becomes a thing of danger. This reversal is not the way life should be. The smoke was more about feelings and inner thoughts, not about everyday existence. If a person's mind is not straight or he is sick, smoking helps to gather thoughts and bring one back. Smoke is really not measurable and neither is the mind, following similar patterns based in feelings.

## *Deer as Holy People*

Deer should be viewed in the same way. They are to be treated not as an everyday animal but rather as one of the holy ones. One reason that the head is so sacred is that its face looks like that of the gods—the nose, eyes, ears, and antlers make them unique. People need to prepare themselves when working with deer. There are certain parts of them that can be eaten and other parts that cannot; some parts are left with an offering; others hold extreme power; one must recognize how each portion should be handled. The deer and buffalo are two animals that are treated this way. The deer also communicates with its tail to the eagle, who brings messages to the holy

*Claus Chee Sonny: "After they had been released from Black God's house, a song was given to the game animals. With this song, with two kinds of lightning, with rainbow, and with the roots of sunlight, they were to travel across the prairie. . . . All traveled across the prairie, kicking up dust and knocking branches off the plants. These plants and this dust today are used as medicine." From Karl Luckert,* Navajo Hunter Tradition. *(Photo by Kay Shumway)*

ones. The elders say that the deer's tail is a plume that matches and speaks with those in the eagle's tail. For instance, the eagle circles higher and higher into the atmosphere above the earth. From there, he learns of the weather and what is going to happen, then signals back to earth. The deer raises its tail to receive the message. A signal might come in saying, "There's snow or rain approaching." Thus, the eagle connects the sky to the land through the deer. I believe the eagle and deer are two of the highest medicine people talked about in ceremonies.

Deer also leave medicine behind for people to use. They eat plants, then regurgitate the mass out; it can later be picked up, dried, ground, and used in the Mountain Smoke ceremony to bring a good way of thinking. As the deer walks around contemplating helpful things, he may be chewing on piñon nuts or some type of fruit like yucca, eating the inside and spitting out the shell or outer covering. People who have their mind cluttered and disoriented with problems need to have straight thinking, just as the deer does. A medicine person will take the things the deer has been chewing, grind them, and put the mixture in the tobacco so that the user will have the same lofty thoughts the deer had when eating it. The Deerway Tobacco is all about restoring sacredness and good thoughts to the mind from depression, from behavior taken to excess, or when acting in an odd manner. Navajos talk about the People's Way (Dine'é k'ehgo) as being correct living. The Deerway is a response to human issues that upset that behavior. Add to this the deer's good hearing and sense of smell, and one can see what a powerful, sensitive animal it is.

When a person is hunting a deer and the animal spins around quickly, turns on him, and stares with ears forward watching every movement, that person should walk away. If one tries to kill it when that happens, it will take his life, or something bad will happen later. The same is true with a jackrabbit. When either animal turns around and gives you the ear, you are supposed to just walk away because they mean business and will use their powers in one way or the other to take you out. The ears, when raised forward, work with the antlers to warn approaching danger, "don't come any closer." It is their Protectionway. If the deer is killed anyway, the animal will curse that person, who will not live long, because the deer is one of the gods and is protected in that manner. Even where a deer urinates is to be avoided. A person never pees in the same place; keep away from smelling its urine or else you will get sick.

My grandfather always talked about the sacredness of the deer and how to respectfully butcher one. They are very different compared to other animals that provide meat. He said it was good to take the hide and meat after it is cut into small pieces, then wrapped in the hide for transport, but he cautioned, "Never take the head or feet; the insides are left on the ground under a tree where plants grow." This is because deer are the keepers of the Ground Ones—grasses, small forbs, and new vegetation. The animal's feet dig into the earth and help the soil to plant and germinate seeds. The stomach and internal organs are laid over a sprinkling of white corn pollen left on the ground beneath the tree, while the head is placed in its branches facing east. Once the head is removed, make an offering. The head is never eaten, and neither are the feet/legs or internal organs. Leave them alone by either depositing them on the mountain where the deer was killed or by taking them to a mountain. The rest of it you put back into the trees and make an offering to it. The head goes to the east, the tail to the west on top of the legs/feet, and in between is where the internal organs go. They are laid to rest with pollen and prayer.

The deer's genitals cannot be cut and neither can the indentations on its hocks in the legs. Otherwise, that person will be crippled early in life. If one cuts below, over, or into the eye, then he will go blind. The nose is also very delicate; if one cuts too deeply into it, he will have problems with his sense of smell and nose bleeds. You can take the nose but leave part of it with the remains. One reason for this careful butchering procedure is that from those things left behind, another deer will grow. Once the head, intestines, and other unused parts are placed on the earth and in a tree, the hunter walks away a short distance. Looking over his shoulder, he will catch a glimpse of the animal getting off the ground and running away. The deer has a new life and leaves a vision that the hunter preserves and which keeps the animal alive.

## *Antlers of Power*

The antlers are considered extremely powerful and to be generally avoided and never played with. If removing hair around the antlers, be careful not to take any of it with you because the antlers are so sacred. Instead, you retain a small portion of the forehead to ceremonially represent the head. The antlers are left untouched because they may have flaky scales on them, which are dangerous to touch. Antlers are never brought into a house because something bad will happen, and they are not to be used to make anything useful, like a tool. They can cause incurable cancer. Look at the inside of one that is cut and see the porous make up—that is what it will do to the bones in your body as they deteriorate internally. Just as the antlers decay and turn white, so too, do a person's bones fall apart and become cancerous.

When antlers start to form each spring, they grow rapidly, having one of the fastest growing tissues known to man. The velvet coating on their outside eventually starts to itch, and so the deer starts scratching against the trees, causing the antlers to bleed. When this happens, it is one of the sacred times because they are changing. Leave them alone when they are in this stage of development. You do not want to get close to the rubbings; even the smell of them can make you very sick. After the deer are finished with their scratching, they shine their antlers, turning them into lightning. The thunderstorm markings of lightning are seen as blackish, yellowish, and bluish colors that form on the antlers. This is another time that they should not be touched, because they have their own way of defeating something. If they are brought in the house, it is for sure that someone will get sick. Whoever brings it in and sleeps in there will have their bones deteriorate in the same way that antlers do when left by themselves. Since antlers are associated with jagged male lightning and are the deer's defense and protection, they have the same ability to harm, just as lightning-struck objects do. Attention needs to be paid to these powers.

Many years ago, my father had an experience with a Navajo man dying from a cancerous tumor in his head. The doctors found it and wanted to remove it, but this man wished to have a ceremony to discover exactly what was happening. My father used star gazing and hand trembling to determine which ceremony would be most effective. After the divination, he told the man that he saw in his house a large mounted elk head hanging over the fireplace. He then asked if this was true. The man said yes. He inquired if the patient was a road man, a ceremonial person, and he was. Father told him that he knew from traditional teachings that there should not be any antlers, heads, or any part of a deer in the house; if he knew this, why was something like that hanging above his mantle? He replied that the head actually belonged to his wife, a non-Navajo, who had shot a Boone and Crockett trophy elk and wanted to display it. She refused to remove it upon his request. This is what was causing the problem. My father told him to get rid of it—"You can't live with it. You can't eat with it. You can't sleep like that"—but he never did, so died of cancer in his brain. A couple of years later, the woman went through the same illness and died. Finally one of their children removed it. These antlers had the markings of lightning on them and so they belong in the air away from people, and not in a house. They should have been respected.

Antlers are also associated with trees. Deer talk about trees and wear their dead branches that stick out on their head, while the white clouds that gather at the tops of high mountains represent their tails. A dead branch from the side of a tree may be used to represent the antlers in a Deerway ceremony. Just as antlers indicate how old and big the animal is, the branches do the same for a tree. The patient needing this rite may be suffering from severe headaches, a spinning sensation, an inability to sit still, urine that turns red and bloody, or difficulty peeing. There may also be issues with one's prostate gland and leaking urine. These illnesses go back to events in the Yellow World where the sexes became separated by a river and the men did not have access to women. The men began to masturbate and perform sex with dead deer livers. This gave rise to sexually transmitted diseases (STDs) that we have today. The Deerway ceremony cures problems with the genitals and sexual reproductive disorders and the prostate gland. If a person fails to take care of these types of problems, they will soon be unable to urinate but have issues with leaking. The patient is taken to the mountain where a tree with branches that look like antlers is selected, the branches are broken off from both the left and right side of the tree, and then they are placed on the corresponding left and right side before the patient. In between is a sandpainting of a deer face created out of gray ash. Black ash is used to represent the nose, white corn pollen the mouth, and little black tips for the ears. The person needing the ceremony now sits on top of this head with the tree antlers on both sides. The medicine man says prayers, using the sacred name for a tree (sadii), which means a representation of all wood, instead of normal terms for specific trees. Prayers, songs, and offerings are left for the deer.

## *Unwounded Buckskin and Sacramental Meat*

The hide cannot be carelessly thrown away. There will be repercussions if you do. The thinking is that if one takes a deer's life, all of the work and effort that goes in to using the meat and hide should be completed. The hair needs to be removed from the skin before doing something useful with it for ceremonies, and it should never be played with. There are two types of deer hide in Navajo thought—one that has been killed by a weapon when hunting and one that has not been pierced by bullets, arrows, or other weapons. The latter is called The Untouched or Unharmed One (dook'aak'ehjí). This has no hole and is more sacred for medicine people to use. If a person is preparing such a hide and accidentally cuts a hole in it, even though unintentional, that is a crossover, and the hide has lost its sacred power. It needs to have experienced no harm in any way and to have never been "touched." If a deer is killed by a car and the skin is not punctured, then it is considered never touched. The hide, not how the animal died, is the important point. These skins are very, very valuable for use in ceremonies performed in a special way. One has to really search for this kind of hide because it produces very good results.

This practice goes back to the time when the holy people were performing a ceremony. They laid a buckskin down and were singing and praying as they walked around it, but the words passed through a hole in the hide. One of the gods stopped the ceremony and pointed to an opening made by an arrow. The others looked and agreed that where the hole was, the deer had died. "Let's not use this one; here is another skin that has no puncture wound so will hold the prayers. The medicine will stay in that area instead of escaping." Today there are those people who try to sew and mend a deerskin with an opening, attempting to contain the spirits, but it is not the same. A hide used in a ceremony also needs to be complete, which means it has to have a tail, ears, legs, and a little cut made just below the ear where the medicine man can insert turquoise and tie the medicine when he is doing prayers. The Blessingway, Protectionway, and other ceremonies use these buckskins. Yé'ii Bicheii masks are often made from the skin of the fawn

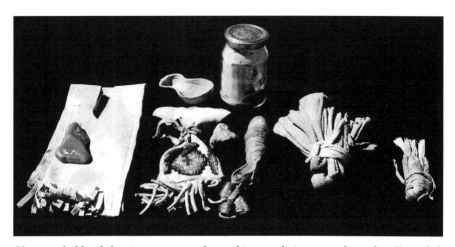

*Unwounded buckskin is paramount for making medicine paraphernalia. From left to right: (1) Buckskin pouch taken with person traveling. Black stone at top (male) and yellow stone (female) help to return with good things. The pouch is used to pray when a traveler reaches the first mountain on a journey. Perry's great-grandmother found the yellow rock returning from Fort Sumner. (2) Medicine pouch with herbs. (3) The blue stone is used to mark seven healing points during the Earthway ceremony and is a mineral offering for bad dreams. (4) This small bundle with four hooves is prayed with during the Enemyway. (5) The pouch holds ntł'iz and yellow, blue, and white ground corn with mixed flowers and plants. These earth offerings are used to correct bad dreams, accidents, and other problems. (6) Within the bound pouches are herbs for a person who faints. (7) The jar holds cattail pollen as an offering to obtain water to drink and good air to breathe when traveling and to prevent allergies. (Photo by Kay Shumway)*

with the fur left on. The white spots on the baby deer's hide are preferred because then they are considered as the holy ones who have their bodies covered in white paint or clay. The two correlate.

Let me share a story about when I was four years old, camping with my family and three others in a small cabin in the mountains. We had just arrived that evening, built a campfire, and then laid down inside in our sleeping bags with a little blanket pulled over the doorway. About three or four o'clock in the morning, we heard something very loud, speeding down the slope of the mountain, so everyone got up. My dad told us to listen as the running animal came closer and closer. Now it sounded like it might be two or three creatures headed directly for our location. Suddenly we heard the cracking noise of something breaking on the south side of the cabin, then the sound of something fighting, struggling. We were scared and did not know what was going on, so we sat still and waited. Perhaps it was a cougar or bear, we just did not know. Then people started piling things in the doorway while dad with his rifle guarded the entrance. We remained like that for the rest of the early morning hours.

With daylight came a clear understanding. We ventured out to find a big, old buck entangled in a wire clothesline stretched between two poles on the south side of the cabin. He had been fighting all night to free his antlers but never succeeded. Dad called his brother and together, they grabbed the deer's antlers, wrestled it to the ground, sprinkled pollen on his nose, then suffocated him with a cloth bag. Next, they took the whole hide. It was a good ceremony. We danced with it and removed the head in a respectful way. We did everything in proper order, with all four families participating. Dad said, "This is the sacred medicine that's going to be in place." Even the meat wasn't supposed to be eaten in a regular way because this deer had come to us for something. Father advised, "You can take the meat, but the bones I want back." The women carved around the bones and butchered the animal right where it died. They stacked all of the meat on a table and put every bone in a big pot. For three days father boiled them until most of the meat was removed, then he stacked them on the table. Four women with knives began shaving whatever remained until the bones were perfectly white, before putting them aside. Father collected the stack of white bones and brought them to a site away from the camp up on the mountain, where he made an offering. Before he distributed any meat to the families, the bones had to be put in their resting place. He told me, "This is the sacred way you are supposed to do it"; it was the first time I had ever seen somebody take this kind of time—a couple of days—to process something in this way. I have never witnessed anything else like this before or since.

This was all because of the sacred way a deer is put together. In the Lifeway ceremony, people eat its meat for its medicinal qualities and often dry it out to make jerky. Later when needed, it can be ground up and used alone or added to other medicines that are mixed and bound together. If these practices of distribution and burial are not followed, there will be sickness that cannot be defeated. The person's body will deteriorate by eating itself. The meat of the deer is very good and considered medicine because of all the plants it eats. This is what was said.

For a Lifeway ceremony, all of the meat is removed from the bones before boiling them for a whole day. A second cleaning of the bones removes little slivers of boiled meat that now serve as medicine. This cooking of deer meat is done in a special way; there are two stories that explain why—one about lightning and the other about fire, who are brothers. When lightning strikes, fire comes to life. At the same time, the thunderstorm that brings the lightning also provides water falling from the sky. The two merge as lightning gives life to the fire, but water puts it out. The Water People, through water, determine that the deer is so sacred because of its antlers and its tie to lightning, that the cooking of the meat should generally be done with fire (lightning) and not by boiling (water). The lightning comes through the fire. Deer meat can also be dried by the sun, another form of fire, but it has to be used as jerky, and if heated, must be put on the fire with other ingredients. Very seldom is deer meat boiled, especially when it is fresh. The blood trapped in the tissues is doubly sacred to the sun but not the water. The blood has to dry within the meat by the sun or else must be cooked by the fire. This is why a lot of people, when they kill a deer, do not immediately butcher it, cut its throat, or in any other way bleed them out. Rather, they hang the body until the tissue gets very red before cutting it up. This way the blood stays in the meat and is not lost. This blood has more power and more sacredness, has a stronger flavor, and contains all of the medicine plants the deer has been eating. Deer and other animals are really just medicine walking around because of their plant food and sacred water from the mountains that they eat and drink. Boiling fresh meat removes the blood, but the water is not drunk. With older deer meat, boiling does not matter as much, but it does lose a lot of its effectiveness.

## *Other Antlered Beings*

Many of the same teachings that apply to deer are also practiced with elk, moose, caribou, and any other animal that has antlers, walks on four feet, and eats small plants and grass. I have already mentioned caribou, who, at the time of White Shell Woman's travel with the people, were assigned to live in the north. They are called the white deer, have gifts that help them to live in that climate, and are said to be able to find new ways to do things. Their guidance from the holy people comes through the front forks of their antlers. From the caribou's throat down to its chest, there is a lot of loose hide, which is said to remind him of when he first became a leader, as in the story told earlier. It holds the vision of what he did to succeed as the lead person, and this is why he was sent to the north—to help the people there obtain new ways of living in that land.

Elk is the animal of the west, is colored yellow, and is associated with twilight, just as the mule deer represents the south and its blue color. When these animals are skinned and their hide tanned, an elk skin has a strong yellowish color (west) as does its hair, the caribou a pronounced white (east), and the mule deer a slight blue tinge (south). The elk is on a higher spiritual level than the deer because of the sacred words it sings. In his mouth is a white shell with a hole in the center that helps him to whistle and sing his holy words, which can be heard for miles. Stories about them teach how they made their songs, exploit their spirituality, and sing their sacred words through a shell inside of them. During the Deerway, when singing elk songs, one can hear their sound and know that the blessing has been correctly given and the elk has returned. You listen for a long whistle like "whooooooooo-hoo-hoo-hoo" sound that stretches through the words. That is when you hear in your mind the song that the medicine man performs and envisions, and he will know that he has healed through the elk returning to help. Even the way the elk carries his face and the extra hide on his front chest speaks of medicine. Healers obtain more of the elk's power by cutting a piece of cougar hide as a strap to hang an elk whistle about the neck; it is blown during the Deerway ceremony. The whistle and strap is called (zéédéílyééh); the medicine man is the only one who wears it. This is how we copy the elk and his sacredness. Medicine people who practice the Lifeway (Iináa'jík'ehgo) and the Flintway (Béshee Biką'jí) have the most stories about the elk and its spiritual powers, because this animal represents healings from the west.

Moose are considered holy ones that are not supposed to be seen. It is said that a bull moose carries the mountains as well as the entire earth. The Big Moose holds all of these things, including the world, in his antlers. He is represented as one of the black gods and is blackish in color, but his antlers are made of white shell. He is referred to as the Big Animal that Holds Everything in His Antlers. When one examines this animal, one sees a place where a person can stand and see the white rocks stand up in a formation, allowing the medicine man to pass between them. The mountains sit up, allow for passage, and then fall back into place. He has this power because of his ability to live and swim in water with his head just above the surface as well as submerged when swimming below. Moose also live on dry land. When underneath, it may arise, just like the water monster (tééh łį́į́'—ocean horse) that came back from the ocean; a person will see his face, his body will be black, and he will emerge from the water. He can live in both places.

Beneath his chin are two powerful goatee-like beards called bells. These are considered one of the holiest objects that anybody could obtain. If a medicine man can get one of these attached to a tanned section of skin and can put his whistle on it, he would be a very powerful person. The moose is considered the most holy and spiritually potent of all creatures with the buffalo as second. This is how medicine people look at these two animals. I do not know of any Navajo person who has one of these bells, and I have never seen one, although it is talked about. It is one of the holiest things that anybody can walk with.

Medicine men also talk about the moose being associated with death, but the average Navajo person does not know anything about this. In the medicine way—the Enemyway and Lifeway—there are teachings about

how miraculous things happen that go beyond life in the everyday world.
For instance, when a medicine man approaches death and his situation could
go in either direction, this is the only time that stories, songs, and prayers
about the moose are discussed. This is when the medicine people start
singing about the elk and the moose and what could happen in the future.
Either that person is going to be run over by the moose or carried to the next
life. These are for medicine people who believe they are dying and are not
sure they will survive. If they know that they are going to die, they always
say the moose is waiting to take them to the next place in its antlers. "I want
to sit in it and he will carry me to the next world." This is never expressed
until the last moments. The moose is considered outside of this realm, sitting
in the dark beneath while his antlers carry the earth. This is what is said.

# CHAPTER SEVEN

# *Creatures Large and Small*

## *Helping the People*

E very culture in the world—bar none—provides a way of first thinking about, then classifying, elements of life important to it. The shape this classification takes depends upon what composes the culture's worldview, how the world was created and operates, and an underlying system of evaluation. Take for example, dominant American society's understanding about animals. Founded on an early Greek system of classification, a technical nomenclature is applied based on physical qualities, which may literally bring an investigator "right down to a gnat's eyebrow." Everything depends upon a creature's noticeable characteristics. Starting with the broadest category of kingdom (animals, plants, fungi, etc.), then moving to phylum where body and genetic characteristics clump large groupings within, say, the animal kingdom; next on to class (mammals, birds, amphibians, etc.), then order (carnivores, primates, rodents, etc.), family (cats, dogs, weasels, etc.), genus (domesticated cats, panthers, pumas, etc.), and finally species, in which individual features and characteristics result in a very specific Latin term that applies only to a single type of creature. All of this is within the realm of science—observable, measurable, and reproducible.

Navajo classification of animals certainly includes observation, but its interpretation and relevance are often far different from Darwinian evolution and the emphasis placed on sometimes microscopic physical differences. Unlike the scientific approach, there is far more dependence on the spiritual/religious explanation that derives from traditional teachings. From this comes a variety of interpretations about the role a single animal may play. Some are tied to physical realms, others to assignments made at the time of creation, still others to the unique powers they hold. In the previous chapter about deer, the classification of domestic versus wild animals carried with it strong taboos, illustrating that the two should not be mixed. Thus, there are many ways to explore the Navajo system of classification, some of which are in keeping with those of Anglos, while others are widely different.

Perry starts his discussion of animals below by suggesting the reader think of creatures along the lines of different Indian tribes, each having its own domain and qualities. Father Berard Haile sees this breaking into four groups: those that walk on all fours, those that creep, those inhabiting the water, and birds or winged animals that fly. These are further subdivided by the place that these animals live. For instance, bear, deer, elk, squirrels, and cougars are considered mountain animals, and although some may frequent other locations such as the open range, the holy people have "assigned" them to certain habitats. Those living in the high country desert of the Navajo Reservation include bobcats, pronghorn antelope, desert bighorn sheep, badgers, jackrabbits, and snakes. Like those in the mountains and elsewhere, each has its own power, responsibility, and place in specific ceremonies that require knowledge of what they have to offer. Otters, beavers, muskrats, frogs, turtles, and fish are water creatures, while all different types of birds— from eagle to sparrow—are denizens of the air.[1] Of all of the animals, only Coyote lacks a specific assignment, making him available to move over every different landscape.

While certain ceremonies feature specific animals and their qualities, elements from different life zones are often mixed. Fur, feathers, bones, shells, stones, and other materials (bile, urine, regurgitated plant matter, pollen shaken off an animal's back, eye liquid from an eagle, and so much more) all have their place in healing. Black God controls all of the animals and makes them available for use, but there are also relationships with the specific over-spirit as well as the physical animal on the ground.[2] Proper prayer and performance allow, in an almost contractual sense, the animal to be taken to provide its power. Perry often mentions the use of different hides, which in ceremonial use are ranked. As he points out, the buffalo is one of the premier medicine animals, and so its hide is considered first and very powerful; next comes unwounded buckskin, then that of the mountain lion because of its strength, and finally the river otter due to his association with water. All bring powerful healing. The names of some of the ceremonies even indicate what creatures from a particular realm might be featured: Featherway, Waterway, Windway, Mountainway, Bluejayway, and Coyoteway for examples.[3]

At the time of creation, the holy people gathered to discuss what life on earth would be like for man. They divided the times of day into four elements—dawn, day, evening, and night—each with their respective qualities and uses: beginning to move, work/activity, coming back together, and rest. As mentioned previously, travel and movement are highly valued in Navajo culture, and so for all of the creatures, how and when this travel takes place becomes tied to the activities of life. The holy people agreed this was good, but Coyote, who often had opposing thoughts, spoke up and said that it was too much to have everyone traveling at the same time. There needed to be more divergent thinking about this plan. He and Talking God discussed the possibilities, after which the two holy people turned to the animals and asked what they preferred. Exactly half of those present, fifty-one, preferred movement during the day, and the other half night, with Coyote abstaining from the vote because he traveled all the time. Talking God and the others agreed there would be equal opportunity for both.[4]

Still, the day and night animals were not satisfied. They decided to join together in a moccasin/shoe game (késhjéé') with more daylight or nighttime going to the winning team. There were 102 yucca spines or counting sticks to represent each of the participating day and night animals, as well as the paths that Sun Bearer took through the sky each year. If one side could win all of the sticks by guessing which of four moccasins a colored yucca ball was under, then they could have more darkness or light. Since this game is played only when dark, the night creatures met the day creatures at sunset. The animals, each with their unique qualities, contributed to the spirited guessing game, which was full of banter and shenanigans with each side singing against their opponents. At least eighteen different animal songs are sung today against competitors. At one point, Owl deceitfully hid the ball in his claws. Squirrel, one of the day opponents, took a stick and hit him, knocking the ball loose, flattening the bird's beak, and causing its claws to assume a clutching position. Coyote, true to his devious ways, ran from side to side, depending upon which group was leading at the time.

The creatures, except for Owl, did not notice the sun rising in the east, but he had the ball and did not want to stop. Finally, the game ended and the stakes—beautiful colored rocks and sand—were hurriedly divided. Some of the creatures were fortunate, like Bluebird, who got turquoise for a color. Prairie Dog took sand. Skunk got ashes, as did Crow, but one of the animals wanted to make Skunk different and so took some white paint and ran it down his back. The animals joked and made fun of each other's appearance. The Eagle took all of the pretty colors left over and mixed them through his feathers. The animals rushed to their homes so as not to be caught by the sun. Mountain Lion had his fur tinted by sunlight, his black mouth being the only part of him that shows his connection to night. Bear also had his fur struck by the red light of dawn as he lumbered back to the mountains. He was in such a hurry that he put his shoes on the wrong feet, and that is the way they are now. Since no single group won the game, today there is still an equal amount of day and night for daytime and nighttime travelers.[5]

Daily and sacred names are another way of classifying animals. Sacred names are used to show respect to the creature, but they are also a way of stepping into the spiritual realm beyond the physical world. Many names are derived from stories in which the creature plays a certain role, or are bestowed because of the animal's notable characteristics. For example, a buzzard (jeeshóó) is referred to as "The Fine Young Chief Who Sways in His Flight Above the Mountains," a porcupine (dahsání) as "The Fine Young Chief Who Penetrates the Mountain at the Hill of the Thorn-bush," and the gopher (na'azísi) as "The Fine Young Chief Walking in the Bowels of the Earth and Shaking the Earth in His Course."[6] A clear understanding of the necessary procedure to assure use and an accompanying attitude of humility go a long way in tying physical needs to spiritual assistance.

John Honie, born and raised on Black Mesa, a practicing medicine man and friend of Perry, offered this story to illustrate the link of animal powers and human needs. A hunter, tired and unsuccessful, became lost in a snowstorm while traveling in the mountains. Two holy people appeared and directed him to "a mountain which was a hogan," and bid him enter. There were many bears sleeping around the circumference of the lodge, but the man was cold, ignored their presence, and built a fire. The animals awoke and told him to put it out and leave; the holy people intervened and directed the bears to help the struggling human, teach him their prayers, and use their pollen when assisting. The animals feared the holy people, so they did as directed, spending the entire night instructing.

> When daylight came again, the hunter had learned all the prayers and songs. The bears told him the meanings of all the words. They told him that the songs and prayers he learned should be used when one is planning to go on a trip. They said the songs and prayers would protect the traveler on his journey. They also said that when someone gets lost or loses something, he should use these songs and prayers to find his way or whatever he is looking for. "When you offer prayers with this pollen, you must pray at the top of a small hill. The pollen should be put on the tracks of bears at the hill top, especially when the sacred wind blows the most."[7]

The hunter returned home with this knowledge to share with others. Power linked to performance brings relief.

Perhaps the most potent yet often impotent of all of the animals in Navajo storytelling is Coyote. Credited with being one of the first and most involved creatures in this world and those beneath, he is also said to be one of the last to exist when the end of this world takes place. Of all the animals in the Navajo pantheon he is best known. His tales are told to children and are given as examples of how not to act, yet he holds strong powers called upon in some of the most important ceremonies. He operates between day and night, vacillates between right and wrong, performs good and evil acts, and controls some of the greatest powers. Thus, he can be both hero and villain. In short, he is representative of the human experience in all of its glory and shortcomings. While Perry often refers to him as the "first teenager," Coyote also controls powers concerning the earth that few other holy people have. The literature about this creature is extensive, but to get a feel for the range of his impact on the Navajo, see *Navajo Coyote Tales* by Berard Haile, *Coyoteway* by Karl Luckert, and the more generalized work by Steve Pavlik called *The Navajo and the Animal People*.[8]

His many names indicate his range of behavior. In Navajo beliefs, home and family and responsibilities tied to both are important. That is part of Coyote's problem—he pays little attention to any of it and when he does, it is often disastrous. Called Slim Trotter, First Angry, First Scolder, First Warrior, The First One to Use Words for Force, The Roamer, Fine Young Chief Howling in the Dawn Beyond the East, or just Ma'ii (Animal), Coyote is constantly on the move with no allegiance to home and no moral compass to guide him.[9] He is often portrayed as a trickster who is sharp in his dealings with others, coming out on the bad side of every interaction. He betrays those who help him, cheats indiscriminately, brazenly and intentionally counters correct choices, and is shunned by most. On the other hand, he is credited with keeping the world functioning, is associated with growth, introduced death as a solution to overpopulation, placed many of the stars in the sky while claiming his own, has a month (October) dedicated to him, is the central figure in the Coyoteway ceremony while appearing in many others, and controls important powers on earth. This dichotomy makes him an interesting character to study.

One example of the importance of understanding the reason for his power is tied to rain. This connection is known among medicine men, but is not often discussed by the general public. As the holy people sat in council listening to Monster Slayer and Talking God speak about how things were to happen with the earth surface beings, Coyote sneaked in to hear the plans. Four times Monster Slayer had him evicted from the meeting; when it was time for the medicine people to enter a brush corral to commence the Night Chant ceremony, four singers lost their voices. Immediately the blame fell on Coyote, and so four times Monster Slayer ordered him to come in and solve the problem, but four times he refused. Threats of violence followed until Talking God suggested that it was better to sue for peace and cooperation. Monster Slayer agreed: "It is well. Let us do as you say. We will make him god of the darkness, of daylight, of the he-rain, of the she-rain, of the corn, of all vegetation, of the thunder, and of the rainbow."[10]

When Coyote learned of the powers he was to receive, he accepted them and entered the "dark circle," then "went up to the east of the great cornstalk, stood facing it on his hind legs, raised his forelegs as high as possible and let forth a long coyote yelp. These acts he repeated at the south, at the west, and at the north; but at the north he followed the long yelp by several short ones." Following this, the singers' voices returned and the ceremony commenced.

In 1999 John Holiday testified of how this power worked. As a thirteen-year-old boy living with his grandmother before apprenticing as a medicine man, he had an "interesting experience." The Four Corners area at that time suffered from an extensive drought that took its toll on the land and its animals. One day a man named Shepherd (Na'niłkaadii) visited their home, asking for employment. Grandmother was not able to hire him but asked if he would perform a rainmaking ceremony, to which he agreed. John was to assist him in getting ready, and so Shepherd gathered a bucket of white clay, mixed it in water, and had the young boy cover his back and other places the old man could not reach. John continued:

> White with clay, he took off running toward a row of small hills leading away from our home. I was curious, so I decided to follow him without being seen. I went down a wash that led to the hills, watching as I ran. Then he stopped and sat down, and I did too. He put something in his mouth and howled like a coyote. He first sat toward the east, then scooted and howled to the south, moved and howled in the remaining directions, then straight up to the sky. That is all he did, then ran back home.[11]

John beat him to the camp, where he helped the man wash off the clay and watched him depart for his home in Dennehotso. Before leaving, however, Shepherd assured the boy that there would be plenty of rain soon. "Within a short time, we saw clouds gather above, and without warning, hail and rain poured down. Water was everywhere, reaching the top of the sagebrush. Our elders were very knowledgeable in these sacred ways back then, but now nobody ever says anything about it." Coyote's powers had been summoned, received, and implemented.

## *Thinking about Animals: Cougar as Example*

The best way to explain how Navajos think about and classify animals is to compare them to groups of Native Americans who have adapted to different geographical and topographical regions and have their own cultural basis. For instance, the Sioux and Cheyenne, living on the plains in buffalo hide tepees, are different from the Hopi living in pueblos in the desert, who are different from the Tlingit in southern Alaska living in cedar board houses. Many of the groups of animals have relatives that may share some similarities and yet are distinctly different like the wolf and the coyote or the deer and the elk, while other groups live in the same habitat but have their own qualities and characteristics. All have their place, and most have their own role and teachings explained through Navajo eyes. What follows is an overview of some of the more important animals not yet discussed.

The cougar (náshdóítsoh—big lion—Puma concolor) is an important mountain animal as was pointed out in another chapter when discussing the use of his bile as medicine and his skin in making a quiver. They are viewed in the Evilway ceremony as high-level and skillful hunters who are in the top hierarchy of important animals. Their skins and other parts are very hard to obtain. Like a cat and bobcat (náshdóílbáhí—gray lion—Lynx rufus), he is known for Paws or Feet That Cannot Be Heard (Bikétł'ááh doo Hodiits'a'í tsiłkę́ę́h). This probably came about when people first saw a bobcat. They named him The Wise One Who Knows His Way Around and How to Do Things—náshdóí. A story tells of Navajos who left a valley and went up to a rocky mesa where they suddenly saw a cougar and wanted to give it a name. They noticed the white color underneath his belly and beneath his head, so the people felt that this represented the dawn and the east. The yellowish color on his back reminded them of a sunset and the west. This is where the morning and evening came together. The White Body holy one from the east gave cougar its white markings on its stomach as well as the white on the badger's face. Both are noted warriors. Someone saw the darkness in its facial features and believed this was the night and the north. Thus, cougar represented three of the four directions, but unlike the coyote who has all four, the blue from the south was missing.

The cougar is fearless and powerful and with one swipe of his big paw can kill a deer. He never backs down. When these qualities are combined with his being The Wise One, he becomes a formidable hunter who is in charge of helping young men to learn how to stalk, kill, and out-think their prey. He was told to teach the young men his skills, but until they kill their first deer, they cannot wear a mustache. Once they have accomplished this feat, he gives permission to wear his, but it must be earned. These are the black markings around his mouth. If the young man is not a good hunter and is an unkind person, he will have to shave it off. The people need to know who their hunters are and that they have the wisdom that characterizes The Wise One.

The cougar's skin is highly prized. I have one that I keep for special occasions such as when I am asked to make a staff for the Enemyway ceremony. When I lay the hide down, people look at it and know that there is a chief sitting before them. You can put a piece of it on your head or on your jacket and it is good. You know you are feared [respected]. If an Enemyway ceremony is being held for a man and he is first in line, then a cougar skin is stretched over the pottery bowl serving as a drum. If the woman is the first in line, then it is changed to buckskin. This is especially true if it is for a chief, statesman, or medicine man—someone of high status—the cougar skin has to be used. Doing this is all about pride and being marked with high respect.

In ceremonies, by putting a cougar or buffalo hide down, you are showing the person's importance as well as that of the ceremony that is being performed. For instance, when my oldest brother had any kind of ritual performed, such as a Protectionway, he either had his mother or sisters or brothers put a buffalo or cougar skin down because he had earned it. When the people surround it during the ceremony, they know what to do and how to show respect. So if you go to a Yé'ii Bicheii ceremony and have somebody sitting there with a buffalo robe, you know there is a medicine man in that group where the medicine is taking place. They represent themselves that way. The clan people, your relatives, will come from miles around to participate when they know medicine men of prominence are going to be holding a ceremony like this. They will sit there and say, "Ah, that's my people, my clan people. I'm going to be there and take my robe with me to pay respect." That is how they used to do that. A lot of people go to North Dakota and other places to buy a buffalo hide or robe and bring it back for this purpose. Even though they did not kill the animal and just bought it, the important thing is ownership and knowledge of the proper way to show respect. It is just like putting on your best clothes when you are doing something important. This communicates a positive attitude.

## *Big and Little Trotters*

The wolf (ma'iitsoh—big coyote—Canis lupus also called Big Trotter) is another important animal who is difficult to find. He is a very private person. Like the cougar, he is always considered a hunter and does not really mix with other species of canines like the coyote or dog. Wolves, as hunters, have a cleaner style of eating and are very intelligent. My father used to say, "If you look at a wolf and he looks at you eye to eye, every once in a while he will turn his head from side to side, trying to figure you out and what you are thinking. Also his tail is shorter than most dogs, and he keeps it high off

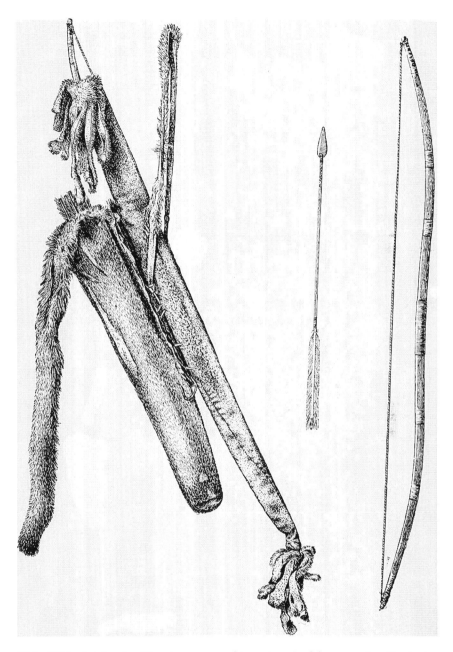

*This 1893 sketch of a Navajo cougar skin quiver and bow-carrier illustrates identification of the mountain lion as a successful hunter with an owner desiring those qualities. A verse from the Stalkingway song recorded by W. W. Hill says, "He goes out hunting, the Mountain-lion am I. With the mahogany bow he goes out hunting . . . through the shoulder that I may shoot. Its death it obeys me."*

the ground but level, never really down or up because he is a hunter. The tail stays right in the center of where his arrows are going to go, or where his kill is going to be." Like the cougar, he is considered a prize. When his hide is removed, it may be used for a quiver; the man who carries one is considered a good hunter. The wolf's bile also can be used in medicine that will help a person to be one of the finest hunters. People will pay good money for that because it is very hard to obtain. The biles of a wolf, cougar, and eagle come from three of the fiercest fighters and hunters and so are powerful.

When a wolf is killed and skinned, the hide is always taken with the head left attached. Some people make the mistake of associating this with skinwalkers, but that is not what this is about. Once the skin is prepared, it is big enough to fit over a person's shoulders, and his legs are long enough to cover one's arms. The head hides half of the person's face, but not so much that he can't see while crawling. The tail drags behind, and so the hunter looks like a wolf to fool the animals being stalked. This animal always has a lot to do with hunting. The holy people appointed him as one of the chiefs because he is intelligent, hunts well, and has a purpose or plan that prevents him from just randomly attacking other animals. He always follows a game plan.

Coyotes (ma'ii—Canis latrans also called Little Trotter) figure very heavily in Navajo teachings. Coyote, the trickster, was born as a holy person on Fuzzy Mountain (Dził Ditł'oi—located above and east of Navajo, New Mexico, and not to be confused with Blue/Abajo Mountain, Utah). Something was crying steadily up on top. As the people watched the mountain and listened to the noise, twilight settled in and the Northern Lights appeared above, moving about and flashing many colors. Then from the east came a white light, from the south a blue light, from the west a yellow light, and then at the end a red light. The people asked, "What is that? There is something up there. What is going on up on Fuzzy Mountain? This looks like the birth of dawn has happened." Some of the people went to see and found a baby wrapped in a long bunch of grass and crying loudly. If one listens today to coyotes talking among themselves, not just howling, they still sound very much like a baby crying. This is where his language comes from. The dawn was born so this is when coyotes are often heard. Once the people saw what it was and how it sounded, they did not want anything to do with it. "We don't need you," but still, it was making the sounds of a baby in need and had the four different sacred colors, and so they decided to help. This is how Coyote began influencing people.

Because of the way this happened, he now has the four colors (hodooniid jiní) on his body, but he also makes human baby noises. His ceremonial name is First Born of the Dawn (yikáísh yizhchį—birth of dawn) or Dawn Child. From the beginning, he was very holy. As he grew to maturity, he was constantly running around, experimenting, getting into trouble, and was intellectually immature. Wolf, who was much wiser, came to him and said, "Coyote, you are very talented. You are a very gifted person and still young, but you do not use in a proper way all of the talents and powers you have been given. You think only about yourself, you see and hear things that you like, but you never consider things from another perspective. The gifts that were given to you such as your ears to listen, eyes to see, mouth and tongue to taste, are not used thoughtfully. You do things that are wrong and you need to learn. No matter what you do on this earth, it is not going to be correct or done in a good way." In this manner, Coyote assumed the role to provide examples of what is right and wrong through his behavior as well as their consequences. They can sometimes be good but more often wrong.

Coyote never really developed his thinking ability. He is like the world's first teenager, with the potential of doing good but not enough maturity to make the right choices. He is always learning new things, which often comes at a price. Sometimes he makes a good call, but most often he does not. His behavior is very humanlike, showing all of his frailties and failing miserably. This is why Wolf told him, "You need to have patience. If you utilize some of these talents and abilities in the correct manner, then your prayers are going to be good, because your language is very special. But the way you are going about things now is not good. You are using sacred language that causes things to happen just to see what and how they are going to change. You are doing this in the wrong way and messing with the order of things. There is always a good way to do things, but you do not see or do it. If you can settle down, have patience, take time out, and be a kind person, you can do a lot of good and be happy. But, you are not like that with your high energy, curiosity, constant busyness, and little sense of right and wrong. You act like a child who gets himself into a situation that he cannot get out of."

Navajos are told to learn from the mistakes of Coyote. Watch what he does and how things happen. If they are not careful, they will end up in the same situation and will learn their lessons the hard way. "He is such a character—learn something from him! If he defeats himself, you stop and say that you should not act like him, then back off a little bit. He was put on this earth for us to learn. He may be a good person, but he gets himself trapped and does not think straight. Since he is always young at heart, he wants to do things quickly, with shortcuts that create problems."

After Coyote emerged into the Fourth World, the holy people warned him that his language was very sacred and that he needed to be careful when he used it. They remembered the problems from the past. "We made so many mistakes that we were forced to leave all of the worlds beneath this one. When you, Coyote, took the baby from the water monster, we were pushed into this world and ended up here. This cannot happen again. It seems like whatever you do, you act like the first born teenager and problems arise. You need to use your language correctly and act in a different manner. Everything that we do in this world is going to be very sacred and the elements and creatures will listen to us and things will happen as we direct it." When Coyote heard this, he wanted to use these powers even more and wondered, "Am I really that holy? Let's see what happens." He looked about and thought, "I would like to see if there is a cloud in the sky to hover over me." And it happened. Every time he said something, his wish occurred and his question was answered. He really liked this. He said, "I wish it would rain so much that the water would come to my knees," and it did. Coyote knew now that he held real sacred power, but he failed to realize, that if he or the people abused it, there could be really bad consequences.

Coyote, just like teenagers, often only thinks of himself and the possibilities that might bring him what he wants. The world is filled with potential, waiting to be tapped, but at what cost? In this way, I see a teenager not thinking about the community but only themselves and what they want. In the end, they often get hurt or abuse something, ending up in jail. That is the way of a coyote, who has the potential to be a good person, but never really uses his full capacity and strength within to achieve beneficial things. Coyote is always on the move. He says, "I'm like this. I'm like that. I travel in the four different directions because I hold their colors. This is how I am known. I will never settle down in one place, but always be on the go, looking for new horizons, new things, new everything. I'm going to be traveling and never have a home, just constantly walking all of the time. There are many hills that need to be looked at, many mountains, creeks, and water holes that need to be visited before I go." He is always on the verge of traveling somewhere new and does not want roots in any one place.

There is an illness associated with Coyote in which the patient shows fear, shattered nerves—shaking and twitching—weakened eyesight, and loss of memory. The Coyoteway, like the Bearway discussed earlier, belongs to the Protectionway group of ceremonies and corrects these problems, although the ritual is now extinct. It was last practiced by Palomino Man near Piñon, where I am from. This is a nine-day ceremony that is too complicated to explain here, but there are Yé'ii Bicheii holy people like Talking God who participate in the healing, sandpaintings of the four coyotes in each of the directions, prayersticks, and body painting. All of this is done because the patient has in some way offended Coyote; his influence has brought sickness that needs to be cast off. Coyote must be respected. This holy person displays a lot of human characteristics that are powerful.

*Coyote is an interesting mix of real intelligence and childish stupidity, of keen awareness and blissful ignorance, and of strong supernatural power and complete impotence. In short, he is a representation of the human experience. He has shaped many activities that have had a profound effect on life from birth to death—in spite of his rarely being invited to help the holy people with planning. (Drawing by Kelly Pugh)*

In many of his stories, he gets into trouble by doing things he is warned against and by taking good things to extremes. Chaos and problems result. Even though he has the ability to help and protect, Coyote often chooses the path of self-destruction that harms his friends and causes concern. People often follow in the same way, hurting loved ones and themselves as they skip down a road that others see as harmful and that leads to a dead end—both literally and figuratively.

Take, for instance, a woman I will call Jane who now lives in the Shiprock area. Her life story is about extremes—those that destroyed her and those that saved her, thanks to the Coyoteway (Ma'ii na'ajiłee) ceremony. When I first saw her, this young woman looked terrible. Black lipstick, many piercings, multicolored hair, while her general demeanor showed that she was not taking care of herself. But the number of doctors she had on her speed dial said something different. In addition to her health cards from three different states certifying she could obtain medical marijuana, and the five psychiatrists she was visiting, there were also medical doctors who prescribed sedatives and medications that kept her drugged and out of touch with reality. Her father watched Jane descend further into the depths of dependency as the situation grew increasingly desperate. Tears and pleas for assistance followed, but the medical community was stumped. No prescription and no counseling seemed to be working. The staff at the hospital referred Jane to me with the hope that traditional Navajo medicine and teachings could reach her in a way that western medicine had not.

After diagnosing her problem through hand trembling, I warned her that the ceremony necessary for healing would not be easy and required extreme measures. "There's a cleansing ceremony that needs to be done, but it is intense, really intense. Herbs, extreme heat, songs, and prayers are all part of the treatment that is performed in a sweat lodge. If you do not want to get better by accepting these things, the ceremony will not work." Jane desperately desired a change and agreed to have the ceremony—the same one that had been performed for Coyote long ago. This is used only after all other medicine has failed and is a last resort because there are few controls once the process starts. Even the medicine man conducting the ceremony has to be initiated enough to have a buffalo hoof rattle.

Coyote was "a teenager," traveling in the four directions, bothering people who cast him out. Although he was not aware of it, he was also collecting different kinds of medicinal herbs that healed people. By the time he reached the Glittering World, he wanted to be like humans and so approached a group of people in a sweat lodge and asked if he could participate. They pushed him out the door, saying that he was one of the holy ones and that he should act like them and not be around earth surface people. True to character, he persisted, asking four times until finally, the people put

*During the Coyoteway ceremony, both Talking God and Coyote attend the healing process. Summoned by the sandpainting and prayersticks, Coyote enters into the event to anoint the head with medicine, to remove and then throw away the sickness, and to conclude by howling into the person's ears. This Holyway ceremony restores the patient from mania and stomach troubles.*

him in the lodge, added many hot rocks, and let him sweat off the medicine on his coat. He screamed and howled at the intensity of the heat and finally passed out. Those outside grabbed his legs and dragged him to a distant spot, then let him awaken on his own. When he did, he saw what the people had done and decided that he should leave and become one of the holy beings.

Jane underwent a similar treatment. I performed it at my home with five women helping me. We boiled many different medicines and had other herbs that she would sit on; the place smelled so strongly of medicine that a person could hardly breathe as it stung the eyes, nose, and body. The dome-shaped sweat lodge held many hot rocks, creating intense heat; there were more herbs placed in buckets of water with more heated stones; the smell from it reminded me of a large container of Vicks Vaporub; vomiting cleansed internally, while the steam and sweating seemed to boil her. She went through the entire process four times. That is why the use of this form of Coyoteway is considered a last resort when no other type of medicine practice seems to work. It took extreme measures to counter her extreme conditions.

Jane emerged a new person as was evident when she returned to the hospital a few weeks later. Her hair was back to naturally black, all of the piercings had been removed, her dependence on drugs and marijuana had ended, and she held a desire to work and be productive—Jane returned to "normal." After a month and a half she had changed so much that she got off all of her prescription drugs, obtained a job, and occasionally came in to speak to people who were struggling with addiction. She is one of my success stories. The Coyoteway is a ceremony that is fading from practice and should not be used without an experienced medicine man, but it is an effective form of healing.

# *Keepers of Beneath*

Badgers (nahashch'idí—The One Who Digs with His Claws—*Taxidea taxus*) are the keepers of the ground and things underneath. They are experts when it comes to understanding the qualities of soil and can indicate to people what kind of dirt to use. When First Man was trying to build a hogan, he asked the beaver to put together the wooden part of the structure. First Man tried many different types of soil, all of which washed off the hogan roof. Finally, he went to Badger, who told him what he needed to use, a red dirt with white specks in it. "This one is really good. Use this because the rain will not soak through and the soil will not run off the roof." It was true, the dirt stayed in place. This is why Navajos say that he is the one who knows about the ground.

One day my father and I were building a hogan. I asked him why we were putting it in this spot that seemed so secluded and undesirable when it came to the view and access. "Why are we putting a house way out here where you can't see things?" He said, "I can't haul the good dirt located here to a more distant place. This is where the good dirt is, and so this is where I'm going to build a hogan." This is an important consideration when selecting a home site. Sometimes, a person does not have a choice. If at all possible, never build a home on blue soil because it is rich in clay that will cling to shoes, is hard to wash off, and is difficult to get a wagon through. Otherwise, you will have to haul in better dirt to put over the clay as a cover. Badger knew these things.

Badger also keeps track of a lot of things going on in the world by listening to what is taking place underground. The vibration from an animal or person can be felt so that he can then send a message to tell the people. This goes back to the time of Monster Slayer and how Badger helped warn of approaching danger. Very few people know this story. When Monster Slayer and Born for Water were waiting to kill Big God (Yé'iitsoh), it was Badger who listened for his heavy footsteps—boom, boom, boom—as the giant approached the Twins. Badger lay underneath the ground telling them, "He's going that direction. That's where he's going." He would keep rising to the surface and alerting them of the enemy's location. This is seldom discussed but is part of the Enemyway teachings, where his songs tell of protection. Otherwise he is rarely mentioned.

A badger also has two helpers that live underground and deliver messages. One of them is a mole (Na'atsǫǫsí—The Busy One—Merriam's shrew) who digs up objects and tunnels underground, piling the earth into a surface mound. While doing this, he brings the moist soil from beneath and places it on top to connect the earth with the heavens. He is communicating with the holy people in the sky to bring water to his location. The wet dirt is the signal for more rain and water already found in the soil. Storms will come. Underneath the mound he sometimes stores things like bits of leaves or grass that he has been preparing. Although he does not show himself, he keeps clean the area outside and inside his home in the mound. Navajo mothers encourage their daughters that if they locate this shrew's home and dig down inside of it, they will find the things (grass, leaves, etc.) that he has stored there that will help the woman to be like him—a tidy housekeeper. By taking these tobacco objects left behind by his door and adding them to mountain tobacco and smoking the mixture, the young woman will always actively maintain a neat and prosperous home. This animal wants to be known for its goodness.

Badger's other helper, a second type of mole, is blind. Its Navajo name "The Sun Does Not See Him All Year Long" (Ahééhéshíįhdéé' naadooboo'íinii—Broadfooted Mole—*Scapanus latimanus*) fits his lifestyle. This brother to the other mole is a medicine animal who knows all of the roots and plants that have healing properties. He originally came from the Black World, is blind, and can return on his own to his place of origin because he knows all the paths and does not need the light to find his way.

Badger has the personality of always being grumpy or angry. As a loner, he does not like having others around, but at the same time, people underestimate his power. He stays low to the ground, has short strong legs, can dig a hole quickly, and has a flat body shape. But if there is a struggle, he can be ferocious and will outfight anything. When the Enemyway was developed, the holy people talked about what offerings should be given to this fierce warrior and how his behavior could be copied by a person trying to survive in battle. Some people said, "Let's make an offering from the bears or cougars. They are fierce fighters." At this time there was a new chief, (name unknown), who was being initiated, and so four people were sent out to bring in the best animals that were known to fight furiously. Badger was one of them, and so after receiving an offering, he agreed to meet with the group. He had his own ceremony and teachings, and even though he was short and unimpressive looking, he proved to be one of the best fighters. If the enemy shot arrows at him, all he had to do was duck down flat on the ground and the arrows flew overhead. Once he arose to go one-on-one with an opponent, he was not beaten. The new chief understood this and told his helpers to stake a leather strap attached to one of his feet to the ground so that he could not retreat but would have to stay and fight his enemies like the badger. He became a powerful warrior who lived a long life defending his people in many battles.

As an old chief who had led his following through difficult wars, he told them, "I am the one that has been made with all kinds of power. I have the bear and cougar in me, but most of all, my face and my painting is all about badger. To my enemy, come and get me. I will fight to my death in a different way," referring to the strap tied around his foot. This is how he challenged his enemies to fight him. He stayed within the circle defined by his tether and defeated all of the foes who came after him. This is how he became the person who stood with badger. Cheyenne Dog Soldiers also used to fight like this, but so did the Navajo. You can see what the saying discussed earlier—when Changing Woman said, "I'm going to bite into the tendons of badger"—means. One should not get close to him, but if you do, there is going to be a ferocious battle. Biting the tendon is like saying "you have the tiger by the tail," and what is there might just be more than you can handle.

*

## *Special Talents, Special Assistance*

Skunks (gólízhii—The One Who Pees in the Air—*Mephitis mephitis*) are considered one of the smartest animals. His distinctive black and white coloring goes back to when the animals were gambling in a shoe game to determine how much night and day there should be. Those animals adapted to the dark wanted more for their purposes, and those wanting increased daylight formed their own group. Skunk sat in the middle saying, "I will take night and day and live on both sides of it. I will wear white and black so that you will recognize me as neutral in this contest." This is why skunks roam about, regardless of the amount of light. As the animals dreamed about their future at the "Holy Hogan" (Tááłee Hooghan) near Dilkon, some learned about the defense mechanisms they would receive for protection. Skunk accepted that his would be a spray, while porcupine dreamed of his quills.

The meat from these two animals, plus that of the cougar, is considered very sacred because they are so difficult for other animals to kill. Most will not even try to attack a skunk, fearing its spray. Skunks are also very delicate and particular eaters, taking only what they want. This is why its meat, like that of the other two animals who have quills or are ferocious in defense, is considered pure. These are the three meats used by warriors to keep the enemy away from them. The enemy is afraid of them because of their defensive nature embedded in the meat. It allows one to fight and know where the enemy is at all times.

My father, one day, was butchering and skinning a skunk he had killed. I was surprised and somewhat shocked, asking how he could do it. He said, "You just have to cut around the scent sac and throw it away so that it does not smell." He held the meat up and asked me to smell it and there was no odor. The meat that came from certain places became part of the medicine used to heal. The meat has to be dried very well before grinding and then mixing it with other meat and herbs. This combination is called zaanił (literally "objects put in the mouth") and used in ceremonies. Skunk meat is one of the sacred meats used in this medicine.

Porcupines (dahsání—The One Who Likes to Be Left Alone— *Erethizon dorsaum*), like the skunk, provide a special meat for the same purposes. It can only be eaten during the late fall and winter when the grass is knocked down, snakes and lizards are hibernating, birds have flown south, and food is limited. People who have it must share it. A story about this occurred during a Mountainway ceremony when food was eaten as part of the healing process. For some reason people were just not getting better, and so they tried to determine what was missing. Deer meat was present, and some people thought that perhaps bear meat should be added, but they knew they should not do this because of his status and also that his meat was greasy. Porcupine spoke up and offered his flesh, saying that it tasted a lot like bear meat without all of the grease. The people agreed and tried it, while the holy ones considered it to be sacred enough for the purposes of healing. This is how this meat began to be part of the Mountainway.

The porcupine's quills are highly prized for decorating medicine objects like pouches and little buttons. They are also used in ceremonies where the quills are woven together to make a small cone-shaped container in which sacred stones are put and then used as an offering to the holy ones. In the same sense, a quill is considered to be an arrow. Some may be braided and then put on the handle of a rattle, then covered with buckskin. When this is done, the quill, like an arrow, will push the enemy away from the patient, defeating the evil that is causing the sickness. If a person pulls one out of a porcupine, it can become a protector just like a flint arrowhead. The porcupine is viewed as one of the most intelligent animals, although he does

*The porcupine, known in ceremonial language as "The Fine Young Chief Who Penetrates the Mountain at the Hill of the Thornbush," is not particularly noted for strong medicinal powers. Porcupine quills were used as decoration and placed on cradleboards to keep evil, sickness, and bad thoughts away from the child. (Photo by Carl Ball)*

things very slowly. He is well known for thinking about a problem before making any move or saying anything. He provides a good example of how actions need to be considered, avoiding a rush to judgment.

An example of this is found in the story of when he was chewing bark off a tree and someone inquired why. He responded that he had an imagination that he used often, even when he was eating. He also watched how other people ate and tried to think what it was like for them. The man said he did not understand what Porcupine was talking about and asked him to please explain. Porcupine directed him to stand next to a pine tree, where the animal cut off some bark. He told the man, "Look on the outer part of the bark and notice how it is very hard and has a blackish-reddish color. Turn it over where the inside is all white. Now keep watching it." He pulled one of his quills and stuck it in his nose, which caused it to bleed. Next he put the dripping blood on the inside white layer of the bark, then placed it in the flames of the fire. It started sizzling and so he turned it over, waited a short while, and then flipped it over again. Suddenly the bark and quill transformed into a stick skewer with roasting meat and a lot of sputtering fat on one side and red meat on the other. He took another stick, poked the cooked meat, and then threw it to the observer, saying, "I'll give you one of my quills when you are finished eating to clean your teeth."

The man got started, and by the time he had finished, the entire portion was gone. Porcupine asked, "Why do you eat bark?" The man replied, "I didn't eat bark."

"You just did. I took it off of that pine tree and you ate it. If you can see me like that then I can see you like this. How did it taste?"

The diner answered, "It tasted good."

Porcupine ended with, "So I guess that's the way my bark tastes, just as good as the steak you ate there," then walked away. The man cleaned his teeth with the quill he had been given and departed as a wiser person, thanks to the teachings of the porcupine, who is always seen as an intelligent individual with many lessons to share.

Rabbits (gah—Something White Is Moving Fast—*Sylvilagus auduboni*—desert cottontail) have been an important food source for the Navajo people in the past. On a number of occasions they saved our people. One time when there was a large gathering for a Yé'ii Bicheii ceremony, a huge storm blew in, dumping six feet of snow and stranding the people. There was no food for man or animal. Some of the warriors dug their way out once the sun began to shine. The dazzling light hurt their eyes, but they knew they needed to do something to avoid starvation. As they started to move about, the men noticed tracks on top of the snow. They decided to follow them, eventually coming upon a hole beneath a rock. Something down below was moving, so they took two arrows, tied them together and put pine sap on the tips. One of the men reached down and put the sticks into the hole, then pushed until he felt a soft body. By twisting the bound sticks, the man entangled the animal's fur in a knot around the wood and pulled out a fat rabbit. The bunny agreed to be part of their food supply and told them that when they hunted rabbits, they needed to look behind the ears of their prey to see if there was a pinkish color. If so, then the animal was healthy and could be eaten. This is not so for a jackrabbit, who is tough and stringy. This is how the cottontail presented itself. So the people hunted these rabbits, searching for their tracks in the snow. The warriors returned to where the ceremony was being held and offered large bunches of rabbits to the starving people. The Yé'ii Bicheii ceremony continued. Everybody ate well and felt good about what had happened, and so they started making songs about the event. This is why some of the Yé'ii Bicheii songs include a rabbit song that tells about their markings beneath their ears, how they are fast with flashes of white that come out of nowhere, and why they are sacred people.

Navajos say that this kind of rabbit will never disappear as some other types might. If a person kills and beheads one, the head should be put in a protected place so that the animal can re-form and turn into a source of food for someone else. If a person eats a lot of rabbit, they will be healthy; I believe it. That is all we used to eat when we were youngsters. Dad used to go out hunting in the winter and bring back six or seven of them. They were so good when cooked over a fire.

Beavers (Chaa'—The Animal with a House in the Water—*Castor canadensis*) are considered the builders. They were the ones who showed First Man how to build a hogan and how it could be done in some of the most difficult places. Look at his home in the water where he lives, stays dry, and raises his babies under difficult conditions. They do not freeze but remain warm. Just like the hogan, his home is made of tightly fitted logs that do not fall apart when storms come and the elements tear at its foundation.

Beavers are very good judges of wood and how to use different types for various things. Navajos say that they were the ones who told the people which tree to use that would last through the season, not rot, and provide implements. Beavers do this by cutting through the bark with their teeth, gnawing into the wood, and eating some of it before making a decision— "this is a hard wood"—then they go on to the next one and say, "this one is different," using their teeth to make a decision. Beaver was also the first person to put the woven wedding basket upside down in a ceremony and to use his tail as a beater. Every evening in a five-night ceremony (Evilway and Lightningway) this is done. Instead of a beaver tail, a drumstick is made out of large yucca plants tied together just like a beaver tail to beat on the basket. He was one of the first ones to put those songs together for the healing ritual, in which he assists, and he is talked about in the hogan songs (hooghan biyiin) of the Blessingway.

There are many other animals that play different roles in stories, but a lot of them do not get much credit. Not until a person really gets into the teachings and events that each narrative has, will one learn about many of them. Take the chipmunk for instance. One story tells of how Monster Slayer killed Burrowing Monster and how Chipmunk volunteered to find out if the creature was really dead. He scampered up onto the chest and determined there was no heart beat and that the evil being was finished. As a reward for his bravery, Monster Slayer allowed him to streak his face and back with stripes of the monster's blood, declaring, "I will wear this as my clothes." Now it is a part of his distinctive markings. Still, few people give him credit because they do not know why he has the outer fur coat that he earned. Unless a person is really involved in the ceremony and knows the story, much gets lost and forgotten.

# CHAPTER EIGHT

# *Domestic Animals*

## *Friendship and Service at Home*

T he two previous chapters have discussed the role of wild animals and made the point that they are classified and kept separate from domesticated ones. In Navajo, a four-legged creature that is hunted is grouped as "dini'" (game animal), which is very close to the word for man "diné." Domesticated animals are referred to as "bilį́į'" or "łį́į," meaning horse. How these terms came to represent these categories is unclear, but there is no missing that the Navajo people became very attached to their newfound friends once introduced by the Spanish. Other than the dog, the Navajo had no domesticated pets until this time. Still, it did not take long for them to adopt and adapt to these new animals and to understand the benefit of having sheep (dibé), goats (tł'ízí), horses (łį́į), cows (béégashii), dogs (łééchąą'í), and cats (mósí) as part of their life. Perry shares some wonderful teachings about each type. This brief introduction to his thoughts touches on a fairly limited literature about all of them except for sheep and horses. The latter two, because of their extensive economic and social impact, are often discussed. This is especially true when considering sheep, which provide raw wool for sale, processed wool for weaving, and animals for food and sale.

The holy people clearly understood how they were blessing the Navajo when they created the first sheep and goats. After Changing Woman/White Shell Woman had finished with the wild animals and specified that they would make themselves available to humans as long as the proper prayers and offerings had been given, this goddess turned to providing a more stable, controlled form of wealth. She made a male and female sheep and a male and female goat using sacred stones (ntł'iz) and "collected waters" for amniotic fluid, some of which dripped into the soil and grew herbs and plants

169

important to these animals. Taking precious fabrics and jewels, White Shell Woman rolled them in small balls, placed them in the corners of the sheep's eyelids and the cleft in their hooves, and pronounced their future to humans: "By means of these you will be able to live on. Time and again it will transform into fabrics of all kinds, into jewels of all kinds. It represents your pets from the tip of which fabrics and jewels of every description will begin to sprout, thus making life possible for you. And you must plead with them, pray to their feet, their head, pray to their bones."[1] Following further instruction, the sheep and goats received their sacred names and began to do her bidding. Perry's explanation starts at a later time when the earth surface people first obtained from the holy beings the animals at "Descending Wide Belt Mesa" (Sis Naateel). Historically, it is interesting to note that this was the first place, according to some accounts, where the Navajos raided a Spanish caravan to capture sheep and horses.[2]

The people also took seriously the charge that Talking God and other holy people gave them when they received livestock. They were warned to use all of the animal, to waste nothing, and to treat them with kindness in a holy way in order to overcome hunger and poverty. In its simplest form, it is all about a multifaceted relationship that boils down to three words: "Sheep is life." One of the Four Sacred Mountains, Dibé Nitsaa, or Big Sheep Mountain, was "made of sheep—both rams and ewes."[3] The holy beings associated with this mountain pour forth their wealth in livestock and are appealed to by herders for supernatural help in prospering. Traditionalist Martha Nez believed, "The mountains were put here for our [the Navajos'] continuing existence. . . . All of the living creatures like sheep, horses, cows, etc., said we will help with furthering man's existence."[4] After discussing the mountain soil bundle with its powers, how the animals' prayers and those of the people bring rain to the land, and why the whole process was interconnected with sacred ties, Charlie Blueyes suggested, "Livestock is what life is about, so people ask for this blessing through dziłleezh [mountain soil]. From the sheep and cattle, life renews itself. Who would give birth in a dry place? This does not happen. You get many lambs and calves from the plants around here. On the tip of these plants are horses, cattle, and sheep. They are made of plants which are sheep."[5]

Compatibility between humans and livestock was an essential ingredient in this relationship. As a person tends the flock, the sheep watch their caretaker. The animals eat to become fat in order to better serve their master when they are killed. If a person takes care of the animals, they will provide him or her with what is needed. Charlie further explained, "The sheep are made of money, gold, necklaces, and many goods. They are carrying pop, flour, and everything we consider wealth and good."[6] Thus, Navajos became intimately aware of each of their sheep and goats. Rather than part of an impersonal herd on the hoof, each animal had its own personality and characteristics. A shepherd knew which ones were most likely to wander, which were weak, and which were docile or belligerent. The owner literally lived with the animals from birth to death and was often present for both.

One part of this ongoing compatibility is to do as the holy people directed by not wasting any part of this "gift." Tall Woman, in discussing the traditional culinary use of sheep, leaves no doubt as to what this looks like. "Goat or sheep meat is roasted, boiled, broiled, baked, fried, made into stew or other dishes, or dried and made into jerky. The goal was to eat almost every part of a sheep or goat except for the gallbladder, wool, horns, bladder, and contents of the digestive tract."[7] She goes on to mention how bones are boiled, the head is baked, and then it is cracked open for the brains while the

> eyeballs, the fat around the eyeballs, the cheek meat, and the tongue are special parts. . . . Most say to pound off the hooves and wash the feet. Then some prefer to bake them in a heated ground pit for at least four hours with a fire built on top, brush off the ashes, and eat the meat. Others prefer to boil them briefly, pull back the skin, and hang them up to sun-dry. After collecting eight to ten dried feet, they will break them in half and re-boil them, eventually adding them to a soup, stew, or hominy, boiling everything again and then eating all the soft parts."[8]

The lungs, heart, liver, and kidneys are delicacies, while the trachea, stomach, diaphragm, and small intestines may be cut up for sausage or eaten alone. The blood, caught in a bowl at the time of slaughter, is used to make blood sausage when mixed with cornmeal, vegetables, meat, fat, and other ingredients, before placing it in the cleaned sheep's stomach and cooked. Even the skin, with the wool removed, may be salted, cut in strips, and cooked to eat as a snack called 'akágí.[9] Using the wool in weaving is another huge application of the sheep's unique products that benefit the Navajo.

Sheep are gregarious animals that prefer staying bunched in a flock as opposed to goats who are more adventurous, harder to control, and less finicky as to what they eat. One or two individuals can control a herd of sheep as they gently graze over the land, and so children might assume this task as early as the age of eight, while an elderly grandmother astride a horse with a few dogs to keep predators away and the animals moving, is also able to control several hundred sheep.[10] As the animals eat and move toward water and better range, the herders guide their movement so that the flock is able to return to home base without having to drive them for long distances. This is an important point. Navajo beliefs prefer that the animals, if at all possible, be corralled by night, since bad influences lurk in the dark. Thus, the sheep are often moved out of the pen at sunrise, allowed to graze, and then put back into their corral by midmorning and taken out in mid to late afternoon for a second feeding. The status of a family, individual pride, and a sense of belonging is reflected in the number and condition of the animals in the herd. Mutton is the meat of choice, eaten at a four-to-one ratio of sheep over goat. "Mutton hunger is a recognized condition of Navajos who must live away from the family herds. 'I want some fresh mutton,' means that the speaker, in fact, does want some mutton to eat, but it also carries the connotation of homesickness."[11] The old practice of singing a protection song, on a daily basis, starts with the first animal out of the corral in the morning and ends with the last one to exit. The relationship continues at shearing time, when each owner takes care of his or her own sheep.

Before leaving the topic of sheep and goats, Perry discusses two different types of corrals—the one to trap wild animals in the mountains and desert and the other that holds wealth on the domestic front. Medicine man John Holiday tells of how the very first domestic corral was dedicated with a marking ritual, sheep songs, and prayers by the holy beings, a procedure still practiced today. "That same corral holds the horses, cows, goats, donkeys, and mules. It is life. It is food. We survive with these foods, and we make a living, and so this is what we teach."[12] Compare this to that of the corral used to trap deer and antelope. Perry is clear that there is a big difference between the two as he describes the death associated with it. For clarity, a brief description of how the game corral worked is presented here.

A leader will collect a group of hunters and determine where there are sufficient game animals to build a corral. After selecting a spot, a circular brush-and-tree enclosure high and large enough to hold the animals is built with two entry ways opposite each other. Then moving outward from the corral approximately a mile, two "entrance strings" or continuous brush wings channel the game into the corral. Next two more lines of brush called "black objects in a line" extend the wings an additional two to three miles out. Once this is ready, the men will spend the night in a "no-sleep" ceremony, singing songs and preparing for the morning, when two riders, armed with torches, go out in search of the antelope on the desert floor. Once they locate them, the grass is set on fire and the men push the animals toward the game corral as they are joined along the way by other riders. The animals, at this point panicked by the fire and pursuing hunters—some on horseback, others running—rush into the corral, where the two doorways are alternately closed and the antelope or deer are trapped. The animals are killed immediately, their carcasses dragged out of the corral and butchered. The enclosure has served its purpose in fostering death.[13]

Horses are animals highly prized by the Navajo. A rather complete study that looks at their creation, powers, connections with health, and ceremonies is found in LaVerne Harrell Clark's *They Sang for Horses* and so is not repeated here.[14] Perry's interaction with his horses, however, underscores the importance of the relationship with domestic animals. He offers examples about how he and his horses respond to each other with devotion. To an outsider, what he describes could be classified as conditioned behavior, where the horse comes at his call to receive food; Perry views it as loyalty. These opposing views are at the center of how differently the Navajo perspective interprets the act of relationship compared to that of the Anglo worldview. Do animals have different personalities, varying needs, and strengths or weaknesses? In the Navajo world, they do, and so are treated as individuals with respect.

Cats and dogs are seen in the same light, serving as protectors. People say they stand between humans and bad things, turning away that which harms. When a medicine man goes to a patient's home to perform a ceremony, however, these protectors are to be removed or kept out of the medicine man's way. It is not good to have them interfere with a ritual. Cats and dogs warn of dangers just before they happen. When they urinate on something in front of you, it is a message, as if to say, "You need to get a medicine man to help you, so that you will not encounter evil."[15] Jim Dandy's family taught that dogs and cats should not be starved, abused, or killed, or else the perpetrator will be cursed and crippled; they have foreknowledge of such events. "The cat is a powerful animal, so the more you take care of it, the more it will take care of you. They are very wise. If somebody is going to visit, the cat rubs its paws in its whiskers. It knows what is going to happen and communicates it so that a person can prepare. My grandmother told me that whenever a cat starts licking itself, she would put a coffeepot on the stove to warm water for whoever was coming to visit."[16] Dogs hold special powers against skinwalkers because canines are not affected by witchcraft. Very few Navajo dogs bite people, but if one does, it is supposed that the animal detected the powers of evil in the victim. For this reason, a medicine man practicing witchcraft could not keep a dog, since the animal would know what the man was like and would not stay. It also has the ability to bring about poverty, as do horses and sheep. Because they understand the voice of man, when a person curses these animals, it is like cursing another human.[17]

Thus animals—wild or domestic—hold powers beneficial to the Navajo in both physical and spiritual realms. As with most power, knowledge or lack of understanding about how to handle and respect it can either put a person on the road to success or the pathway to harm. Domestic animals, while not major actors in the creation of the world, obtained a role as important as those raised in the wild. They hold the riches and the wealth that sustain the people in their daily lives.

## *Sheep and Goats: Holders of Wealth*

There is a combination of spiritual and practical relationships with all animals. Take sheep for instance. They are associated in prayer with young ladies just as horses are connected to young men. Each has an area of responsibility in a ceremonial sense, outlining the female and male division. In the Blessingway songs that tell about this, there is always a second lyric that speaks to these responsibilities. The holy ones provided sheep as a main source of food for the Navajo people, saying that if we take care of them, they will take care of us. The story goes back to a time when there was a white sheep standing on top of Descending Wide Belt Mountain/Mesa (Sis Naateel—located eighteen miles west of Cuba, New Mexico), where Rock Crystal Boy (Tséghádi'ndínii Ashkii) sang his song. In it, he called the sheep in a holy, spiritual way. He sang nélooshdéí—calling a sheep in a spiritual way. People asked "Why? What are you saying? That's not even a Navajo word!" but the god answered, "I'm calling the sheep. There's a food that's going to be in line with you, that you will learn to walk with. These animals are called sheep." And from there he sang his songs: Nélooshdéí nélooshdéí nélooshdéí ei yiná hąą'igi nilah hąą ąągi lah nélooshdéí nélooshdéí nélooshdéí ei yiná hąą'igi nilah hąą ąągi. This is calling the mountain sheep in a spiritual way in a ceremony. Although they cannot be seen, they are there, in the ceremony, participating and renewing the promises to take care of the people. Each animal has its own distinct way of being there and taking part.

This is how he began singing, then he said, "On Belt Mountain the sheep are standing on top." He called the sheep down, and as they descended, they sang. When they arrived, the holy people explained that these animals had wool for humans to make rugs, dresses, and other types of clothing. They were provided with the understanding that when butchered, all of the sheep would be totally used, nothing wasted, not one part of them thrown away. The sheep agreed to give their life so that the hide could be used for bedding, wool for weaving, and meat—all of it—for eating. The feet, head, everything inside was to be used with nothing of value to be discarded. Individually and collectively, the sheep would grow in number, act tame, and permit themselves to be herded with the understanding that if they had good care, they would take care of their owners. This is how the sheep were presented by the holy beings. The mountain sheep provided the lower form of domestic sheep, but still look over them and are responsible and so are prayed to. This is also true of mountain goats and their relationship to the goats kept in a corral.

*No animal has had as much impact in defining what is today considered traditional Navajo culture than sheep. From making one "mutton hungry" with a wistful look toward home to the weaving of the famous Navajo rug and blanket, sheep dominated the cultural and economic scene until after the livestock reduction of the 1930s. Here two women have carded the wool (tool resting in pile), and are now twining it to tighten the yarn before going through the final stage of weaving a blanket.*

When selecting a sheep to butcher, some people say that one will stand out as if offering itself. Once the animal is chosen, a small bit of that sheep's wool is plucked off and put in the mouth of another sheep, usually female, in the belief that this will serve as a continuation of the one that is giving its life for others. Its posterity will continue and be born the following year. There is a prescribed way of killing and butchering a sheep. Its throat is cut and the blood caught in a pan for blood sausage, the head faces to the north but is not entirely severed until after the hide is removed, and the cutting up of the animal follows an exact sequence. There are no shortcuts or things performed out of order. If it is done in another way, it is considered rude and breaking with tradition. The spine, back, legs, and internal organs all follow a prescribed pattern of removal when butchering.

Sheep meat is considered normal food, unlike that of deer, buffalo, and other medicine animals already discussed. Medicine animal bones need to be taken to a special site, but not those of sheep, which can be put aside in some nearby bushes or a quiet place where they return to the earth. When butchering, however, all of the bones need to be removed from the hide, because they belong to the animal, and once it is killed and used for meat, the bones need to be completely released with not one left behind. Every bone is supposed to go back to the earth, according to the directions given at the time of creation. If a bone is left inside of the animal, then the rule is broken. The head, once removed, is singed and baked in a hole in the ground filled with coals, but even after being eaten, it is put back with the plants and the herbs to show respect. If a bone is broken while it is still in the skin, this can affect the person working on the sheep and can cause problems with his or her own bones. The hooves on the legs are chopped off and the skin removed, but everything has to be maintained in one piece. The legs are placed on one side of the animal and the bones and feet on the other side. The feet can be cooked in the ground and eaten. In the old days, the hooves were boiled and the tacky liquid used as glue to fletch arrows and reinforce bows.

Although sheep are considered regular food, there are also some ceremonial restrictions where certain parts of the body are used as medicine. It is done when a sick person has to have specific foods taken away. This is called the Sacred Boiling of Different Parts of the Sheep (ałta'ná'ábééžh). During the Windway ceremony, if a person is bothered by headaches, ulcers, stomach problems, and other internal discomfort, they are told to abstain from eating certain foods like sheep intestines, stomach, brains, and other parts. Like a human, sheep have seven distinct sacred areas that are part of their physical and spiritual makeup. They are called the Seven Senses (tsosts'idi ha'oodzíí') and are found from the ankle, to the knee, to the hip, to the shoulder, to the elbow, to the wrist, and then to the neck, in that order. Each one of these has its own prayers, and so from each one of these a small portion is cut. During the first ceremony, which is performed four times, they are removed from the patient's diet. Later, a second ceremony heals that person and allows them to again eat those parts that now provide healing power. A woman who is living a sacred life is selected to take small portions from each of the seven areas, including a sheep's ears, legs, heart, intestines, and other specific places where the medicine is made from a butchered sheep. She boils them together, places them in a small cup, and gives it to the patient. The opportunity to eat this food is restored.

Goats are another source of sustenance, related to sheep, but are viewed as inferior or second-class animals when the two are compared. The story of the sheep standing on top of Sis Naateel Mountain is tied into this. The people below spotted the first goat and at first thought he was a moving rock in a field of snow until they saw his horns. He moved over to where the sheep were standing. These animals were different, with a different kind of wool. The goat moved in a different way, was faster and agile, and was more like a mountain person when he descended. Even though his hair was silkier, he acted wilder, and he was less settled, the sheep decided to adopt the goat as a relative. A sheep's and goat's spirits are different. Goats are leaders and explore their surroundings, while sheep are followers and content just to graze. Goats will lead a flock of sheep into the wilderness if the herder is not careful, and so they have to be watched. They teach sheep new behavior and want to be in front of the flock, leading it to new places. While the sheep are more highly valued, have their own song (which the goat does not), have their meat used in ceremonies (which the goat cannot), and are considered holy ones, there should still be at least one or two goats with each flock. This is because goats lead, are unafraid, and go away from the herd of sheep to spot danger. If they find it, they will return to the flock and take them to safety.

## *Cows, Horses, and Donkeys*

Cows, like goats, do not have a lot of teachings. Their sacred name in Navajo is interesting. It translates as the Living Thing in the Water That Munches on Plants. This comes from the story of the water monster's horse (Tééh łį́į'), the pet of the water monster that guards his home. The people say that one of these animals came out of the water and became adapted to the land. Its big nose, large horns, strange noises, and weird face are what the monsters that live in the water look like. It dug into the earth with its horns, and so it also received the name of Déélgééd—The Horn That Digs into the Ground. When the people first saw them, they performed ceremonies to keep them peaceful and at a distance.

The horse, on the other hand, is a sacred animal and has many songs. It is thought of as a domestic creature that does not belong to those that are wild. The creation of the horse started when the holy ones were making animals like the deer, bear, and so forth out of clay. As they were finishing, they wanted to remove some of the material that was stuck to their hands, so they tried to rub it off. As they rubbed, they formed strips and rolls of clay that they brushed off by the doorway. The materials came together to form a horse that stood up and walked away. As the holy ones cleaned their fingers, rubbed their hands, and dusted off the remaining flecks of material, which at this point was becoming increasingly dry, the clay-like substance turned whiter. Soon there was enough material to form a donkey, who like the horse, stood up and walked away. This is how the old people used to talk about it in the medicine way.

The prayers about a horse speak of its hooves being made from mirage stone (hadahoniye') and its fetlocks, just above the hoof, as the wind. The mane that rests upon its shoulders is said to be the black wind from the north.

Its teeth are made from white shell while its eyes are considered to be of black jet. Like the deer and the rabbit, a horse's ears are considered messengers, and his tail is what guides him away from danger and indicates how fast he will be able to run. When blessing a horse with speed and protection, these same areas are followed in this order. Starting with the front hooves, the person moves to the shoulder, then to its mouth and nose, and then to the mane. The prayer follows along the entire back to the tail, ending with its back legs.

As the horse is replaced by the automobile as the main means of transportation, Navajos bless their cars. Many of the same principles and thinking are applied through protective songs and prayers. When blessing a vehicle, one starts with the tires, just as one begins with the hooves and legs of a horse. Instead of putting corn pollen inside as it is put in the horse's mouth, the steering wheel, brakes, and all of the working parts on or below the dashboard are blessed with prayers and the smoke of mountain tobacco and then herbs to keep evil away. These plant materials are mixed in water, then sprinkled internally and externally. An eagle feather is often hung from the rearview mirror as an added protection. At the time of the smudging and blessing of the car, this life feather is taken down and purified by passing it over coals of burning juniper bark; the car is blessed with it before tying it back on the mirror. The life feather provides guidance for everything that you are doing and protects the occupants from harm.

Many years ago, I used to raise a lot of quarter horses. There were two stallions that I had for over ten years, and I could really communicate with them. I was particularly close to one horse. We really understood each other. He might have been up in the mountains, and I may have been gone for days, but when I came home, I would clap my hands a few times and yell, and in moments he was flying down the slope at full speed, appearing in my pasture with the other horses as quickly as their legs could carry them. The stallion would then go to my doorstep as if to say, "I want my grain." I would get some, and he would start pushing me with his nose and saying, "hmmm, hmmm" as I talked to him. After he had finished, the horse would put his nose on me and really rub up and down, showing his appreciation. I, in turn, massaged his feet and legs, which he really enjoyed. There was always good communication. One time, my brother took this horse to the trading post, something happened, and the horse ran home with packed groceries on his back. The next morning he was knocking at my doorway. My wife opened the door and found Tonka waiting, saddled up with the groceries still intact. That is how loyal he was. I believe communication and loyalty between humans and animals are real.

Although horses may be used for food, they are still considered very, very sacred animals. It walks with mirage stones on its legs, its mane is like a thunderstorm, and its bridle is a rainbow that gives direction. He understands a great deal through his ears and learns much of what is going on around him when he listens. They help him to communicate. The horse is so sacred that it has its own warrior status, so that when it goes to war, it is fighting just like his rider. The two become one, working to defeat the enemy. This is why a horse is given his own feather and may be painted with protective designs before going into battle. They provide safety and recognize him as his own warrior. The horse was given four colors—red, white, blue, and yellow. Some people painted lightning on its body, indicating how it was going to strike the enemy. An owner needs to constantly be looking out for his horse. Most Navajos took pride in their horses and tried to have a nice woven saddle blanket with silver on the bridle, just as today we try to drive and take care of nice cars. Horses took us everywhere we wanted to go.

Horses were eaten during the winter months—around January and February—when colds and flu were about. Their flesh is considered medicine because of all the plants and herbs they eat; none of it was wasted. The reason horses are considered so sacred is because they have a lot of songs and prayers given by the holy ones. They are highly respected and are themselves considered to be holy creatures. No other animal has songs like a horse. Still, when hunger and starvation strike, it was necessary and appropriate to eat a yearling or two-year-old horse, but the old ones were left alone. Blinders may be placed on its eyes before a blow to the head with an ax kills it. Warriors who lived nearby might help with the skinning so that they could obtain the sinew that runs from the head and neck all the way down the back to the tail. When the butchering was completed, they received some of this to put on their bows as reinforcement to make them stronger and more powerful. They would boil what they needed then wrap it tightly around the wood. It quickly hardens like it was glued on. When finished, the weapon is called a Black Bow, which has nothing to do with its color but rather indicates its physical and spiritual power as found in traditional teachings.

While horses are very sacred animals, the donkey (dzaanééz—Long Eared) is even more so. After most of the creatures had been made and one of the holy people finished forming the horse, he began to scrape off the last of the clay stuck on his hands and fingers, and the black dirt under the fingernails. He rolled the scrap material into a ball and threw it in the ash pile, where it dried, took on the light gray color of the ashes, and emerged as a donkey. Out of this residue the donkey fortunately obtained many of the good qualities that other animals had received during their creation. The fingernail dirt became the donkey's black stripes on his four legs and along his back. Like the deer, antelope, elk, raccoon, and other animals from the

*Horses, mules, and donkeys have served the Navajo people as a primary means of transportation for approximately three centuries. Like sheep, goats, cattle, and chickens, these animals were introduced by the Spaniards in the 1600s; as with many innovations in Navajo culture, they have been adopted and adapted to the People's cultural needs.*

mountains and desert who had similar markings, the donkey became a medicine person. He holds much of the healing power that animals on the mountain hold. In some ceremonies (an abbreviated Evilway—marking with ashes), the patient is given four black markings, the same type that the donkey wears on his legs. He also has the black mark from the Evilway ceremony over his shoulder. So he is represented in a number of rituals, even though his involvement had not been initially planned. The donkey is colored like the ash used in ceremonies. Its white nose comes from the corn pollen from which it is made.

Although he stood at the end of the process of creation, he also obtained a blessing from the eagle. Like the deer and jackrabbit, his brothers, he received two eagle feathers for ears, which the horse never received. The jackrabbit and donkey also have a similar type of flesh with the same texture and whitish color because they belong to the holy ones, while the horse has very red meat and does not. The donkey also wears a different fur coat than the horse. Donkeys are considered one of the holy medicines, as is a horse, but he is a little bit more special because of his two "feathers." He is a walking medicine person that is a holy one, who holds special medicine powers as the last medicine animal to be made and one who has many riches.

Thus, Navajos consider him a very valuable animal. They say if a person wants to raise a lot of horses, sheep, and goats, there must be at least one donkey with the herd. A livestock operation is not complete unless there is one. They are part of the family and will add wealth to what is being raised. If you have one, people will say, "Oh, this is a wealthy family. They carry this." Donkeys have the mildest attitude and do not fight or buck. They are pleasant to be with and feel self-assured because they know who they are and what they have. Their presence in a horse herd maintains its sacredness. It is the last medicine horse.

## *Dogs and Cats: Guardians of the Home*

The teachings about dogs started when the holy people were getting used to some of the new things in their environment. Early one morning, there was a barking coyote in the distance, but then came a second unfamiliar noise with a very different tone. Instead of the short yapping of a coyote, they heard a long unfamiliar howling. The people asked, "What is that? Something to the east is calling," but no one could identify the sound. At this time, the Yé'ii Bicheii were living with the people, and so Talking God sent one to find the answer to what was making this unfamiliar sound. The holy being went to the east, found a strange looking animal, and brought it back to the group. He said, "This looks different. It doesn't look like a coyote or a wolf. This creature moves in another way and is constantly wagging its tail and holding it differently. And look, its tongue is always hanging out of its mouth. What's wrong with this thing? I will say, however, that he is very friendly, but still he barks too much." The people were not sure what to do with it, and so they left it tied away from their homes and let it sit alone for a while. They wanted to observe this creature to see if they wished to have it around.

The dog was lonely and constantly barked. It did not take long for the people to get fed up and planned to get rid of it. "Why does he have to bark all the time?" the gods asked. "Let's kill it and get it out of here." They put a leash around its neck and started to haul him away, but when the dog heard they were going to end his life, he offered to explain who he really was. "I come from a place where the sun lives. My eyes can see spirits that you cannot. I know when somebody is coming to you, and that is the reason I bark all the time. If an individual or a spirit is approaching your camp, I will warn you. I can see through the darkness like nobody else can and will detect bad spirits out there. When I know one is around, I start to bark, and that is why you hear me all the time, but then they flee because they know they have been spotted. I am here to be a protector."

The god, who had brought him in, stood there and thought about it, admitted that the dog had a point, and so took him in with the understanding that he would only bark when he saw something that could bring harm. The animal agreed, promising to become more relaxed and not bark unless he was sure that he saw something worthy of warning. A few days passed, and the dog started barking again. The people went out and looked at him with his ears pointed forward, standing alert, giving his warning. Sure enough, someone was coming. Everyone accepted that these were useful qualities and that the dog should remain to warn of approaching danger—whether physical or spiritual.

Now he needed a name. Coyote had already received his: The One Who Cries in the Morning or Dawn (yikáí yitah yichaa'í). The people understood that a dog was different than a coyote, and so they decided to name him The One Who Sees Beyond the Ashes or Ash Pit. He has this name because when a person dies, their spirit goes to the north, just as when things that are used up, such as ashes from a fire, are put to the north of a home. The dog's name indicates that it will alert when spirits approach from the north—the same direction that the dead come from. The dog keeps them away and is considered part of the family. His everyday name is not as special—The One That Poops Around (łééchąą'í). Dogs are considered to have good thoughts and a positive energy. They know a lot, can understand things, and have their own spirit. As mentioned earlier, dogs communicate things they are thinking, what they want, and their intelligence. If a person is going to kill a dog, that animal will know. This sense of things unseen is one of the reasons that dogs are not to be abused. They have the ability to curse someone if mistreated. This is no different than when people beat or are mean to another human. The dog wishes the bully would go away and stop the abuse, just as a woman beaten by her husband wishes that he would stop, leave, and not return. Domestic violence is about treating humans like animals, but the animals do not like it any more than a person does. They have feelings, as do we.

Dogs can even the score and curse a person when least expected. Let's say a man runs over a dog while his wife is pregnant or working with a youngster during the child phase. Suddenly the infant gets sick, vomiting and declining in health no matter what kind of medicine it is given. The medicine person might diagnose the cause through hand trembling or crystal gazing and determine that the child needs the Dogway ceremony. Symptoms may include bloating, constipation, dizziness, and stomach problems. The offended dog is "remade" by taking steamed corn, drying it, and then moistening it so that it can be formed into the shape of a dog perhaps three or four inches long. Turquoise is placed in this figure's ears, nose, mouth, and tail, then prayed over by the medicine man, who eventually leaves an offering to the offended spirit. This is a renewal or restoration ritual that removes any ill will that might have arisen from the dog's death or serious mistreatment. The child's illness is healed and the problem settled. A lot of people may not see the need or believe in this ceremony, but medicine people understand animals and know that they are very intelligent and aware of human conditions.

Domesticated animals, like wild animals, have their own personalities and ways of communicating. Cats, dogs, horses, sheep, and even baby animals show emotions of love and fear and everything in between as they interact with humans. If you are good to them, they will trust you and follow your direction as they understand it. The more you are around them the better they get to know you and anticipate what you want them to do. For instance, a dog left behind at your house welcomes you home by jumping around and leaping into your lap. They are happy you have returned and express love and loyalty by their enthusiasm. If you have a spare moment to sit down, talk to them, and explain what you want, they will sit, listen, watch, and try to respond.

Cats are beautiful people that are highly poised. Their story starts when they appeared unannounced one day at a hogan and immediately took their position on the top (roof) by the smoke hole. That is where they belong. People inside kept looking up when first they saw a tail, then a face and ears, then the entire cat peering down. First Man asked in a dream, "Why is this

*Dogs are protectors. Whether around the home to warn of strangers or the approach of evil influences, or as a watchdog to keep coyotes and other predators away from livestock, they play a welcomed role. Some Navajos insist that the dogs guide their sheep, keep them together as a flock, and feel a real responsibility to work for their masters.*

person up there? What is he supposed to be doing?" The gods told him, "He is the one known as The Foot That Makes No Sound, because he will sneak up to you without any noise." The gods taught more, saying, "The hogan represents the mountain where most cats that look like him are found. This is a small animal compared to cougars and bobcats, but he is going to sit on top of the hogan at night and capture any evil dreams that might be coming through the smoke hole to someone sleeping in the home. This is how he protects and guides family members while they slumber. Dreams are associated with the night and things of darkness. Some come from the stars as a means of communication, others come from places that are not good. They may linger and wait so that when the time is right, they can get into a person's home through the smoke hole. The cat appears to be sleeping there, but even though its eyes are closed and it is purring, it is really on duty checking all that is trying to enter. If a bad dream comes, the cat will capture it and put it on its tail, where there are a number of rings. Once on his tail, he is able to sleep it away. He is going to take care of you and your dreams." He may lie there, guarding by the chimney as a medicine person, but you should not let him into your house. This is how my father explained it to me.

People say that Cat is the keeper of all of those creatures that have patterns and crawl like snakes, turtles, and other small animals. His body, from the top of his head running down to the tip of his tail is that of a snake; its fur often has a reptile pattern. His forehead has the head of a snake while his flexible spine and tail are the snake's body; this is why a cat is so fast on its feet and able to bend and twist in many directions. People say that if he gets mad at one of the snakes, a single slap with his paw will kill it. That is how bad he is. I believe this because I have seen it. There was a big rattlesnake that had his head up and was ready to strike a one-year-old cat that was a lot smaller. He got mad at the snake, watched for the right moment, then struck him on the jaw one time with his paw and killed it. He was so much faster—he hit with lightning speed. I could not believe it and did not understand how he did it. I examined the soft cat's paw with its retracted claws, but there did not appear to be any way he could have done it. My father explained that cats actually do that kind of killing with a claw behind the other ones—a dew claw that is found only on the front paws. Since the cat already has a snake design on his back, he is much faster than a regular snake.

The cat symbolically sits on the top of the hogan and is a protector, just as there is a holy being who sits on the mountain and protects animals. My father one time was singing a song that I did not recognize, and so I asked him about it. He told me to listen to it as he sang it again and then he would explain. He started: "shits'íís yiką́ą danooyééł ei ę̀ę shei nei yą́ą ąą shits'íís yiką́ą danooyééł ei ę̀ę shei nei yą́ą ąą shits'íís yiką́ą danooyééł ei ę̀ę shei nei yą́ą ąą shits'íís yiką́ą danooyééł ei ę̀ę shei nei yą́ą ąą," meaning "There is a holy one that sits on top of me and I live with that. I'm one of the animals; this hovers above and cares for me." This caretaker appears in the form of mist, fine rain, and a rainbow that hides the protector who lives around the mountains. These are the defenders of all animals; they come in a mist-like cloud that circles high places. They leave only a small amount of water, just enough to form a dewy covering on top of the trees, grass, and rocks. Father said the caretaker of all animals in the mountains leaves it there. The holy one on top is there watching over those he is responsible for.

One of the good things that cats do is hunt for mice, which in Navajo thought are considered very negative. They come into a house when it is not clean or cared for, and so the people living in it have to always be looking out for them. Everything should be done to prevent this animal from entering the house. A mouse is considered an informer sent by people involved in witchcraft. He will take things like a person's hair, a little bit of their clothing, or something else that they have been in contact with from that person's home and sell it to those who are performing witchcraft against them. The mouse gets paid to come and get it and take it back. Mice are talked about and observed but are not allowed to come into a home. If they do, then they are killed immediately. There is no second chance for a mouse, whereas if a snake enters the home, it is put outside and told not to return. There is no second thought about killing mice. When you watch a mouse, its eyes do not blink. The way that they are set in its head, a mouse's constant stare, and its way of entering graves make it just like a dead person. Navajos fear them and feel like they are looking at a ghost that has come to visit.

## *Corrals and Cages: Protecting Wealth, Enabling Death*

Animals, whether wild or domestic, interact with humans. Domestic animals need to be controlled, cared for, protected, and treated as wealth and part of the home. Every Navajo camp has a corral built for this purpose. In contrast, wild animals have to be located, driven, captured, and killed in order for them to be useful for people. Navajos also built corrals for this purpose, but they are associated with capture and death. This corral for wild animals was first built in the mountains and called neidzį́į́n, which means a Place of No Return, where captivity and death occur. Anything that goes into it will become food or will die and never come back to life. This is a scary word and situation. People avoid going into one except for killing and dressing the trapped animals; nothing is performed inside because the place has a spirit and is concerned with death. Stay on the outside.

The people talked about how First Man and other holy ones built the initial corral out of logs in places in the mountains where the deer could be fooled and trapped before they knew what was going on. The hunters sat on the outside and shot the deer before they escaped. This is how the first corral started; later it was brought down from the mountains and into the valleys where the people lived, but these kinds of structures are never built close to a home because they are associated with killing and death. They were so effective in trapping animals that the people began to feel uncomfortable about what they were doing. They agreed that these enclosures should not be used all of the time, but only if it was necessary to get meat. When the neidzį́į́n was used, they prayed and sang to the animals: "Today you will sacrifice your life for us, so we will live again on this earth," communicating with the deer in this way.

At this point, the animals stayed in the corral and began talking among themselves. They said, "These people, who put this thing together, think of themselves as our masters, but being trapped in a closed circle like this is not a good thing. We'll curse them that they will be rounded up just like a herd of horses and put in a corral called a reservation. Through this they will understand what they did to us, when they reflect on the past." The animals set the curse and told the Navajos, "Watch, watch. You will go through the same thing that we are going through. You will be rounded up and will sit around in a pen on the land that will be called a reservation. See how you like it. You will try to move to the cities where there are new laws, but it is not going to work for you." Through this story, Navajos can understand their current situation, which is also true for other Indian groups living on reservations. Navajos do not go beyond the mountains to do things that need to be done but are stuck on their plot of land.

This is how the first type of corral was used, but it is the opposite of the ones found around Navajo dwellings. These are considered to be homes and places of safety for the livestock and wealth. A sheep corral is called dibé bighan (sheep's home) and is built differently than the one used for hunting. This is opened every day—morning and night—to let the animals in and out. They return home for safety and are guarded by dogs and their owners. This is the place where they live and eat; what happens here represents some of the good things that are taking place for their owners and family. Positive things like lambing, wool shearing, even butchering are done in a good way. This is how domestic life sources were structured, as opposed to the things that take place in the mountains and untamed areas.

The corral is a blessing and is formed in the same way that a Navajo home is built. It has a doorway with a post on either side, as in a hogan, and is connected to important elements of life. When going out of the corral, the post on the left represents turquoise, hard goods, the south, daytime, male qualities, and Turquoise Boy (Dootł'izhii Ashkii), while the other side represents white shell, soft goods, the east, dawn, female qualities, and White Shell Woman. The animals' life is in a circle, protected from everyday influences and harm. Each morning they leave the safety of the corral and meet challenges, but they return home in the evening to be safely guarded again. This is the same with humans when they go into their home or a sweat lodge. As people or animals pass between the two doorposts, they are blessed with male and female wealth. The livestock belongs to its owner who cares for them, but the inner thoughts, the inner feelings always go back to the pattern where turquoise represents the male and white shell the female. When going through the entrance, the wealth of hard goods and soft goods are enticed to come to that person and are physically represented by the sheep being cared for. The songs and prayers offered in the corral prepare the person for what he or she will encounter when going about daily business. Good thoughts will bring good things.

*The sheep corral (dibé bighan—sheep's home) reflects a number of the same values that Navajos ascribe to their own home. It is round and made of wood, the entryway faces east, the gateposts represent the wealth derived from hard and soft goods, and it is a place of prayer. Care for these animals is a constant concern.*

As you can see, many of these animals, whether they are big or small, have a lot of power and need to be shown proper respect and care. An important issue for the Navajo people today is how to treat them. More specifically, the tribe has a zoo in the Navajo Nation capital, Window Rock, in which many of the wild animals are caged and held in captivity instead of being allowed to live a normal life in nature. These animals are watching and know what is happening. There have been heated arguments about this, and most medicine people agree that this should not be. They have insisted that the animals be freed, but their desire has been overridden so many times that it seems hopeless. We have tried to explain that these creatures should not be trapped and kept as prisoners. They should have the same freedom that we Navajo people want for ourselves.

This argument goes all the way back to 1978 when the American Indian Religious Freedom Act (AIRFA) gave Native Americans the right to worship as they wished, with no outside interference. Spiritual rights became its central theme. This act said that Indians, as natural people, could pray and perform ceremonies as we saw fit, and it legalized the use of sacred peyote. Religious freedom belongs to everyone. My grandfather and father were still around then and talked about what all of this meant. Part of that discussion included our relationship with animals and how, as medicine men, they were opposed to zoos and other ways that animals had to live in unnatural settings, especially on the reservation. After listening to my father, grandfathers, and other people, I knew that as the zoo became a reality, it violated traditional beliefs and practices. There was a large protest march with many of the medicine men coming together with signs opposed to what was happening. The other side argued the zoo was for the children, the development of the young people. But the elders were saying, "No. You can't do that because it takes us back to the time of the Long Walk and Fort Sumner. If you were the animal sitting there, how would you feel?" It was just like our elders in the old days, asking why they were being caged at that place with its unfamiliar surroundings, divorced from their land. Animals have their own lands, trees and plants, means for obtaining food, and way of life. Why should they be caged and kept away from that? Who says that as a human being, as a Navajo, you know best for them, can choose the type of food they eat, or control all aspects of their life?

The medicine men reasoned that if these animals were going to be caged, they should at least be fed the mice, snakes, and other things they ate before they were jailed, not processed food. We are treating them like prisoners, sitting there, and yet they are our people. We come from them, and so why are we caging them? It's not right. The argument grew with traditional views attacked, overridden, and defeated. The Navajo Nation president vetoed our request. The linear thinking of Christianity entered in and offered the explanation that won out. Even today, there are still a lot of medicine men who do not like it and think it is wrong to create something like a zoo.

This same kind of thinking is found when people pen their horses right around their house. Most people live in areas where there is enough room and grass that the horses can graze freely in the open without having to be penned up in a small metal rectangular corral. When there is land available for them, animals should not be caged. Perhaps they need to be kept in a corral for a couple of days, but otherwise, they should be given freedom. This reminds me of how one day my youngest brother had just completed a ceremony held at another brother's home. The older brother had four horses that he kept in a corral all of the time. He used them for roping competitions at rodeos and was constantly on the road with them, heading for the next event. My younger brother had just come out of the ceremony early in the morning and stood there, his eyes fixed on these animals. We all asked, "Why are you so serious? Why are you standing there so quietly looking at the horses? What's on your mind?" Younger brother turned to his older sibling and said, "It doesn't bother you?"

"What bother me?"

"Your horses. Do you believe that horses have their own minds, eyes, ears, and sensibilities that a normal person has? I think they know what they're doing. If you were a horse, would you want to stand in that six-foot by eight-foot metal corral and walk in a circle all day? How would you feel?" My older brother considered what was said, and by the time they had finished talking, he had tears running down his face. He went to the corral, opened the gate, and turned them loose to graze, saying "That's better now. I feel better about this. I know I wouldn't like it if you closed the door on my house and kept me walking inside. We have our own places to go and things to do." As people think about the stories and teachings concerning animals, they realize that these creatures do have a mind, feelings, and different things they want to do. They should not be caged.

# CHAPTER NINE

# *Fish, Fowl, and Reptile*

## *Inhabitants of Earth, Water, and Sky*

Sprinkled throughout the chapters of this book and its accompanying first volume are traditional teachings about various creatures ranging from birds and mammals, toads and turtles, to ants and caterpillars, eagles and crows. Mention has also been made of the four levels of healing with songs and prayers based in relation to the ground and progressing upward to the sky; there has also been discussion of Navajo classification. In this chapter, as Perry looks at the wide-ranging topics of birds, reptiles, and insects, the reader gets a very quick glimpse of the understanding of a people who not only lived close to nature, studied the habits of some very obscure creatures, and noted many of their individual characteristics, but also shared stories and teachings that ensured these beings played a significant role in the Navajo worldview.[1] Far too complex in breadth and depth to substantially analyze here, a few examples of how they are viewed and why their powers are used is offered.

Medicine people often classify birds into four broad categories generally grouped according to where and how they fly in relation to the ground.[2] As Perry mentioned previously, there are four levels of prayers and songs used to heal people, the more serious the illness, the higher the level above the earth. As part of this hierarchal scheme, the lower the level, the less intense the appeal and the simpler the remedy. The higher one goes, the more complex and serious the illness, with birds from those levels assisting in the healing. Starting at the top, eagle, as master of all birds, flies above, reaching as a messenger the most powerful of the holy beings inhabiting the heavens; two types of hawks, with some usually flying higher than others, reside in the next two regions, appealing to the holy ones in those realms; finally, small birds that flit about close to the ground operate on the lowest level. Within these four levels, birds are categorized according to where they live—around the sun, on mountain tops, on rocks, in trees, on the ground, or in the water. Physical characteristics or habits also suggest the names they receive.

A similar naming process is applied to insects. Anthropologists Leland Wyman and Flora Bailey compiled *Navaho Indian Ethnoentomology* in which they identified 5,551 insects.[3] Approximately half of these creatures had generic names while many others were mislabeled or unknown to the people asked to identify them. As with the titles of birds, one-third of the bugs and insects that were recognized received their name from their behavior, another third from physical attributes (color, size, shape, etc.), a fourth based on where they lived, with the remainder of the names untranslatable due to an ancient derivation.[4] When thinking about the relationship between insects and the Navajo world, many of these creatures are categorized in some meaningful way such as being dangerous, pests, medicine (human), veterinarian cures, food, sandpainting images, witchcraft, or mythological. Wyman and Bailey provide extensive information on moths, ants, spiders, grasshoppers, and bees.[5]

In this brief space, the eagle, waterfowl and fish, salamanders and snakes will receive the most attention, since Perry emphasized their importance. Starting with a discussion of eagle life feathers, he addresses this important source of individual protection. Washington Matthews observed that a "life-feather or breath-feather (hiiná biltsós) is a feather taken from a live bird, especially an eagle. Such feathers are supposed to preserve life and possess other magic powers. They are used in all the rites."[6] These were first introduced by Spider Woman, who gave each of the Twins one for their journey to meet Sun Bearer. They were small enough to be held in the hand for protection or to fit in an individual's corn pollen pouch. In the past these feathers were obtained by digging a pit to camouflage a man inside who secured a live rabbit outside as bait for an eagle. When the bird attacked its prey, the man grabbed its legs and pulled it down captive into the pit. Then the desired feathers could either be plucked and the bird released, or it could be smothered with corn pollen and a hood. According to Gladys Reichard: "The longer the bird struggled, the more potent were its parts in a ceremony. The feathers represent strength, speed and motion, deliverance; the pollen exposed to them stands for light and life, that is, the sheen of the feathers."[7] Another way to secure live eagle feathers was to climb to a nest and pick one from a baby eagle.[8]

In ceremonies an eagle bone whistle called a "spirit carrier" is used to summon the holy people and to send or carry prayers to them. Eagle feathers are worn in the headdress of Talking God and Hogan God—twelve of them were received as payment for helping the Twins in defeating some of the monsters. Some life feathers were tied in a special knot before being placed in a pouch carried by the person seeking protection. Medicine men use the help of birds, such as eagles, who see far away during divination. They catch a bird alive, put corn pollen in its eye, then take the resulting "eye water," mix it with finely ground rock crystals, and apply it under the diviner's eyes for "the clearness of the crystal and the far-seeing vision of the eagle."[9] Birds, such as herons, turkeys, magpies, quails, roadrunners, and those of the night, also aid with "far-seeing" eye water.[10] Born for Water gathered eagle down to make prayersticks, other holy people used it to fletch arrows, and others obtained it for hair ornaments. "All the other gods received either tail feathers or down feathers from the eagles. Every sacred article was provided with some kind of eagle feather and the Navajo still use the sacred objects so trimmed to this day."[11]

But it was Monster Slayer who was directly saved by his life feather when a giant monster bird snatched him in her claws and flew to Shiprock peak to dash the young warrior against the rock, turning him into food for her young below. Instead, he floated gently to the formation with his life feather and later defeated the bird.[12] The prayers and the words the Twins received from Spider Woman gave the life feathers efficacy. Without knowledge of the prayers, the power could not be set in motion. Gary Witherspoon reminds us that "control of a particular diyin dine'é [holy person] is accomplished by knowledge of his or her symbols (particularly his or her name), knowledge of his or her offering, and knowledge of the smells, sights, and sounds which attract, please, and compel him or her. The correct songs, prayers, and symbols are irresistible and compulsive. A Navajo does not supplicate or worship his gods; he identifies himself with them and both controls their power and incorporates their power within himself."[13]

Other birds are also important and hold their own powers. For instance, any type of bird that has wings that can spread like a fan are associated with winds, clouds, and moisture, as are insects like dragonflies and moths. The cry of the kill-deer, snipe, plover, and mourning dove summon rain, as does the croak of a frog tied in a corn field.[14] Franc Newcomb provides three reasons why birds who live on water control similar powers that should not be trifled with: "The flesh of ducks, geese, swans, and other water-birds must not be eaten. There is an especially large group of taboos that protect all birds that swim and all birds that wade. First there are all the taboos that apply to creatures which walk on the earth; second there are all the taboos that apply to those having the power to fly through the air; and added to these are the taboos which apply to water creatures. So there is no time during the year when the flesh of water-fowl may be eaten."[15] Those who did so were shunned, may be accused of being a witch, and were indirectly eating another source of tabooed food—any kind of fish, shellfish, or eel coming from the water. They are all part of the water monster's domain. Many have a rainbow on their underside and so are protected by Father Sky and should be left alone. To eat this food could cause the person to look like that creature or have problems with their joints.[16]

Another being associated with rain is the mud puppy or mud dog, a salamander that is found where it is damp. The powers of this amphibian are appealed to during a Chaashzhiní (Mud Dancers) ceremony, which may be part of the Enemyway and which serves as a request for moisture and to heal people suffering from fainting spells and pain. It is performed as a prayer, which brings heavy rain showers. The teaching for this says that when there is a downpour, a person can go to places where water collects in streams and rock basins and find these water dogs, frogs, and tadpoles swimming like fish or resting in damp cool spots. They bring the rain, come with it, and are not to be killed, but left alone.

At one time these were people, just like the water monsters and water babies. They were holy people, and so by acting like them, they bring storms and bless the Navajo with their power. They represent rain, wet earth, and fertility; these are the blessings that a mud dog shares with the people when they call upon these powers. Participants in the ceremony become what they are representing and obtain their assistance while also getting toughened up. Just as with Coyote, when he calls for rain, it happens. They are the Water People and must be respected.

Jim Dandy tells of his experience when participating in a mud dance ceremony.

> Once there had not been rain for some time, a real dry season. The people performed an Enemyway ceremony that I participated in then held a mud dog blessing. They said a short prayer before we went out and dug a large hole, perhaps ten feet in diameter, then added water mixed with herbs until it was filled with mud. Stripped down to loin cloths, a number of men went running after the people, brought them back to the mud hole, and threw them in. My sister was making fun of me while I was on horseback, feeling just so light, quick, and strong because of my involvement in this ritual. The ceremony also helps a person to think fast. With this added strength it was easy to grab someone and toss them in the pit. We took her, even though she was dressed in fine clothes and beautiful jewelry, and threw her into the mud and water. She became a mud dog like the rest of us, grabbing others and pushing them into the hole. Following the round up, a prayer

was said and people placed on a rolled blanket, swung back and forth then tossed into the mud as the participants sang. This is a blessing not only for rain but also for those who need to be healed from sickness or are under stress. We become the medicine, the holy people, helping to get that person well. After obtaining as many as you can to assist, the people line up to receive their blessing by putting a little bit of mud on them with a prayer. Individuals line up for a long time to receive this. The ceremony is exciting and a lot of fun to watch.[17]

Perry's final subject is that of snakes. A good comprehensive overview of Navajo practices concerning snakes is found in Steve Pavlik's *The Navajo and the Animal People*.[18] An excellent example of how Navajos deal with snakes on a daily basis is provided by Tall Woman, who had a number of encounters. As a young mother, while living by Chinle Wash, she was busy feeding some horses when a rattlesnake lunged out of the alfalfa she was cutting and bit her. Tall Woman's mother blended a concoction of herbs in water that was applied to the swelling arm, while her husband waited until the wound began to heal, then hired Fingerless Man to perform a five-day Beautyway ceremony to remove the serpent's ill effects. "From then on, the snakes respect you and you respect them; they don't bother you, after you've had a Beautyway."[19] This ceremony is part of the Holyway group and is "firmly associated with snakes (and sometimes with lizards and certain water creatures) and deals with illnesses attributed to snake infection, such as rheumatism, sore throats, skin rashes or sores, and other problems."[20]

A few years later, there was a second incident, when Tall Woman was living in a ramada (chaha'oh) and sleeping outside. She had been careful to follow the traditional practice of applying an herb called nábįįh (*Conioselinum scopulorum*—Rocky Mountain hemlock parsley), the root of which is ground and added to water before sprinkling it around the hogan and shade. Its strong-smelling odor is believed to keep snakes away. One was not deterred and settled in a hole supporting part of Tall Woman's loom. The reptile struck and tried to make its escape, but Frank caught it and dispatched it with a shovel. She felt that he should not have done that, but he reasoned that the snake was acting out of order because of the previous ceremony, which served as an agreement that should have been honored. Again, the couple waited for a partial healing before having, this time, a five-day Windway ceremony. Following a bout with infection and a visit to a clinic, Tall Woman got better and life returned to normal.[21] Snakes, as with so many creatures, large or small, powerful or seemingly inconsequential, have a place and responsibility within the natural world of the Navajo. And like humans, they have personalities, can accept or reject a relationship, and can bless or harm those they come in contact with.

# *Eagle, Master Bird*

In Navajo thought, many birds are connected to the heavens, hold strong spiritual powers, and serve as messengers. The eagle (atsá—It Clinches Its Food) especially embodies these qualities and is aptly associated with distance—he can see far away, fly for miles, and soar high in the sky. His ceremonial name translates as Yellow Beak Chief. Eagle represents and holds many of the powers found in the heavens and is the only bird that can fly quickly through the atmosphere to see what is happening without his eyes being bothered by tears. He visits the holy people in the sky and yet returns to earth to live his life. That is why anything that belongs to him—his bones, body, feathers, claws—represents one of the holy ones, almost like an angel. Anything that comes from this bird is used to easily make connection with those people—easier than anything else. He is the messenger from the ground to the heavens.

An eagle feather and eagle bone whistle are used in crystal and star gazing and serve as the means by which a question or request is sent to a star. The medicine person asking for answers is given a view through the eyes of the eagle to learn what has happened. This is the only person who has that vision. The whistle opens up the medicine and alerts the holy people that their presence and assistance is desired. It also helps spread the medicine and power to the sky when it is blown into a bowl containing a healing solution. Communication between the eagle and deer has already been discussed. Eagle feathers always stand for life and are used as a force for good. This is considered one of the highly important and powerful medicines and is used to decorate the prayerstick (k'eet'ááną́ą́) dedicated to Talking God (K'eet'ą́ą́ yáłti').

One of its most important uses for an individual is that of a life feather (iiná bitsee'—plume). Golden eagles are preferred by medicine men over bald eagles for their plumage. The life feather is taken from beneath an eagle's tail while it is still alive or when one is found detached in a nest. If the loosened feather has not touched the ground, it is still viable. This plume is normally found beneath the twelve main tail feathers and must come from this exact location, because that is where the holy one sits. The large tail feathers above are divided into six gods sitting on one side and six on the other. Half of them are the ones who visit the heavens, and the other ones visit the ground and the water. They are considered to hold the qualities of a thunderstorm because they have black tips. Just as when a storm is approaching, the person standing on the ground will see a very dark bottom

*Golden eagle feathers belong to the most powerful bird, a direct messenger to the gods. The bundle on the left is held by a patient, while the feathers on the right are placed in the ground. By walking through them, evil is kept away and the patient is restored. Both sets of feathers are used in the Evilway, Enemyway, and Lightningway. (Photo by Kay Shumway)*

that is black, while on top there will be clear skies. That is how the storm touches the ground, and the same is true with the ends of the eagle's feathers. The tail with its plume always represents the feelings and thoughts of life—they never sit still. The top part of the tail is slick and shiny, but underneath, where the plumes look like they are in a ball, the feathers are not settled. It won't sit in one place. This is where you will find a plume with a tip on it long enough to serve as a cushion. It is said this is the first part that touches the ground or that creates life while the eagle sits on its nest, keeping the young ones alive. It is the blanket they use to cover their eggs, keeping them holy until the eaglets are ready to come out. This is the role of every mother, to keep life safe, protected, and cushy.

During part of the Mountainway ceremony when a piece of cloth on a stick is burned, the ashes from it become holy and can be used to cure the sick. Later, two eagle feathers are tied on the stick to represent life. The holy ones who visit the ceremonial corral during the day will be dancing with it for the people that night. The spirits will be dancing as the songs are sung to the accompaniment of the drum. The stick with the feathers represents life renewal. This is why the cloth is burned but the feathers, standing for life, are not. The song tells about the cloth coming back, but it is the feathers (life) now tied to the stick that really represent returning.

Obtaining eagle feathers today is very difficult. Even if one finds a dead bird, the law makes it hard to get permission to take the medicine parts needed for ceremonies. The process requires submitting an application to wildlife refuges in the U.S., Canada, or Alaska. If they have a bird's body available, then they will ship it to you. But first you have to have a medicine man's license, showing the feathers will be used for spiritual purposes or in paraphernalia that is being created. In the old days, getting eagle feathers was easier, and a lot were used to make war hats, but that is not so today. Even just displaying a feather in your car or carrying one around, especially off the reservation, is enough to get you stopped. Police want to know where and how you obtained it.

Eagles and owls are brothers. This goes back to the time when Monster Slayer killed the Monster Birds (Tsé nináhádleehí) that lived on top of Shiprock. Once the two parents were defeated, there were two young ones that needed to be dealt with. Monster Slayer grabbed the first one and twirled it about his head, turned him into an eagle, and charged him with positive qualities to help the earth surface people (humans) in the future. The second one received the same treatment and became Owl. He received some of the negative tasks that he still performs today. Like his eagle brother, Owl is a messenger but not of good news. He is not involved in any type of healing ceremony, and he works with his cousin, the vulture, in the realm of death.

At the time Monster Slayer turned them loose, it was also decided that one of the birds would be a day creature; the other was to be night. The holy ones talked about it and gave eagle a white head and black body. Owl received gray and white colors. The white of the eagle was more intense, and so he was given to early light and received the name The One That Carries the Early Morning Dawn, which holds both day and evening colors. He works during the day and sleeps at night; Owl rules the night and sleeps during the day.

# *Birds and Bats of Evil*

I am not sure why Owl has such a negative life, but they say he was involved in some cursing, part of which was reversed, and so received some of it back to become part of his personality. He would sit there and watch the cursing take place and would know what was going to happen. Then he would tell it to the vulture, who sent word of it back to the heavens. Owl was able to predict who would die and who would live that day. When word came back from the holy people, Owl would then spread the news to the earth surface people, that one of them would soon die. The same is true now when an owl comes around one's house. You know something will soon happen concerning the dead, both past and future. This is not good when Owl visits because something tragic will take place. He is the representative of death as is the vulture. Do not let him near your house or animals. If you see him coming close, he is telling you a story of what is going to occur.

My uncle (father's brother) was a powerful medicine man. When I was about two years old he passed away. I guess another family member was using witchcraft and acting as a skinwalker. He stole my uncle's moccasins to work against and curse him, just before he died. A month after the funeral, family members began having visits from an owl; my father said the bird was insisting he wanted his shoes back. Dad did not know what he was talking about—lost moccasins made no sense—so he turned to star gazing. He saw an image of my uncle's moccasins hanging in a burial place. Another medicine person went to the spot, found them, and brought them back. My father tied them to a tree and made an offering. The owl returned, took the moccasins, and never came back.

One of Owl's cousins is the vulture who is always associated with death and evil. A story is told about a young man who liked to pretend he was hurt and dying just to receive others' attention. He acted as if he had killed himself, put blood around his mouth, and then lay on the ground with a stone on top of his heart. People would come running to give help, cry, and pray for him. Then he would laugh and make fun of them for believing his trick. One day he played this game when vulture was there. People knew this bird understood a lot about life and death so they asked him if this time the young man was really dead or was it just another joke. Vulture replied, "No. I just went to the heavens and he was not talked about there. No one knew of his death, and so he is just playing one of his games." The people were angry and asked, "Can you do something about this behavior?" Vulture answered, "Knowing that he doesn't want to live on this earth, but only plays games with life, we will give him something that he can really play with and see how he likes it." The young man's body began to rot with cancer, and he suffered slowly in a horrible death as the vulture sat beside him. The bird admitted to him, "I gave you this illness because you like to act like you are losing your life. So if you want to play this way, we can see how you like it when it is real. Maybe you like it; how do you feel?" The young man repented, begging vulture to remove the sickness and restore his health, but the bird had no medicine that could act as cure. "You chose this to be your life and so I gave it to you." Next he warned the people, "If you're going to act this way, this is what's going to happen. Be very grateful for your life. It is precious. Don't play with it. The Creator has provided your life; one time I will spare your life, but if you want to play with it, there will be some kind of disease, given to you by the holy ones, who will take it. You can play with that. I will be the one who brings cancer or other illness to you. When the holy people say, 'This one doesn't like to live this way, so work with him on it,' I become the messenger. Not everyone will die, because people learn to appreciate life again, but others do not and just pass away." Life is

*Eagles and owls are said to have derived from the monster bird (tsé nináhádleehí), who snatched Monster Slayer in her clutches to feed her offspring nesting on Shiprock. After killing the two adult birds, Monster Slayer sent the two babies off with different instructions as to how they were to interact with humans. Bats are said to have come from the leathery wings of this monster. (Courtesy San Juan School District Media Center)*

precious and should not be played with. Some people get the message, while others are depressed and want to commit suicide. People should live as long as they can and find happiness in their existence. Life is a gift.

Another flying creature, this time a mammal that is tied in with the birds that came from the Tsé nináhádleehí living on top of Shiprock, is the bat (Jaa'abaní—Buckskin Ears; its sacred name: At the Celestial Home in the House of the Dark Clouds Where He Was Reared). They are to be feared even though they do not attack. Still, these ugly beings have a mouth like a wolf, the head of a dog, strange looking ears, and usually a body that does not have hair but a leathery skin, which makes him a really odd-looking animal. He was designed like the old flying monsters (tsé nináhádleehí), who when they were killed, left their wings behind, which the bat now uses. These are not like bird wings but are made of skin that look like something that came out of the rocks where the monster birds lived. The same is true of his big fangs. He is always considered "the dark person," one that will attack you if you are not careful. Do not bother him while he is sleeping, because unlike a normal animal, he sleeps upside down so that his mouth is always ready to bite something below. This is why he is feared.

A second reason that he is feared is because, as in the Coyoteway, they say that he has the same kind of face as a skinwalker. This is what he looks like. He is ugly and is associated with death, darkness, and nothing good. One day a medicine man captured one and told him, "Because you are feared so much, I'm going to take my corn pollen, sprinkle it on you, and then shake it off. I will use this shake-off as my protector so that every time I go to the spirit world, I am going to put it in front of me when I walk through to the other side. That will be the medicine I use as a shield, as a protector." This was because the bat was feared. He's not to be connected with anything in the Blessingway.

There are two types of bats, one that is white and the other that is black. The white one has his own story that is connected to that of the Great Gambler (Nááhwiiłbįįhí—The One Who Wins You) who lived in Chaco Canyon during Anasazi times. Great Gambler had a number of betting games that he would use to beat people and then enslave them once they had lost. One of those games was the Navajo stick game (tsidił), which uses three pieces of wood with black on one side and white on the other. The people had grown tired of their enslavement by this harsh ruler, and so they plotted to defeat him at his own contests and win their freedom. In this particular game, the three sticks were bounced off a rock and the white bat ensured that they would fall to the ground with the white side facing up. This happened, and the person betting against the Gambler won every time, freed the people, and cast out the evil Gambler. Thus, the white bat has his own story, which is a positive one.

If there is a bat that flies into your home, it should either be chased out or killed. The home needs to be blessed again, and the person that sees or kills it needs to go to the sweat lodge and have a Protectionway ceremony performed. When a bat enters a home, he ruins all the good things that are at work there. His fangs and the residue of whatever else he has had in his hands could be harmful because he is never considered a clean person, but always a disease carrier that eats bad things. To cast out this presence, the house is blessed with a short prayer and a sprinkling of corn pollen in the four directions. Some people may use a lightning-struck piece of wood, sprinkle herbs about, and use smoke to purify the hogan and return the harmony. Wherever people were sitting at the time, pollen is sprinkled and then washed off to get rid of the presence.

Crow in Navajo is called Gáagii, while his sacred name means The One That Will Turn on You and Cannot Be Trusted. This name is sometimes given to a human who acts this way; it is not complimentary. Crow did not have to be like this. People say he was one of a group of birds who was supposed to be helpful, but he refused to be like that and wanted to stay with his friends the buzzards. Other birds urged him not to be with these scavengers, to be on the good side and helpful, but Crow would have nothing to do with them. If he was going to be that way, the helpful birds refused to let him be part of their family and no longer wanted him. He joined the scavengers, who were not good, were always in search of something dead, and were acting in an antisocial way. Everything that he did opposed proper behavior, and to make matters worse, he would lie about it. His behavior in the story of the hidden deer is a good example of how he knew what had happened, ate meat and lied about it, and became a tattletale as soon as he escaped from his captors, who were trying to fix a bad situation. He was never to be trusted. He is known for waiting until something bad happens and then flying around, telling everyone about the incident, spreading gossip. He even gives information to the enemy.

This is why medicine men call him The One That Has Red Knees (Gaagiiłchíí' dziztihsí), meaning somebody that is never trusted and will do away with you. Crows will take your things and give it or sell it to someone who will use it against you. For this reason, he is not allowed to be in any part of the Blessingway or any other ceremony except the Enemyway that deals with fighting and death. In this ceremony, his feathers are used when working with ashes, casting out evil, and defeating the enemy. The crow's beak is employed in this ceremony to curse those who are causing trouble. His body is taken along with his spirit and wrapped in buckskin, then directed with the words "we are going to turn you, who have taken something from us and given it to the enemy. Now, we're going to use your body to go back over there and curse them." This is done in a symbolic, spiritual way to push the evil back on the ones who are causing trouble. Crow never has had a positive story or a good reputation.

## *Feathered Friends*

Hummingbird is also a messenger, but unlike Crow, he shares good information and is truthful. He is viewed as an investigator, constantly looking for answers and flitting about. This bird is the one who knows where people are located and their current circumstances, almost like a busybody or gossip, knowing everyone's business. He visits every little corner of everything, trying to learn what is good for him. Each flower, when it needs to be pollinated, its current color, where the last moisture in each plant is located—there is nothing too insignificant for Hummingbird to know. In the story about bringing the rains back to Mother Earth, Hummingbird knew right where to go to contact Frog. Sitting in the middle of a dried pond under a curled piece of mud for a sunshade, Frog was living on the last moisture available. Hummingbird knew this, smelled it, and investigated. When he approached Frog he was told, "The last of this water does not belong to you. We own this mud chip that is sitting upside down. We're sitting in here. You can't touch it. We are the keeper of all the moisture here, so if you want us to help you, then go and talk with our superior person down the line—Water Monster." Through Hummingbird, the other animals were able to make that connection and have the water return.

Hummingbirds learn a lot by flying everywhere and are difficult to see. They may appear out of nowhere, briefly explore an area, and then are gone. You cannot touch them and once their movement is detected, they vanish. Compared to other birds, they are built and act differently and are almost like some new technology—quick and efficient. Hummingbird feathers are really good medicine and are used in bundles associated with Talking God, but their feathers are very hard to obtain.

Turkeys are called tązhii, which is a reference to the hanging flesh that droops over the side of the beak, which is called a snood. They are considered very, very smart birds who have a lot of teachings. His role in the emergence—the last bird to enter this world from the one beneath, the white tips on his tail feathers left by the rising waters that chased him up the reed, the shaking of his feathers that brought many different kinds of seed into this world for Navajo use—are all examples of why he is so highly respected. Turkey is said to think about a lot of things before they happen. He can see far into the future and determine what is going to take place. He prepares himself, always thinking, always watching, and so his tail feathers are used in almost every ceremony. Any kind of ritual that is going to be about the good way or something positive in the future will have his tail feathers, which assist in seeing things before they happen. This is why his feathers are used to fletch arrows and are on the traditional war cap along with those of the red tail hawk. They help things to move forward in the future and bring success. As mentioned previously about the decorated prayerstick for Talking God (K'eet'ą́ą́ yáłti'), turkey feathers are also placed on the staff in the Enemyway with two or three on top. There is a lot of dawn and evening sunset reflected in his tail, which talks about how a person's success stories took place. His meat is said to be very sacred and in the old days was never used as a daily food like it is today. Turkeys were rarely caught because they are crafty, running around and then escaping by flying. He belongs to the same family as ducks and geese and other birds that are edible, have good eyesight, and are always on guard.

There are many stories about Turkey and his association with agriculture, food, and good things. One tells of when the birds held a large social but did not invite him because they considered him clumsy and not that appealing. One evening, everyone participated in a huge gathering, where all were dressed in their finest and exhibited their dancing skills. The birds followed the traditional squaw dance step, going around in a circle, showing off their best feathers, and admiring each other's colors. The dancers became increasingly animated and proud of how fine they looked, convinced they were breaking new records in beauty. Turkey, on the other hand, got pushed farther and farther to the back of the crowd, antagonized with comments like, "You don't even have any colors or know how to dance. Just get behind." He became increasingly angry until someone offered the challenge, "Let him dance. Let him show us something. Let's see how he does." Everybody started laughing, yelling, "Let him have the floor," and so he went into the middle of the crowd and started lightly trotting around, throwing his tail feathers first to one side, then the other, then spreading them in a grand array of different colors as he dipped and glided around the circle. As if that were not enough, an approaching thunderstorm was moving toward the dancers with its boom, boom, boom. Turkey started to dance to the sounds, following the beat, just as is done in dances today with a drum. All of the other birds were surprised saying, "Oh, my gosh. He's making the whole thing move," as the lightning illuminated his feathers. He actually was a very beautiful bird, and the way he danced and put his steps, feathers, and body movements together amazed them. At that moment, he became the inventor of Indian dance—the first one to start dancing the way he wanted to—encouraging the other birds to follow in his footsteps. He invented the powwow dance move now called the canoe step, which is a basic movement used by dancers today. Traditional Navajo dances like the Round Dance are still performed, but this was the beginning of powwow dancing as put together by all of the birds that had come in from the east, south, west, and north. They were later copied and modified by different Native American tribes, depending upon the region they inhabited. At this time there was no such thing as a Navajo way of doing things. How the birds got together then is how people come together for a powwow now with dancers today acting just like the birds did back then. They are there to compete, look beautiful, show off their own traditional dances, and be admired. Thanks to Turkey and his teachings, the drum has become part of it, and new steps have been devised, with face and body paint an addition. Turkey was the one who showed dancers how to paint themselves. His head is colored red, with blue around his eyes, and further down his body is purple. People decided this looked good and began adding colors to their face.

Geese are called díłí, which means they are very difficult to overcome or capture. Although they fly in formation, geese are constantly shifting direction, are wary, and are hard to sneak up on. These birds are able to give an individual direction in a physical and spiritual sense if one is searching for an answer. Depending on what one is thinking about, geese will appear and provide a response to a question as well as indicate a direction to follow. In the past, medicine people sought them out, then watched for an answer. The solution was spiritual in nature as one searched to understand the problem. The answer often is found in the future or as an interpretation of a vision. People say these birds only come in a way and at a time when they are truly needed. A person might puzzle over an issue for a whole year, pondering the situation and thinking about a solution, before they suddenly look up and spot a flock of geese flying above. Their formation, the direction of travel, and other elements of their flight signal what needs to be done. These kinds of answers are only rarely given.

One day, a medicine person struggled to know what to do. He had been told that there was a lot of medicine that he needed in a certain location. Somebody else said he should go in a different direction to find what he was looking for. The medicine man did not know where to go, while he also worried about the horse he was riding because of the treacherous landscape that lay ahead. He was confused and questioning his options. That night he had a dream in which he heard, "Something's going to happen today. Look around and be observant." Next morning there suddenly appeared a large flock of geese flying in an arrow formation in one of the two directions. That was the answer this medicine man needed, and sure enough, there were plenty of the plants he was seeking right there. This medicine way with geese allows people to understand things not normally clear.

*While ducks, geese, and other waterfowl have powers because they are Water People, Turtle is considered the chief of this domain, controlling much of the water medicine. He is also able to collect medicines on land. He knows both sides, but is prominent in Waterway ceremonies (Tóyee) used for people who have had a near-drowning experience, who have paralysis, or who need rain. This turtle shell can be used to drink medicine in any ceremony. (Photo by Kay Shumway)*

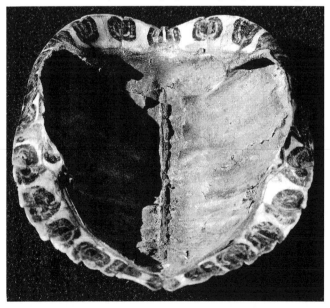

Ducks (naal'eełí—The One That Glides on the Water), to a lesser extent, can do the same thing, but they are not as powerful. They can, however, tell a person where water is located and how close one is to moisture. Cranes (dééł) are another fowl, and like all of the creatures—frogs, fish, turtles, and so forth—that go into the water to eat water-type herbs, they are considered water or rainbow children. Cranes are called Along the Side of the Water, and have long beaks and legs that help them feed in ponds and marshes. Their feet are all the same, allowing them to swim or hunt beside the shore and in shallow water to find things to eat. This is the pattern of the Water People. They are all rainbow children.

These teachings go back to the old days, maybe to the 1920s or earlier. In those times, people paid a high price for goose meat, which was considered holy and a ceremonial food for rituals such as the Lightningway. Duck and turkey flesh were also special because of their sacred nature. Today, they are easily found in grocery stores, so their meat is not viewed as special. If you tell a young Navajo person about these things, they say, "whatever" and do not care or know anything about it. Compare this to someone who is ninety years old. There is a very big difference in terms of understanding and respect. The same is true when seeking for spiritual direction.

# *Getting Bugged*

In Navajo thought, insects are part of the story with birds. They came from the First World to serve as food for birds in subsequent worlds and to represent life itself. Take ants for instance. They are always moving, building their homes, smelling something, and sometimes annoying you. People shoo them away, but they come back with determination and bother you to a point that lets you know you are still alive. They are a nuisance pestering you but also keep you going. One day there was a man who was totally stressed out. His elders told him to sit by the river and seek a sign that would lead to understanding his situation. Something would come to him like a medicine man, but he needed to sit there calmly with his clothes off, arms across his chest, and deal with his sickness. He was exhausted and could barely move to feed himself, but he knew he would receive help. Suddenly a fly appeared and flew right up his nose. This started the man hitting and digging himself to get the fly out while people nearby watched his nose move from side to side. "Look. He moved. He moved. Look at him. What did that to him?" they said before they realized it was a bug. Next mosquitoes came and started biting and sucking blood from him. He swatted them left and right, his arms flailing about to keep them off and away. To do this, he really had to move around to help himself. By now he was fed up with sitting there naked and decided to go home; this was not the treatment he had expected. A medicine man appeared and told him that it was the insects that had helped move him from inaction and helplessness into a person who was now focused on taking care of himself. Even though they had pushed him around and forced him to do something, they had also healed him of his problem.

At another time, I told you of the ants and their ceremonies that bring people back to life and of the caterpillar who was depressed about its existence, climbed a tree, built a cocoon, and emerged a beautiful butterfly with a changed outlook. The Navajo depend on this same caterpillar to determine how much moisture will be received in the coming year. People look for him in the fall, and if he is found to be very green, then he is sprinkled with corn pollen so that he will bring an abundance of snow and rain to help future crops to grow and the animals to find lots of grass. If he is gray in color, we grind certain plants and paint him with the green color, put little red markings on his topside, sprinkle him with corn pollen as well as put some in his mouth, and provide a small ceremony so that he will change the amount of moisture we will receive during the winter season. After this, he is placed back in a tree. His green color means there will be a big snow. He is a very important being that can really assist the Navajo. This is the same type of offering and ceremony that is done for the frog in the dry pond that we send to bring water back to the land.

Navajos talk about different insects that have a purpose, meaning, and teaching that are important to know. For example, there was a young girl who had a big scab on her leg, filled with pus, that was very sore. Nothing seemed to heal it or remove the pain and so her family members talked to the Bear Clan people, who asked what they were using. When they heard, they told the family members not to worry—that the bears had taught them how to heal this kind of wound. The medicine man sent them in search of an old tree that had been lying on the ground for a long time, broke it open, and found fly eggs—maggots—and put them on the wound. In a day and a half, the wound was cleaned, sanitized, and on the road to healing. Sure enough, it healed quickly. Bear has his own way of talking and thinking about this type of medicine, so he used flies to heal the infection. This story comes from the Bear People and is a good example of how insects can help earth surface beings. My father used to say that no matter where you go in this world, there are going to be insects. They burrow down into the ground, crawl on top of it, live in the wood of trees and in shrubs and flowers, and fly in the sky—everywhere there are insects. When the weather warms, they come out, and when winter arrives, they hide, but they are always present.

# *Horned Toads and Snakes: Creatures of Power*

One of the most powerful, yet smallest creatures in Navajo beliefs is the horned toad (na'ashǫ'ii dich'izhii—Rough Skinned Reptile; sacred name: Nihah sęęsi Tséłkéí—Wart of the Earth Boy/Girl), who is often referred to as grandfather. The name, if translated literally, means Snake with Rough Skin even though he is neither a toad nor a snake. His pointed head is said by some to resemble an arrowhead, and along with his tail, is seen as similar to that of a snake. He is one of the most special creatures with his eighty-seven horns or points that protect his back and attract strong spiritual powers. Navajos call him grandfather because he is able to solve problems, help, and protect when they are in need. There is nothing bad about him, for he always is kind and protective of young children but also looks after everybody. He thinks with a mature view and is very involved in the Enemyway. He had emerged into this world fearless and continued to not be intimidated by evil forces and monsters at work all around. His story is one of bravery and protection, and that is what he continues to represent.

There are a number of narratives about him; one tells of how he earned his title, "grandfather." This occurred during the time when Navajo-eating monsters roamed the earth, a number of whom were particularly effective in chasing down and killing the people. One day, a flying monster (Tsé nináhádleehí) who lived on Shiprock pursued a dozen children fleeing to a pile of rocks for protection. The monster bird hovered over the cringing boys and girls as they tried to escape its powerful beak. Crying, frightened, and confused, the children moved up the rock seeking more protection. In desperation, some of them called for help screaming, "Grandpa, where are you," hoping that one of their elders would hear and come to their rescue. Suddenly a horned toad appeared and reassured them, "Don't cry. Just stand behind me. I will deal with this monster." He climbed to the very top of the rocks and flashed lightning from the horns on his head. Then he pulled one of his arms, which caused another flash that came out his other arm, then pulled on his back legs as more electricity surrounded, then engulfed him. As the monster bird circled, Horned Toad began directing this electricity at it, warning the bird to keep its distance. Other lightning, friends of the monster bird, saw what was going on and approached in large black storm clouds. They attacked the horned toad, but were no match. He was so powerful that they admitted defeat and departed. All of the other attacking forces also recognized his power and left. The thankful children began calling him "Grandfather." This is how he earned that title.

More and more stories about his powers developed. At one point he was a farmer who raised corn and talked to it to help it grow. He spoke to the elements, told them how he was put together and had been born through their power. He explained that he was to be the master of the ground people and shared some of these rights with Snake, but he remained the primary one in charge and so had most of the responsibility and respect. The people started to live with him, and whenever anything went wrong or they needed help, they would seek out Horned Toad, who taught them. He reminded them of the emergence, the fight against the earth surface monsters, and how they no longer needed to fear for their lives. The people appreciated this very special friend and developed Protectionway ceremonies with the children, who wrote songs about their grandfather. He is always there for his children and is a protector of the people.

Today, they say if you find a baby horned toad, you are supposed to pick him up and let him scratch you with his claws on your chest just below the throat. These are markings of protection. Then give him a little bit of corn pollen as an offering and in thanksgiving, and let him go. If you find

*Size is not always an indication of power. Maker and wearer of arrowheads, associated with lightning, and protected by flint armor, the horned toad serves as a "grandfather" who defends a Navajo person lucky enough to find one. He is also able to remove leg pains, nurture crops, and guard a helpless baby in a cradleboard. (Photo by Kay Shumway)*

one that is stillborn and has its placenta on it, shake corn pollen on it, then remove the placenta, dry it off, and keep it for its power of protection. It is called the "hide" and is considered a prized possession. My grandfather paid seven cows and four horses for one of them; that is how highly esteemed it is by medicine men. The placenta is mixed with other medicines, a five-night ceremony is held that further blesses it, then it is placed in a big medicine bundle. This object cannot be shared unless people pay a high price. It is used to either chase babies out of the womb during a difficult birth or to correct deformities of the newborn. This is what that object does, but it can also cure other illnesses and is considered one of the holiest of all medicines. It is very, very rare to find. That is why real medicine men will pay a high, high amount of money for it. I do not have it.

There are two major types of snakes (tł'iish; its sacred name: Bits'íís Yeiyigáałii—One Who Walks with His Body) found in Navajo teachings. The chief of the snakes is the bullsnake (diyóósh) who is called The One That Walks Away with the Corn Pollen. This is seen on his body where there are yellow and black markings on top. They do not bite and are not poisonous, but they can go certain places that no other animal can go, such as climbing straight up a rock to the top. He can go anywhere as one of the headmen of the snake people and one who walks with corn pollen on his back. But he also has the darkness on top in some of his markings. The snakes that carry yellow colors are usually those that go with the ceremonies.

Compare the bullsnake to the rattlesnake. The rattler makes noise as a warning that he is about to strike, but he only does that when he feels heat and movement. He can't see beyond his feelings. He goes right through them and strikes with no remorse. A lot of snakes do not have much color, mostly gray, and those are the ones to fear. They did not receive their colors because of their personalities—no charm or charisma—while the ones with bright colors represent springtime, flowers, and the goodness of other things. The rattlesnake, on the other hand, is just too mean and does not like people around or want to be touched. This snake is like the yucca plant. Yucca does not allow anybody to touch it, and if you try, you will be stuck with a sharp point.

Sometimes rattlesnakes are pictured in sandpaintings when they have injured or sickened a person by their presence. They are designated by the colors of the east, south, west, and north with different designs on their back. The tail and the neck always have four stripes of white or blue or yellow or black. The surrounding edge of the snake has its complimentary color. If it is a white snake, it will be outlined in black and have stripes of black; if a blue snake then it is outlined in yellow. On the first night while the person is still sick, the snakes' tongues are red. On the second day, when the Blessingway ceremony is performed, the color of the tongue and the outline of the snakes' form is yellow, like corn pollen, which means now the snakes are harmless. The patient is in harmony and his health restored.

If a snake is found in a hogan, it needs to be chased out. If it keeps coming back, then it should be killed. A second or third visit indicates something is wrong and it is coming there for a reason. The first time the snake is just removed and the house is cleansed using snake root (ch'ildiilyésiitsoh—big dodge weed). This plant is boiled, and then it is sprinkled by the doorway. Pour the juice all around it. If the snake crawls through, something is not right and it needs to be killed. The snake can be a messenger and can be sent with the power of witchcraft. They can have a lot to do with sorcery. People who practice witchcraft may send it to bite a person or put one in the victim's car, but first it comes as a messenger. The second time it appears, someone is going to get hurt.

My grandfather taught that there is a prayer that sends the bullsnake over the ground to erase the markings and tracks of those who are doing evil things. The snake is told to slither over and erase the tracks of those who have buried a witchcraft object. This is left behind to curse a particular person. They say that a bullsnake is directed to that area to clean up the tracks of the evil-doer and to remove the power of that which is there to harm. The bullsnake received corn pollen to chase the evil away. He will go with that evil to make sure it does not return, just as it is said to chase away rattlesnakes. The bullsnake was once a different person, but when he received the task to act in a good way as a representative of the reptile people, he changed. There was a prayer attached to this responsibility that goes with the snake's yellowish (corn pollen) color. If someone is planting a corn patch, this snake will come and bless it. Although he may crawl away, he will make sure there is a lot of yellow, blue, and white corn that grows there. He will never attack, will be there to share a story, and will warn you if there is danger around. He is a friend.

# *Notes*

## *Introduction*

1. River Junction Curly, "Version III," in *Blessingway: With Three Versions of the Myth Recorded and Translated from the Navajo by Father Berard Haile, O.F.M.*, ed. Leland C. Wyman (Tucson: University of Arizona Press, 1970), 616.

2. Berard Haile, O.F.M., *Soul Concepts of the Navaho* (Saint Michaels, AZ: Saint Michaels Press, 1943, 1975), 69.

3. Ibid., 64, 67, 77.

4. Slim Curly, "Version I," in *Blessingway: With Three Versions of the Myth Recorded and Translated from the Navajo by Father Berard Haile, O.F.M.*, ed. Leland C. Wyman (Tucson: University of Arizona Press, 1970), 154–55.

5. Frank Mitchell, "Version II," in *Blessingway: With Three Versions of the Myth Recorded and Translated from the Navajo by Father Berard Haile, O.F.M.*, ed. Leland C. Wyman (Tucson: University of Arizona Press, 1970), 402.

6. Karl W. Luckert, *The Navajo Hunter Tradition* (Tucson: University of Arizona Press, 1981), 19.

7. Ibid., 39.

8. Farley Mowat, *Never Cry Wolf* (New York: Bantam Books, 1963, 1984), 88–94.

9. Gary Witherspoon, *Language and Art in the Navajo Universe* (Ann Arbor: University of Michigan Press, 1977).

10. Ibid., 63–149.

11. Ibid., 71.

12. Ibid., 76.

13. Ibid., 77.

14. Ibid., 80.

15. Mircea Eliade, *The Sacred and the Profane: The Nature of Religion* (New York: Harcourt, Brace, and World, 1957).

16. Ibid., 11–12.

17. Mitchell, "Blessingway," 462.

## Chapter One

1. Robert W. Young and William Morgan, *Navajo Historical Selections* (Lawrence, Kansas: Bureau of Indian Affairs, 1954), 14. Note: the following quotes from this source were provided by unnamed Navajo medicine men who were providing information on "The Traditional Navajo Country" during a series of oral interviews.

2. Frank Mitchell, "Version II," in *Blessingway: With Three Versions of the Myth Recorded and Translated from the Navajo by Father Berard Haile, O.F.M.,* ed. Leland C. Wyman (Tucson: University of Arizona Press, 1970), 362.

3. Young and Morgan, *Selections*, 15.

4. Ibid., 464.

5. Slim Curly, "Version I," in *Blessingway: With Three Versions of the Myth Recorded and Translated from the Navajo by Father Berard Haile, O.F.M.,* ed. Leland C. Wyman (Tucson: University of Arizona Press, 1970), 238.

6. Young and Morgan, *Selections*, 17.

7. Charlotte J. Frisbie, *Navajo Medicine Bundles or Jish: Acquisition, Transmission, and Disposition in the Past and Present* (Albuquerque: University of New Mexico Press, 1987), 57.

8. Ibid., 69.

9. Ibid., 69–73.

10. Charlotte J. Frisbie and David P. McAllester, ed., *Navajo Blessingway Singer: The Autobiography of Frank Mitchell, 1881–1967* (Tucson: University of Arizona Press, 1978), 200–207.

11. Charlotte J. Frisbie, ed., with Rose Mitchell, *Tall Woman: The Life Story of Rose Mitchell, A Navajo Woman, c. 1874–1977* (Albuquerque: University of New Mexico Press, 2001), 188–89.

12. Frisbie and McAllester, *Navajo Blessingway Singer*, 202.

13. Ibid., 203.

14. In Leland Wyman's *Blessingway: With Three Versions of the Myth,* the author writes, "'To steal oneself' means to have sexual relations without the knowledge of one's parents [which] is a shameful thing (for the parents, not for the girl) because it deprives the family of a possible son-in-law as an economic adjunct." Wyman ties this phrase into the illicit sex between Changing Woman and Sun Bearer (p. 420).

## Chapter Two

1. Gladys A. Reichard, *Navaho Religion: A Study of Symbolism* (Princeton, NJ: University of Princeton Press, 1950), 609.

2. Ibid., 491.

3. Caroline B. Olin, "Four Mountainway Sandpaintings of Sam Tilden, 'Ayóó Anííłnézí," in *Navajo Religion and Culture: Selected Views—Papers in Honor of Leland C. Wyman*, edited by David M. Brugge and Charlotte J. Frisbie, Papers in Anthropology no. 17 (Santa Fe: Museum of New Mexico Press, 1982), 51–52.

4. Klara Bonsack Kelley and Harris Francis, *Navajo Sacred Places* (Bloomington: University of Indiana Press, 1994), 36–37.

5. Ibid.

6. Robert S. McPherson, Jim Dandy, Sarah E. Burak, *Navajo Tradition, Mormon Life: The Autobiography and Teachings of Jim Dandy* (Salt Lake City: University of Utah Press, 2012), 187–88.

7. Franc Johnson Newcomb, *Navajo Omens and Taboos* (Santa Fe: Rydal Press, 1940), 60–64.

8. Sydney M. Callaway and Gary Witherspoon, *Grandfather Stories of the Navajos* (Rough Rock, AZ: Navajo Curriculum Center, Rough Rock Demonstration School, 1974), 15–21.

9. John Holiday and Robert S. McPherson, *A Navajo Legacy: The Life and Teachings of John Holiday* (Norman: University of Oklahoma Press, 2005), 92–97.

## *Chapter Three*

1. See (arranged in alphabetical order) Sally Pierce Brewer, "Notes on Navaho Astronomy" in *For the Dean: Essays in Anthropology in Honor of Byron Cummings* (Tucson: Hohokam Museum Association, 1950): 133–36; Berard Haile, *Starlore Among the Navaho* (Santa Fe: William Gannon Press, 1977); Nancy C. Maryboy and David Begay, *Sharing the Skies, Navajo Astronomy: A Cross-Cultural View* (Bluff, UT: Indigenous Education Institute, 2005); Trudy Griffin-Pierce, *Earth Is My Mother, Sky Is My Father: Space, Time, and Astronomy in Navajo Sandpainting* (Albuquerque: University of New Mexico Press, 1992); Alfred M. Tozzer, "A Note on Star-Lore Among the Navajos," *Journal of American Folklore* 21 (January–March 1908): 28–32; Mary C. Wheelwright and David P. McAllester, *The Myth and Prayers of the Great Star Chant and the Myth of the Coyote Chant*, Navajo Religion Series, vol. 4 (Santa Fe: Museum of Navajo Ceremonial Art, 1956).

2. Franciscan Fathers, *An Ethnologic Dictionary of the Navajo Language* (Saint Michaels, AZ: Saint Michaels Press, 1910), 37, 354; Gladys Reichard, *Navaho Religion: A Study of Symbolism* (Princeton, NJ: Princeton University Press, 1950), 470–75.

3. Franc J. Newcomb, *Navaho Neighbors* (Norman: University of Oklahoma Press, 1966), 165.

4. Buck Navajo, interview with author, December 16, 1991.

5. Ibid.; Cecil Parrish, interview with author, October 10, 1991.

6. Berard Haile, *The Upward Moving and Emergence Way: The Gishin Biye' Version* (Lincoln: University of Nebraska Press, 1981), 140; Franciscan Fathers, *An Ethnologic Dictionary*, 41; Washington Matthews, *A Part of the Navajos' Mythology*, American Antiquarian Society, 1883, Special Collections, Harold B. Lee Library, Brigham Young University, Provo, Utah, 6–7; Ada Black, interview with Bertha Parrish, June 18, 1987.

7. Haile, *Upward Moving*, 140; Buck Navajo, interview; Ernest L. Bulow, *Navajo Taboos* (Gallup, NM: Southwesterner Books, 1982), 1.

8. Griffin-Pierce, *Earth Is My Mother*, 153–73; Mary C. Wheelwright, ed., *Navajo Creation Myth: The Story of the Emergence by Hasteen Klah* (Santa Fe: Museum of Navajo Ceremonial Art, 1942), 66; Linda Hadley, *Hózhǫ́'jí Hane' (Blessingway)* (Rough Rock, AZ: Rough Rock Demonstration School, 1986), 20.

9. Matthews, *Navajos' Mythology*, 7–8.

10. John Holiday, interview with author, September 9, 1991.

11. Ibid.; Bertha Parrish, interview; anonymous medicine man cited in Griffin-Pierce, *Earth Is My Mother*, 138.

12. Franc Johnson Newcomb, *Navaho Folk Tales* (Albuquerque: University of New Mexico Press, 1967), 83–88; Guy Cly, interview with author, August 7, 1991.

13. Newcomb, *Navaho Folk Tales*, 85–88; Buck Navajo, interview; Ada Black, interview with author, October 11, 1991.

14. John Holiday and Robert S. McPherson, *A Navajo Legacy: The Life and Teachings of John Holiday* (Norman: University of Oklahoma Press, 2005), 198–99.

15. Robert S. McPherson, Jim Dandy, and Sarah E. Burak, *Navajo Tradition, Mormon Life: The Autobiography and Teachings of Jim Dandy* (Salt Lake City: University of Utah Press, 2012), 166–67.

16. Rhoda Kascoli paper, "Navajo February Snows," used with permission, in possession of author.

17. Franciscan Fathers, *An Ethnologic Dictionary*, 47–48.

18. Leland C. Wyman, *The Windways of the Navaho* (Colorado Springs: Taylor Museum, 1962).

19. See Robert S. McPherson, *Sacred Land, Sacred View: Navajo Perception of the Four Corners Region,* Charles Redd Center for Western Studies Monograph Number 19 (Provo: Brigham Young University Press, 1992), 87–97, for an explanation of how Big Wind, among other elements, destroyed the Anasazi.

20. Joe Manygoats, interview with author, December 16, 1991; Ada Black, interview with author.

21. Ada Black, interview with author; Shone Holiday, interview with author, September 10, 1991.

22. Mary C. Wheelwright, *The Myth and Prayers of the Great Star Chant and the Myth of the Coyote Chant* (Santa Fe: Museum of Navajo Ceremonial Art, 1956), 22–23.

23. Karl Luckert, *A Navajo Bringing-Home Ceremony: The Claus Chee Sonny Version* (Flagstaff: Museum of Northern Arizona Press, 1978): 198.

## Chapter Four

1. Vernon O. Mayes and Barbara Bayless Lacy, *Nanise', A Navajo Herbal: One Hundred Plants from the Navajo Reservation* (Tsaile, Ariz.: Navajo Community College Press, 1989), 80; Franciscan Fathers, *An Ethnologic Dictionary of the Navajo Language* (Saint Michaels, AZ: Saint Michaels Press, 1910, 1968), 414; Clyde Kluckhohn, W. W. Hill, and Lucy Wales Kluckhohn, *Navajo Material Culture* (Cambridge, Mass: Harvard University Press, 1971), 361–63.

2. Kluckhohn et al., *Navajo Material Culture*, 191–95; Franciscan Fathers, *An Ethnologic Dictionary*, 467–73.

3. Robert S. McPherson, *Sacred Land, Sacred View: Navajo Perceptions of the Four Corners Region* (Provo, UT: Brigham Young University Press, 1992), 56–57.

4. Marilyn A. Martorano, "Culturally Peeled Trees and Ute Indians in Colorado," in *Archaeology of the Eastern Ute: A Symposium*, ed. Paul R. Nickens, CCPA Occasional Papers 1 (Colorado Council of Professional Archaeologists, 1988), 5–21; Marilyn A. Martorano, "So Hungry They Ate the Bark off a Tree," *Canyon Legacy, A Journal of the Dan O'Laurie Museum* 1, no. 1 (Spring 1989): 9–12.

5. Mayes and Lacy, *Nanise'*, 72; Franciscan Fathers, *An Ethnologic Dictionary*, 211, 318; Charlotte J. Frisbie, *Food Sovereignty the Navajo Way, Cooking with Tall Woman* (Albuquerque: University of New Mexico Press, 2018), 122, 317; Kluckhohn et al., *Navajo Material Culture*, 23–26, 33–35.

6. Mayes and Lacy, *Nanise'*, 5, 30, 37, 134; McPherson, *Sacred Land*, 57.

7. Mayes and Lacy, *Nanise'*, 30, 134; Frisbie, *Food Sovereignty*, 84; Franciscan Fathers, *An Ethnologic Dictionary*, 66; Kluckhohn et al., *Navajo Material Culture*, 171–72; Franc Johnson Newcomb, *Navajo Omens and Taboos* (Santa Fe: Rydal Press, 1940), 67.

8. Newcomb, *Navajo Omens*, 67–68.

9. Mayes and Lacy, *Nanise'*, 78–79; David M. Brugge, "Western Navajo Ethnobotanical Notes," in *Navajo Religion and Culture: Selected Views*, edited by David M. Brugge and Charlotte J. Frisbie, Papers in Anthropology no. 17 (Santa Fe: Museum of New Mexico Press, 1982), 95; Franciscan Fathers, *An Ethnologic Dictionary*, 243.

10. Frisbie, *Food Sovereignty*, 122–23; Robert S. McPherson, *Both Sides of the Bullpen, Navajo Trade and Posts* (Norman: University of Oklahoma Press, 2017), 127.

11. Franc Johnson Newcomb, *Navaho Folk Tales* (Santa Fe: Wheelwright Museum, 1967, 1990), 192–203.

12. Frisbie, *Food Sovereignty*, 78; Mayes and Lacy, *Nanise'*, 55.

13. Frisbie, *Food Sovereignty*, 140, 149–50.

14. Nedra K. Christensen, Ann W. Sorenson, and Deloy G. Hendricks, "Juniper Ash as a Source of Calcium in the Navajo Diet," in *Journal of the American Dietetic Association* 98, no. 3 (March 1998): 333–34.

15. Gladys Reichard, *Navaho Religion: A Study of Symbolism* (Princeton, NJ: Princeton University Press, 1950, 1970), 49, 515, 517.

16. Robert S. McPherson, Jim Dandy, Sarah E. Burak, *Navajo Tradition, Mormon Life: The Autobiography and Teachings of Jim Dandy* (Salt Lake City: University of Utah Press, 2012), 55, 63, 81, 128, 208, 238, 240.

## *Chapter Five*

1. Good sources to study the use of plants as food and medicine are found in the following works (arranged alphabetically by author): Flora L. Bailey, "Navaho Foods and Cooking Methods," in *American Anthropologist* 42, no. 2 (Spring 1940): 270–90; Sam and Janet Bingham, *Navajo Farming* (Chinle, AZ: Rock Point Community School, 1979); Charlotte J. Frisbie, *Food Sovereignty the Navajo Way, Cooking with Tall Woman* (Albuquerque: University of New Mexico Press, 2018); Charlotte J. Frisbie, ed., with Rose Mitchell, *Tall Woman: The Life Story of Rose Mitchell, A Navajo Woman, c. 1874–1977* (Albuquerque: University of New Mexico Press, 2001); Willard W. Hill, *Agriculture and Hunting Methods of the Navaho Indians* (New Haven, CT: Yale University Press, 1938); Vernon O. Mayes and Barbara Bayless Lacy, *Nanise': A Navajo Herbal: One Hundred Plants from the Navajo Reservation* (Chandler, AZ: Five Star, 1994); Leland C. Wyman and Stuart K. Harris, *Navajo Indian Medical Ethnobotany* (Albuquerque: University of New Mexico Press, 1941); Wyman and Harris, *The Ethnobotany of the Kayenta Navajo*, Publications in Biology 5 (Albuquerque: University of New Mexico Press, 1951).

2. Adapted from Franc Johnson Newcomb, *Navaho Folk Tales* (Albuquerque: University of New Mexico Press, 1967, 1990), 39–41.

3. Frank Mitchell, "Version II," in *Blessingway: With Three Versions of the Myth Recorded and Translated from the Navajo by Father Berard Haile, O.F.M.*, ed. Leland C. Wyman (Tucson: University of Arizona Press, 1970), 349.

4. Gary Witherspoon, *Language and Art in the Navajo Universe* (Ann Arbor: University of Michigan Press, 1977), 92–93.

5. George Blueyes in *Between Sacred Mountains: Navajo Stories and Lessons from the Land*, edited by Sam and Janet Bingham, (Chinle, AZ: Rock Point Community School, 1982), 23–24.

6. Charlie Blueyes, interview with author, August 28, 1988; Mary Jelly, interview with Aubrey Williams and Maxwell Yazzie, January 21, 1961, Doris Duke Oral History Project #772, Special Collections, Marriott Library, University of Utah, Salt Lake City, 16–18.

7. Robert S. McPherson, *Sacred Land, Sacred View: Navajo Perceptions of the Four Corners Region* (Provo, UT: Brigham Young University Press, 1992), 57–58.

8. John Holiday and Robert S. McPherson, *A Navajo Legacy: The Life and Teachings of John Holiday* (Norman: University of Oklahoma Press, 2005), 282.

9. McPherson, *Sacred Land*, 54; Franc Johnson Newcomb, *Navajo Omens and Taboos* (Santa Fe: Rydal Press, 1940), 43–45; Hill, *Agriculture and Hunting Methods*, 20–35.

10. Slim Curly in Wyman, *Blessingway*, 239.

11. Holiday and McPherson, *A Navajo Legacy*, 318.

12. Wyman, *Blessingway*, 30.

## *Chapter Six*

1. Karl W. Luckert, *The Navajo Hunter Tradition* (Tucson: University of Arizona Press, 1975).

2. Ibid., including versions translated by Berard Haile; Washington Matthews, *Navaho Legends* (Salt Lake City: University of Utah Press, 1897, 1994), 184–94; Franc Johnson Newcomb, *Navaho Folk Tales* (Albuquerque: University of New Mexico Press, 1967, 1990), 182–91.

3. W. (Willard) W. Hill, *The Agricultural and Hunting Methods of the Navaho Indians* (New Haven, CT: Yale University Press, 1938).

4. Ibid., 132–33.

5. Ibid., 117–21.

6. Robert S. McPherson, Jim Dandy, and Sarah E. Burak, *Navajo Tradition, Mormon Life: The Autobiography and Teachings of Jim Dandy* (Salt Lake City: University of Utah Press, 2012), 192–94.

7. John Holiday and Robert S. McPherson, *A Navajo Legacy: The Life and Teachings of John Holiday* (Norman: University of Oklahoma Press, 2005), 358.

8. Barre Toelken, "Traditional Navajo Arts in Southeastern Utah," *Blue Mountain Shadows* 7 (Winter 1990): 37–38.

9. Gladys Reichard, *Navaho Religion: A Study of Symbolism* (Princeton, NJ: Princeton University Press, 1950, 1990), 426–27; Hill, *The Agricultural and Hunting Methods*, 144; Franciscan Fathers, *An Ethnologic Dictionary of the Navajo Language* (Saint Michaels, AZ: Saint Michaels Press, 1910, 1968), 172, 412–13.

10. Robert S. McPherson, *The Journey of Navajo Oshley: An Autobiography and Life History* (Logan: Utah State University Press, 2000), 150.

## Chapter Seven

1. Franciscan Fathers, *An Ethnologic Dictionary of the Navajo Language* (Saint Michaels, AZ: Saint Michaels Press, 1910, 1968), 138–42; 156–57.

2. For a more detailed example of this relationship, see Karl W. Luckert, *The Navajo Hunter Tradition* (Tucson: University of Arizona Press, 1975).

3. See Gerald Hausman, *The Gift of the Gila Monster, Navajo Ceremonial Tales* (New York: Simon and Schuster Press, 1993).

4. Frank Mitchell, "Version II" in *Blessingway: With Three Versions of the Myth Recorded and Translated from the Navajo by Father Berard Haile, O.F.M.*, ed. Leland C. Wyman (Tucson: University of Arizona Press, 1970), 369–73.

5. Charlie Blueyes, interview with author, August 28, 1988; Henry Jackson, interview with author, February 3, 1989; see also Aileen O'Bryan, *Navaho Indian Myths* (New York: Dover Publications, 1956), 62–63.

6. Franciscan Fathers, *An Ethnologic Dictionary*, 172–75.

7. Vada Carlson and Gary Witherspoon, *Black Mountain Boy, A Story of the Boyhood of John Honie* (Phoenix: Navajo Curriculum Press, 1974), 31–33.

8. Father Berard Haile, O.F.M., *Navajo Coyote Tales: The Curly Tó Aheedlíinii Version* (Lincoln: University of Nebraska Press, 1984); Karl W. Luckert, *Coyoteway: A Navajo Holyway Healing Ceremony* (Tucson: University of Arizona Press, 1979); and Steve Pavlik, *The Navajo and the*

*Animal People: Native American Traditional Ecological Knowledge and Ethnozoology* (Golden, CO: Fulcrum Publishing, 2014).

9. Gladys Reichard, *Navajo Religion, A Study of Symbolism* (Princeton, NJ: Princeton University Press, 1950, 1990), 422–26; Pavlik, *The Navajo and the Animal People*, 123–24.

10. Washington Matthews, *The Night Chant, A Navaho Ceremony* (Salt Lake City: University of Utah Press, 1902, 1995), 203.

11. John Holiday and Robert S. McPherson, *A Navajo Legacy: The Life and Teachings of John Holiday* (Norman: University of Oklahoma Press, 2005), 85–86.

## *Chapter Eight*

1. Slim Curly, "Version I," in *Blessingway: With Three Versions of the Myth Recorded and Translated from the Navajo by Father Berard Haile, O.F.M.*, ed. Leland C. Wyman (Tucson: University of Arizona Press, 1970), 245–46.

2. Laurance D. Linford, *Navajo Places: History, Legend, Landscape* (Salt Lake City: University of Utah Press, 2000), 279–80.

3. Slim Benally, interview with author, July 8, 1988.

4. Martha Nez, interview with author, August 2, 1988.

5. Charlie Blueyes, interview with author, July 8, 1988.

6. Charlie Blueyes, interview with author, June 7, 1988.

7. Charlotte Frisbie, *Food Sovereignty the Navajo Way, Cooking with Tall Woman* (Albuquerque: University of New Mexico Press, 2018), 220.

8. Ibid.

9. Ibid., 224.

10. James F. Downs, *Animal Husbandry in Navajo Society and Culture* (Los Angeles: University of California Press, 1964), 31.

11. Ibid., 37–38.

12. John Holiday and Robert S. McPherson, *A Navajo Legacy: The Life and Teachings of John Holiday* (Norman: University of Oklahoma Press, 2005), 278.

13. Edward Sapir, *Navaho Texts* (Iowa City: University of Iowa Press, 1942), 325–29.

14. LaVerne Harrell Clark, *They Sang for Horses, The Impact of the Horse on Navajo and Apache Folklore* (Tucson: University of Arizona Press, 1966).

15. Holiday and McPherson, *A Navajo Legacy*, 279.

16. Robert S. McPherson, Jim Dandy, and Sarah E. Burak, *Navajo Tradition, Mormon Life: The Autobiography and Teachings of Jim Dandy* (Salt Lake City: University of Utah Press, 2012), 205.

17. Charlie Blueyes, interview with author, August 28, 1988; Jim Dandy, interview with author, December 4, 1989; Franc Johnson Newcomb, *Navajo Omens and Taboos* (Santa Fe: Rydal Press, 1940), 52.

## *Chapter Nine*

1. For the best single source in identifying all creatures inhabiting Navajo land, from bears to birds to snakes to snails, see Sebastian Wittig, *Naaldeehii* (Blanding, UT: San Juan School District, 2015). This book is written entirely in Navajo, but for non-native speakers, it is still an invaluable reference for animal types and the correct spelling of their names.

2. For those interested in a variety of teaching tales about birds, see Franc Johnson Newcomb, *Navajo Bird Tales Told by Hosteen Clah Chee* (Wheaton, IL: Theosophical Publishing House, 1970); Newcomb, *Navaho Folk Tales* (Albuquerque: University of New Mexico Press, 1967); Louisa Wade Wetherill and Harvey Leake, *Wolfkiller: Wisdom from a Nineteenth-Century Navajo Shepherd* (Salt Lake City: Gibbs Smith Publisher, 2007).

3. Leland C. Wyman and Flora L. Bailey, *Navaho Indian Ethnoentomology* (Albuquerque: University of New Mexico Press, 1964), 10–11.

4. Ibid., 20–24.

5. Ibid., 26–27.

6. Washington Matthews, *Navaho Legends* (Salt Lake City: University of Utah Press, 1897, 1994), 232.

7. Reichard, *Navaho Religion*, 533.

8. For a description of this process and the accompanying myth see Franc J. Newcomb, "Origin of the Navajo Eagle Chant," *Journal of American Folklore* 53, no. 207 (January–March 1940): 50–77; W. W. Hill and Dorothy W. Hill, "The Legend of the Navajo Eagle-Catching-Way," *New Mexico Anthropologist* 6/7, no. 2 (April–June 1943): 31–36.

9. John Holiday, interview with author, February 24, 2001; Jenny Francis, interview with author, March 23, 1993; LaVerne Harrell Clark, *They Sang for Horses: The Impact of the Horse on Navajo and Apache Folklore* (Tucson: University of Arizona Press, 1966), 105–6.

10. Berard Haile, *The Upward Moving and Emergence Way: The Gishin Biye' Version* (Lincoln: University of Nebraska Press, 1981), 79, 83.

11. Franc Johnson Newcomb, "Origin Legend of the Navajo Eagle Chant," *Journal of American Folklore* 53, no. 207 (Winter 1940): 64, 73.

12. Washington Matthews, *Navaho Legends* (Salt Lake City: University of Utah Press, 1897, 1994), 129.

13. Gary Witherspoon, *Language and Art in the Navajo Universe* (Ann Arbor: University of Michigan Press, 1977), 61.

14. Franc Johnson Newcomb, *Navajo Omens and Taboos* (Santa Fe: Rydal Press, 1940), 55.

15. Ibid., 56.

16. Robert S. McPherson, Jim Dandy, Sarah E. Burak, *Navajo Tradition, Mormon Life: The Autobiography and Teachings of Jim Dandy* (Salt Lake City: University of Utah Press, 2012), 187.

17. Ibid., 168.

18. Steve Pavlik, *The Navajo and the Animal People: Native American Traditional Ecological Knowledge and Ethnozoology* (Golden, CO: Fulcrum Publishing, 2014), 240–71.

19. Charlotte J. Frisbie, ed., with Rose Mitchell, *Tall Woman: The Life Story of Rose Mitchell, A Navajo Woman, c. 1874–1977* (Albuquerque: University of New Mexico Press, 2001), 164.

20. Ibid., 429.

21. Ibid., 176–77.

# Index